STA 0216

14.95

# BASS ANGLERS GUIDE

# BASS ANGLERS GUIDE

*Where to Find and How to Catch the Big Ones*

## Max Hunn

Stackpole Books

Published by
STACKPOLE BOOKS
Cameron and Kelker Streets
P.O. Box 1831
Harrisburg, Pa. 17105

Photographs by Kit and Max Hunn

Printed in the U.S.A.

**Library of Congress Cataloging in Publication Data**

Hunn, Max.
  Bass anglers guide.

  Includes index.
    1. Largemouth bass fishing. 2. Fishing—Florida.
  3. Fishing—Georgia. 4. Fishing—South Carolina.
  I. Title.
  SH681.H83   799.1'758   82-3368
  ISBN 0-8117-0216-2   AACR2

# DEDICATION

*To my devoted wife, Kit, who wasn't an unhappy "fishing widow," but instead an active angling partner always ready to help; and to the memories of the countless hours we spent fishing and enjoying the great outdoors.*

# Contents

# Acknowledgments

Without the expert advice and assistance of the following fishermen, this book would not have been possible. To the following I express my heartiest thanks for all your help during the pleasant hours we've spent fishing.

Buck Bray, Citrus Springs, Dunnellon, FL; Marty Butler, Lake Seminole, GA; Danny Bell, Santee-Cooper, SC; Dennis Botts, Abbeville, SC; Russell Blackmon, Santee-Cooper, SC; Ron Bobrow, Lake Seminole, GA; D.C. Brown, Santee-Cooper, SC; Hurley Badders, Anderson, SC.

Forrest and Glen Baker, New Albany, IN; Tony Cox, Lake Talquin, FL; Jim Canaday, Freeport, FL; Chip Campbell, Okeechobee, FL; Wendell Chavis, Charleston, SC; Warren Crabtree, Santee-Cooper, SC; Grady Clark, DeFuniak Springs, FL.

Frank Drose, Santee-Cooper, SC; Bill DeLisle, Immokalee, FL; Tom Eanes, Santee-Cooper, SC; Jon Farmer, Suwannee, FL; Jim Fowler, Okeechobee, FL; Larry Fetter, Leesburg, FL; Jim Fulmer, Lake Murray, SC; Al Glaze, Wewahitchka, FL; Ben and Gerald Holley, Crestview and Chipley, Fl; Chuck Hall, Panama City, FL; Tom Howerton, Lakeland, FL.

*11*

Sam and Mike Hanvey, Anderson, SC; Lou Hart, Lake Seminole, GA; Bill Hughes, Anderson, SC; Thad Hentz, Lake Murray, SC. Dick Hale, Silver Springs, FL; Roger Hall, Charleston, SC; George Jacobek, Blue Cypress Lake, FL; Hoss Johnson, Murrell's Inlet, SC; Bill Kerfoot, Cape Coral, FL; Jerry Lunsford, Lake Wales, FL; Terry Linton, Wewahitchka, FL; Lon Maas, Belleview, FL; Justin and Rocky Morgan, Silver Glen Springs, FL; Carl Maxfield, Charleston, SC; Roy McQuaig, Valdosta, GA; Joe Middleton, Blue Cypress Lake, FL; Duncan McQuade, Panama City, Fl.

Jim Nix, Lakeland, GA; Chico Neyrey, Murrell's Inlet, SC; B.J. Newsome, Panama City, FL; Nip Purvis, Lakeland, GA; Dean Poucher, Bluffton, SC; Steve Plein, Tavares, FL; Hank Parker, Lake Norman, NC; Ed Perry, Anderson, SC; Ben Robertson, Charleston, SC; Steve Shackle, Santee-Cooper, SC; Tommy Sing, Murrell's Inlet, SC; Jerry Sims, Lake Seminole, GA; Bill Smith, Lake Murray, SC; Austin Tharp, Panama City, FL; Tom Thaxton, Santee-Cooper, SC.

Danny Whaley, Abbeville, SC; Jack Wingate, Lake Seminole, GA; Fred Wilson Jr., Okeechobee, FL; Vince Williams, Kissimmee, FL; and Jim White, Lakeland, GA.

# Introduction

Largemouth black bass fishing has been popular since the nineteenth century when the development of the revolving spool reel, and the forerunners of today's lures first appeared on the market.

While it is undoubtedly often easier to catch lunker bass with natural baits, much of the appeal of the sport of bass fishing has been and is in luring the bigmouths into hitting artificial lures made of wood and plastic. Today, bass fishing is a highly developed sport, and no other fish has received the attention—scientific or otherwise—that ol' bigmouth has.

The construction of hundreds of new reservoirs following World War II helped spread and develop bass fishing fever. Built purportedly for flood control—often a disguise for other special interests—and for hydroelectric power generation, these huge reservoirs afforded waters for bass fishing where there had been none before.

With and without man's assistance, the bass responded to the thousands of new acres by multiplying rapidly, and with the greater abundance, fishermen began seeking the largemouths with greater and greater intensity.

Americans, with their innate competitive urge, soon began competing. At first, the competitions were between fishing partners, then in small groups, and finally in the 1960s, the idea of large, organized money tournaments developed.

When Ray Scott successfully formed the Bass Anglers Sportman Society at Montgomery, Ala., he aroused the competitive instincts of thousands of bass fishermen, and B.A.S.S. tournaments soon became the ultimate of pro bass fishing.

With the development of tournaments that spurred greater interest in bass angling, the fishing tackle industry jumped on the band wagon. New lures, rods, reels, and accessories flooded the market. Bass fishing became a big-time sport and resulted in vast publicity and a rapidly expanding membership in the bass fishing fraternity.

Interest in bass fishing reached unheard-of peaks, and the bass anglers perusing various magazines dealing with the numerous bass tournaments not only read about the newest lures and tackle, but also about famous lakes, reservoirs, and rivers throughout the nation.

Bass fishing became more than just a weekend affair within a few miles of home. Anglers travel hundreds, even thousands of miles either to compete in tournaments or more often to sample the waters they had read about usually seeking a trophy bass.

But as veteran bass fishermen know, and beginners quickly learn, fishing strange waters is far different than fishing at home. No matter how extensive their fishing expertise, they found that they needed certain basic information about a given lake. Advance planning was more than merely selecting a destination.

They quickly discovered they needed specific details about the new, strange waters. Yes, the bass were there, but each fishing water is different. Some are clear. Others are murky. Some are grassy. Some are deep with submerged structure. Others are shallow with little structure. Bass change locations during every month of the year, and certain locations are much better than others if you know when to fish.

Visiting anglers learned it is necessary to adjust their tactics. You can't use the same lures month after month after month. Some waters produce best with top-water lures. In others, the bigmouths hit when crank down or spinner baits are used. Almost universal, of course, are plastic worms, but even their sizes and colors can be surprisingly important.

This book was written to provide such detailed knowledge of the waters of the Southeastern states—South Carolina, Georgia, and Florida—where some of the finest bass fishing waters are found.

Each chapter provides specific information on how to fish each lake or river the year around; the type of cover normally encountered; the type of structure; the most successful type of lures; and the individual details that only local anglers know, but which can mean the difference between success or failure.

When planning a trip to one of the famous bass holes in the Southeast, check the specific chapter as to the best time of year to go or to find out what you can expect to encounter during your trip, and whether or not you have the proper tackle. Watch for the individual quirks of the various waters. Do this, and your chances of success will increase a hundredfold.

Tight lines and good luck!

# 1

# Grand Bassing Along
# South Carolina's Grand Strand

It doesn't seem possible that a resort area visited annually by thousands of vacationists would have a secret fishing hole.

It doesn't seem possible that behind the facade of a glittering Atlantic beach resort are hundreds of miles of rivers and creeks where largemouth black bass up to 10 pounds are frequently caught.

But this unusual situation does exist along South Carolina's Grand Strand, the beach resort stretching fifty-seven miles from the North Carolina state line to Myrtle Beach and southward to Georgetown.

It might seem that Grand Strand anglers are trying to keep this freshwater fishing bonanza a secret, but they are not. Largemouth black bass fishing is almost ignored because vacationers and native South Carolinians do not realize what's at their back door. With a grand beach and excellent saltwater angling at their front door, few residents and visitors even consider the freshwater fishing possibilities. But that's their error.

To understand why so many bassmen neglect the Grand Strand, you have to understand the geography of the area. While driving U.S. Highway 17, the coastal route which runs along the Strand, it's hard to realize that you are on a peninsula. Inland is the Intracoastal Waterway, which, while a saltwater route, here follows the fresh Waccamaw River. To the east is the broad Atlantic. To the west is the Intracoastal. The tip of the peninsula is at Georgetown, where the Waterway and the Waccamaw are joined by the Pee Dee and Black Rivers in Winyah Bay.

The bigmouths are not only caught in the Waccamaw River, but also in the numerous creeks such as Jericho, Thorofare, Schooner, Sand Hole, Cow House, Bull, Squirrel, as well as in other nameless creeks. Many of these creeks connect with the Pee Dee River, a fact that influences where and how you fish in the creeks and in the Waccamaw. Also many of these twisting creeks run through land that in the eighteenth century was used for rice cultivation. Now the deteriorating rice paddies are good fish breeding grounds, as well as logical places to fish.

Although I had visited the Grand Strand area many times, it wasn't until I studied the NOAA Small Craft Chart for the area (No. 11534) that my curiosity was aroused about the possibilities of freshwater bassing. The chart is designed for boatmen who use the Intracoastal Waterway, which runs from Maine to Florida, and it shows numerous freshwater creeks and rivers that offer bassing possibilities.

I began asking questions about bass fishing, but failed to get any solid information until I met a pair of saltwater party boat skippers—Captain Hoss Johnson and Tommy Sing. Both are natives of Murrell's Inlet, and they like to bass fish to relax from their daily work of skippering Atlantic party boats from Murrell's Inlet, just south of Myrtle Beach.

Through them I met Chico Neyrey, a swing guide who handles saltwater and freshwater parties. He's an inlet, small boat guide for those who like saltwater angling for flounder, sea trout, and channel bass. But he also guides anglers to the "back door" Grand Strand bass fishing. Also through Chico, I met Paul Cribb, an ardent, local bass fisherman.

After conversations with them, it was obvious to me that there was good bass fishing behind Myrtle Beach. Chico's biggest weighed 8 pounds, 4 ounces and Paul's record is 7 pounds, 3 ounces, while Hoss Johnson's heftiest weighed 7 pounds, 6 ounces. Although these bass usually do not reach the double-digit weights that Florida fish do, you can expect to encounter bass weighing from 7 to 10 pounds.

However, bigger fish have been caught by local table anglers using jigger poles. The local foursome know of an 11-pounder that couldn't

When fishing the numerous creeks and rivers of the Grand Strand for largemouth black bass, both buzz baits and spinner baits are useful when tossed close to the banks and retrieved over grass beds. Chico Neyrey hand lands a Grand Strand black bass that he hooked with a noisy buzz bait.

resist the jigger technique. They also know of a 13-pound, 8-ounce bigmouth that got caught in the intake of a local power plant.

The four local anglers know the quirks of the little-fished waters. They were glad to guide me, and in three days in the spring, we poked into more out-of-the-way fishing holes than you could imagine exist. We caught black bass in unlikely locales, and our experiences demonstrated the importance of the Pee Dee River's height in successful angling. We found that the ideal time to fish the Grand Strand is when the Pee Dee is at normal height. As a result of a series of interconnecting creeks, the Pee Dee has a direct influence on the Waccamaw River. When the Pee Dee is flooding, it sends a torrent of muddy water seaward, not only down its main channel, but also through the interconnecting creeks, and it is a big influence on the Waccamaw.

Whenever you plan to fish the Grand Strand area make certain you know the height of the Pee Dee. Forget any hopes of highly successful bass fishing trips if it is at flood stage.

If you do attempt to fish when the Pee Dee is at high water, as we did, do not expect any great success unless you can find clear water. It is possible to do so, but you may have to spend a lot of time cruising. Fishing definitely is work and a gamble with high water conditions.

The influence of the Pee Dee is but one of the quirks of fishing this area. Another is the importance of the tides. Although all of the water is strictly fresh, nevertheless it is all tidal influenced. Rising and high tides hold the water back in the rivers and creeks, while falling and low tides allow them to flow normally. A dead high tide is very unproductive, for it prevents or minimizes the flow of the freshwater streams, and moving water is vital to bass fishing success.

You can improve a trip's success by knowing what sort of tides to expect. You can check the tides for Georgetown, which are the most influential, being at the mouth of the main rivers. Locals can advise how many hours to allow for the same tidal action inland.

When I questioned my four local contacts as to which tide is the best, there was a difference of opinion. Paul favors the first two hours of the flood, while the others prefer the last three hours of the ebb. In either case, it's a good rule to plan to fish the last three hours of the ebb, and the first three of the rise. Success will be greatest during this period.

The importance of falling water is easily understood when fishing the rice paddies. On high tide, the paddies flood and provide a sanctuary for bait fish. But when the tide turns, the bait has to return to the creeks. The bass know this, and they concentrate around outlets from the paddies to feed. If you fish such outlets on a falling tide, your chances of success are good.

The changing water level caused by the tides also requires you to adjust your techniques. With high water, you find the bass are close to the banks, and you have to cast your lures with great accuracy under and around a variety of obstructions.

However, as the water falls, the bass have to move back into the main part of the creeks, and you must fish accordingly.

On the last of the ebb, it is almost fruitless to cast close to the bank, unless you're certain there is a deep hole there where the big-mouths can hide. Nine out of ten times, they have headed for the deeper channels. If they are in the extremely shallow, falling water, they are spooky.

The Grand Strand's back door affords a wide variety of fishing terrain. Cruise up the Pee Dee River, and you encounter black water tributary creeks that often twist through beautiful cypress swamps.

The cypress knees, fallen logs, and other debris are perfect bass hideouts. The Waccamaw has cypress knees and logs, but it also has stretches of lily pads and grass beds. Here also is the deepest water.

Fishing the creeks near the old rice fields offers different terrain—flat land with ancient canals draining into the creeks. Around the mouths of the canals, you find old logs and timbers—always potential bass hideouts.

Often the creeks in the flatlands have lily pads and grass beds affording cover for the bigmouths. Success here is governed by the depth of the water. Often the water is too shallow for bass except on a high tide.

The year-round fishing pattern does not change very much. Because of the cold weather, there is little fishing during January. However, by mid-February the local anglers begin seeking the largemouths.

To do this, you fish the creeks with the deepest water—up to 20 feet, still deeper in others—for the bass are suspending in the deepest holes and warmest water they can find. However, you still fish the edge, not necessarily in the center of the deep holes. Often the holes are near the bank. With cold water, naturally, you have to fish your lures slowly. The bass are sluggish. Also you have to fish deep. This is a period when deep-diving crank baits are effective, as well as worms with slip sinkers, and even spinner baits bounced off the bottom.

Lure colors aren't too unusual. Dark green-backed crank baits with either crawfish or pink-colored bellies are effective. Chico has had success with pearl crank baits with a crawfish colored underside.

This combination comes close to matching the natural shiners, one of the main items in the diet of these bass.

Plastic worm colors are standard, and the general preference is black, blue, and chocolate. Most anglers fish them with the regular weedless Texas rig, but Hoss Johnson finds he has more success fishing with worms that have exposed hook, despite the additional grass collecting that results.

All types of spinner baits are used, single and double blade, with either silver or copper blades, with a variety of skirts, even a chocolate-colored one. Chico developed this idea, and for some unknown reason the chocolate color is very effective during the cold months.

In the April-to-June period, fishing locations change, and so do the lures. Now you can fish the shores around the grass beds with water from eighteen inches to three feet deep early and late in the day. During the middle of the day, you work steep banks where there is good cover with 3 to 5 feet of water.

Obviously, the water depth influences what lures are used. When fishing the grass shorelines, the successful lures are buzz baits, rubber frogs, and Jitterbugs. When fishing the rice paddies, you work a worm around the mouths of runoffs from the old fields.

When fishing water 3 to 5 feet deep, crank baits are used such as Rebel's Deep Wee R, or Bagley's balsa Killer B, along with both single and double blade spinner baits, and even buzz baits. Blades are either silver or copper, and skirts white, black, blue, yellow, and mixed combinations.

Plastic worms are used if the water is not too swift, in both six and nine-inch sizes. The six-inch, however, is favored by most anglers. One-quarter, and three-eighth ounce leads are used, the weight depending upon how fast the water is moving.

April through June is also the period when the single and double top-water propeller lures are effective, and the colors are sometimes a bit odd. For example, Tommy Sing caught a 3-pound bass on one of our trips with a green, double propeller Devils Horse. It was an odd green color, but the bass did not seem to mind.

During this period, you can use shallow divers such as Rebel minnows and Bagley's Bang-O-Lure. Big bass will strike viciously at surface lures. Hoss prefers to use a broken-back Rebel when fishing the grass beds during these months working the lure slowly to avoid fouling in the grass. However, he caught his biggest bass with a straight-back, black and gold, Bang-O-Lure.

Fishing techniques don't change during the July-to-September period. You are fishing the same locations with the same lures, varying your selection depending upon water conditions. Remember to fish the shallows on the falling water early and late, and fish deeper during the day, as the fish move according to the tide.

The last quarter of the year varies. October is a good month, following the previous fishing pattern. Then as the cold weather comes, fishing success declines. Most of the fishing is in water from three to eight feet deep with crank baits in various colors being the prime lure. Worms also are used, the colors being the same as before.

The Grand Strand's back door has an enormous number of fishing holes, and you would be smart to hire a guide. I've found only two. They are Chico Neyrey and Chase Heath. You can reach Neyrey c/o Swing Guides, P.O. Box 709, Murrell's Inlet, SC, 29576, telephone (803) 651-2125. The telephone number is for Capt. Dick's Marina because Neyrey is a swing guide. He also takes parties fishing in coastal creeks for saltwater fish.

You can reach Heath c/o Wacca Wache Marina, Rt 1, Murrell's Inlet, SC 29576, telephone (803) 651-2994. You also can reach Neyrey at Wacca Wache. He books from this marina, too.

If you cannot locate a guide, there is nothing to prevent you from exploring with your own boat. If you do, then the most central launching site is at Wacca Wache Marina, which has a concrete public ramp.

Back door bassing is a well-kept Grand Strand secret now, but it won't be long when the word gets out. The bass are there, and currently there's little fishing pressure.

# 2

# Bulls Island—Sea Surrounded Bass Hole

Can you imagine catching largemouth bass as big as 12 pounds from a pond on a sea-surrounded island three miles out in the Atlantic?

It's hard to believe this can be done, but it can if you fish Bulls Island in the Cape Romain National Wildlife Refuge, about twenty miles north of Charleston, South Carolina. Bulls Island is only a short distance from the bustling seaport where the gray ships and nuclear power subs of the U.S. Navy glide through the busy, commercial harbor where Fort Sumter (the place where the Civil War began more than a century ago) still stands today.

It's not only fishing in an unusual location, but fishing that produces unusual results. There are times when it is so simple it seems like spearing fish in a barrel. Then there are times when the bass seem to have a bad case of lockjaw. Fishing can be red hot, ice cold, or something in between. It's definitely unpredictable.

Having fished the island several times, I can testify it can be tough angling. However, I also have fished it successfully with Bulls Island experts such as Wendell Chavis, Roger Hall, and Ben Robertson.

The trip that stands out in my memory with these South Carolinians saw us catch and release forty-odd fish. Although none of the bass were over 2 pounds, still that's a lot of largemouths, and on light tackle a lot of fun. But were the South Carolinians impressed? No way!

Their low opinion of that day's catch was understandable. Earlier in the month, Chavis, Bob Tyndall, and Glen Garrett caught and released 150 bass in one day. Now that was really fantastic fishing! They scored using electric sneak boats, casting either $\frac{1}{16}$ or $\frac{1}{32}$ ounce jigs, or four-inch plastic worms of various colors.

Naturally, a 150-fish trip makes a forty-odd score look mediocre, but that's par for fishing Bulls Island. If you can locate the bass, figure out what they will hit, you can get plenty of action in this freshwater bass hole surrounded by the sea.

But if you can't locate the bigmouths, and they are difficult to locate at times, or you can't entice them into striking, you can collect a big fat zero on Bulls Island.

When things click, Bulls Island fishing is as near angling heaven as you can imagine. Not only are there fish in abundance, but not all of the bass are kindergarten size.

Despite the lack of accurate records of big bass caught on Bulls Island, it is certain that 11 and 12-pound bigmouths have been landed. Even bigger fish may be dying of old age because the fishing pressure isn't that great.

Al Silver Sr., a veteran Palmetto State angler, can testify that there are big bass in Bulls Island ponds. He has two wall mounts from the island. One is an 11-pound bass, the other a 12-pounder. He caught these trophies jigger fishing several years ago.

Roger Hall's biggest bigmouth caught on the island weighed 9½ pounds. His prize couldn't resist a black, plastic worm, However, Roger is certain there are larger bass in the ponds, but they haven't reached trophy size by carelessly opening their mouths. It takes luck and skill to land them.

Bulls Island's ponds undoubtedly are some of the most unusual bass fishing locales in the United States. There are few coastal islands that harbor freshwater largemouths. I know of one similar setup at the St. Vincent National Wildlife Refuge off Apalachicola in the Florida Panhandle. There may be others, but they are not common.

From the moment you begin planning a Bulls Island fishing trip, you have to be ready for special problems. This is no haul down to a ramp, launch, and go fishing arrangement. No, indeed! It requires planning.

Just getting to Bulls Island is a feat. You have to launch on the South Carolina mainland: either at the Refuge Headquarters at Moore's Landing near Awendaw; at the little fishing village of McClellanville; or at Sewee Campgrounds.

The National Wildlife Refuge ramp is nearest to Bulls Island, *but* it's no place to launch or haul out with a dead low tide. There is a six to nine-foot tide along this section of the Atlantic coast, and low tide is a problem in many places. At Moore's Landing, the ramp and approach become nothing but soggy, slimy mud impossible to reach by boat. However, on a half-in to a full tide, this ramp is useable.

Sewee Campground ramp is three miles farther north than Moore's Landing, but it's an all-tide ramp, and so is the one at the little town of McClellanville still farther north.

The most logical choice is to use the private Sewee ramp (nominal fee) and cruise down the Intracoastal Waterway to the marked channel leading to Bulls Island. Obviously, you make a trip to Bulls Island only with good weather.

The U.S. Fish and Wildlife Service has marked the twisting channel most of the way through the marshes and shell banks from the Intracoastal, but the last part of the cruise is across unmarked Bulls Bay. In the Bay, you need to know where you are going.

Tides are vital in scheduling a Bulls Island trip. Not only is launching a problem, but the tides govern when you can get in and get out of the Island's fishing area. You need a minimum of a half tide—rising not falling—to cross Bulls Bay and run Jack's Creek to the dike which retains the fresh water in the ponds on the island. On dead low tide, Jack's Creek goes dry, as does much of the nearby bay.

You work to reach the Bulls Island fishing. You run three miles of winding, saltwater marsh channels, and up narrow Jack's Creek to the dike.

When you arrive at the dike, you remove and park your motor on shore, and manhandle your boat over the dike to launch on the freshwater side. Only electric trolling motors are permitted in the fishing ponds.

Trolling motors provide sufficient power for maneuvering a small, aluminum johnboat, or the sneak boats that are becoming popular, *but* don't go without a spare battery. Ben Robertson and I had only one battery in our boat, and it went dead. We had to paddle back to the launch site. Fortunately, there was no wind, but it was a long, long paddle. Roger Hall had been in the same fix on an earlier trip. Paddling is no fun, especially if there is a wind.

To really appreciate the experience of fishing Bulls Island, it helps to know the area's background. The Cape Romain National Wildlife Refuge was established in 1932, containing approximately 34,000 acres of woodland, marsh, and water in Charleston County, South Carolina. In addition, 30,000 acres of open water nearby is closed to migratory waterfowl hunting by Presidential Proclamation.

Oddly, Bulls Island—named for Stephen Bull, one of the leaders of the first English colonists in the area—was added to the refuge in 1936.

The island is an ancient barrier reef, low and rolling, approximately two miles wide and six miles long with extensive vegetation. Over the centuries, the nearby restless Atlantic has washed away a lighthouse, a cape, and hundreds of acres of forest. Inland are large ponds, where thousands of waterfowl gather each winter.

The fishing area consists of 610 acres of water and grass in four ponds so interconnected you can move easily from one to the other. Officially, they are known as Jack's Creek Pond, and Ponds 1, 2, and 3. Jack's Creek flows across Bulls Island to a culvert gate through the dike which enables the creek waters to spill across the salt marshes into Bulls Bay.

The history of the island's bass fishing begins in 1929, when Gayer G. Dominick, then owner of the island, introduced black bass to the ponds. The bass thrived, and fishing was excellent until 1953, when the ponds were flooded with salt water to eliminate an overabundance of cattails.

For the next five years, fishing ceased to exist because of the high salinity of the water. But by 1958, the water had become fresh enough to permit restocking with bluegills, redear sunfish, and black bass.

Test samplings three years later showed poor bass reproduction, but adequate panfish. After two more years of poor bass spawns, 25,000 fingerlings were stocked with 275,000 bluegill fry.

Two years later, fishing became fantastic. Oddly, although you could catch your bass limit in an hour, there was no satisfactory reproduction by the bass and it became obvious that regular stocking would be necessary.

In 1966, 2000 six-inch hybrids (cross of white bass and stripers) were stocked, and the following year, 5,700 more hybrids. However, few hybrids have been caught. Either the ponds are not suited to the crossbreeds, or anglers do not know how to fish for them.

In 1976, bream and redear fingerlings were stocked, while in 1977, 6,100 black bass, and 4,600 striped bass were added to the ponds. In the next few years, some lunker fish may be showing up on the stringers.

Bulls Island ponds are open for fishing during daylight hours only from March 15 through September 30. The rest of the year, the island is off limits to provide the migratory waterfowl an undisturbed wintering area. This, of course, decreases the fishing pressure, as does the remote location.

Although the ponds cover only 610 acres, your first problem is finding the fish, and they do move. The deepest water is near the dike where the control culvert is located, and this area is usually the most productive during warm weather. But there are times when you can hook a bass anywhere.

There is a grass problem that limits your choice of lures. During the winter, the grass dies back, and it's a minimal problem during April. This is the best time to use small, top-water propeller lures, or shallow divers, particularly the balsa types such as Bagley or Rapala. The ponds are very shallow: maximum depth in some places is 15 feet.

After April your main lure is the plastic worm—4 to 7 inches long— or tiny, one-sixteenth or one-eighth-ounce jigs with various colored skirts. White is the most popular, but do not hesitate to experiment. In August and September, spinner baits buzzed across the top of the grass sometimes are effective.

The thick grass challenges your handling of a plastic worm. You do not just flip it into the grass. You have to drop your worm dexterously near the edge of the grass line, and tease the bass into thinking that it's a meal. The majority of the largemouth lurk in the shoreline grass, but they will come out in the open momentarily for a pseudo meal.

Although the average bass usually is not a trophy, for some unknown reason these Bulls Island bass are extremely hard fighters. By using six to ten-pound test line, and matching your rods, you're guaranteed a fighting fish whatever the size of your foe.

Like their mainland brethren, Bulls Island bass can be fickle as to worm color preference on a given day. Take a full worm box with you, and do not hesitate to change color if the action doesn't develop quickly. Black generally is the most effective color in the normally clear water, although we found smoke gray was the key color on several trips.

Bulls Island regulars have discovered that there are other factors influencing the island bass. They've found success diminishes after a heavy rain. Their theory is the sudden influx of fresh water turns the bass off, either because of the change in salinity—the water normally is a bit brackish—or because the rain washes in an extra food supply from the banks, and the bass will not hit pseudo meals. Whatever the cause, bass fishing is off for forty-eight hours after a significant rainfall.

Another factor is water depth. A sudden drop in the water level of the ponds gives the bass lockjaw. Chavis and I experienced this one trip. The water control gate was damaged, and the water dropped quickly, and so did our fishing results.

When the bass are particularly coy, Chavis has found that using a tiny jig on a fly rod is a very successful method of teasing bass into striking. This was the key to his success on our second trip.

Wendell uses a seven to eight-foot fly rod to drop the tiny jigs into holes in the grass. He doesn't cast. It's more like flipping, but not as active. He uses his long rod much like a bream fisherman working a lily pad field with a cane pole.

Once the lure is in the grass hole, he raises and lowers it vertically several times, thus imparting a tantalizing fluttering motion to the jig's skirt. This technique entices the bass into grabbing the jig, but he doesn't always land them. Landing a struggling fish from thick grass isn't easy.

One of the major problems with Bulls Island fishing is your choice of boat. It's no place for a heavy one—bass or otherwise—because you have to carry your craft over the dike to launch in the freshwater ponds. Because of this you want as light a boat as possible.

Yet your boat can't be too light nor too small because you have to run three miles of Intracoastal Waterway, marsh, channels, and Bulls Bay. You need a small boat that will handle reasonably rough water. Don't forget the weather can change during the ten to twelve hours you're on the island. Naturally, you have to check the weather forecast carefully in advance.

Most of the Bulls Island veterans use fourteen-foot aluminum john-boats, light enough for two men to handle, powered by fifteen to twenty-horsepower motors. Such motors aren't too heavy to be removed from the boat and left on the special rack the Fish and Wildlife Service provides at the dike.

Some of the most ardent island anglers such as Hall and Chavis have developed a special technique. They haul sneak boats to the island in larger boats. If the tide is low, they anchor the big boats in Bulls Bay and proceed to the island in the sneak boats propelled by electric trolling motors. Naturally, they carry two batteries. No paddling Nellie home for them.

Even if you are fishing a sea island in a Federal Wildlife Refuge, you need a South Carolina freshwater fishing license. South Carolina's bag limit is ten bass daily.

Before making a Bulls Island trip, it is wise to do two things. First, arrange to go with an experienced island angler; second, get the latest information on what's happening. A good source is the Refuge Manager, Cape Romain National Wildlife Refuge, Route 1, Box 191, Awendaw, S.C. 29429.

It is real adventure to fish Bulls Island. Whether you score or not, it's a fishing trip that will live long in your angling memories.

# 3

# Black Bass
# In the Rice Paddies

Little did the eighteenth-century colonists who built the great rice plantations along South Carolina rivers realize that the crumbling remains of their back-breaking toil would result in unusual largemouth black bass fishing in the twentieth century.

In the seventeenth and eighteenth centuries, the production of rice was a major economic factor in South Carolina. Huge plantations lined the banks of the Cooper, Combahee, Edisto, Ashley, Santee, Wando, and other rivers that drained into the Atlantic.

The low river lands of these huge plantations were converted into rice paddies with dikes being built to shut out the river. Canals were dug to permit controlled flooding of the rice fields, and the rivers themselves were used for transportation.

But when the rice cultivation declined after the Civil War, the huge plantations virtually were abandoned. The old rice fields now are untended. The dikes are crumbling, and the rivers sweep in and out over the shallow flats. At high tide, there are three to four feet of water in the old paddies. At low tide, only inches of water remain. Often, many go dry.

However, today, this is the terrain of the rice paddy bass. Here the bait fish roam, and the bigmouths regularly prowl for meals that often include properly presented lures.

The fact that these ancient rice paddies harbor bass up to 12 pounds is not widely known outside of local angling circles. South Carolina bassmen, of course, know of these "honey holes," but for some reason this angling has never been widely publicized.

Surprisingly, even the number of South Carolina anglers who are experts on this type of fishing is limited. It's river fishing requiring special techniques. Many anglers prefer to fish huge lakes such as Santee-Cooper, Murray, Greenwood, Clark Hill, or Hartwell, all within easy reach of South Carolina fishermen.

I've had some very interesting experiences on these rice paddy rivers. On one trip, while fishing the Combahee near Beaufort with Dean Poucher, I caught my limit of bass—ten fish a day limit—on two successive days during a hot July. The mercury soared, but these rice paddy bass cooperated in the middle of the day when the sun was really scorching.

Even more spectacular was another trip, this time on the Cooper River which flows through Charleston. I landed eight bass in a couple of hours using seven different top-water lures. The bass were feeding recklessly on top. They clobbered a yellow Rebel popper; a black and silver Finlandia (balsa) minnow; a frog back Dalton Special; a yellow and green Shadrack; a gold Redfin, plastic minnow; a black and white magnum Torpedo; and a silver and black, homemade minnow-type lure. Would they hit anything? No. Several other lures failed to provoke strikes. Whether there was that much difference in the lure action, or whether it was merely coincidence, we never were able to decide. Nevertheless, lure choice can make a difference in fishing the rice paddies.

Equally impressive was another trip that I made with Carl Maxfield, Wendell Chavis, and Ben Robertson to fish the Cooper River only fifteen-odd miles above the bustling seaport of Charleston.

This was a trip when buzz baits flipped tight against the shoreline produced. In less than two hours, we landed seventeen bass weighing up to 3 pounds, and left, according to the local anglers, before the fishing was right.

While none of the fish I've landed were in the heavyweight class, there are big bass caught from rice paddy rivers. Carl Maxfield's largest is a 10-pound, 2-ounce bigmouth. He caught the bass with a green and white Devils Horse in October, one of the prime months for probing the paddies.

Undoubtedly, there are bigger bass lurking in the South Carolina waters. The largest Carl has heard of coming from the Cooper weighed 15 pounds, 3 ounces. That's a real wall mount. He also knows a local angler—a fly-rod specialist—who landed an 11-pound, 15-ounce bigmouth with a pink popper.

Reports of such fishing successes could lead you to believe this rice paddy bass fishing is easy. It isn't. You have to know the quirks of this particular river fishing, or you can fail.

There are three major factors governing success in the Low Country rivers, namely: knowledge of the tides; knowledge of the fish drops; and knowledge of the most suitable lures.

Inland fishermen, unfamiliar with fishing tidal-influenced waters, often encounter problems. It's not the time of day that governs, but the tide. Forget about dawn and dusk patrols *unless* they happen to coincide with favorable tides.

Although you are fishing fresh water, the rivers of South Carolina are influenced by the Atlantic tides as far as fifty miles inland. This water fluctuation is the key to success. If you do not fish the right tide, you don't get fish. Even during the hottest weather, the tide is important.

The best tide is an ebb, preferably about half out. The importance of an ebb tide can't be overemphasized. If the ebb occurs at midday, the bass will hit. If it falls at midnight, the bigmouths hit then.

You can catch a few fish on the first hour of the flood tide, but the odds are much better during the last two hours of the fall.

It was this fact that caused the South Carolina anglers to moan and groan when we had to leave early on the 17-bass trip. We left when the tide was only one-third out, and the local anglers knew the fishing would get better as the tide ebbed more.

Naturally, you have to make tidal corrections depending upon how far up the river you're fishing from the Atlantic. The tide will fall at a different time upstream than it will at the river's entry into the sea. There can be as much as eight hours difference depending upon the distance involved.

Another important facet of this rice paddy fishing is knowledge of the "drops," as South Carolina anglers call the fishing holes. Although all rice paddy terrain looks excellent, there are certain things to remember in seeking the best fishing waters.

Naturally, the depth of the canals, which you can fish, particularly on high water, is important. But even the canal fishing is tricky. The best angling is at canal junctions, not in the straight sections.

It's customary to begin fishing inside the dikes (if legally permis-

The abandoned rice paddies of the eighteenth and nineteenth century rice plantations along South Carolina's rivers are natural largemouth, black bass holding areas. Since the rice paddies are influenced by the tides, the best time to fish them is when the water is falling forcing the bait fish to retreat from the shallows into the main river channels.

sible, which it isn't in many instances) if the tide is very high. This angling, however, cannot compare with the success when fishing the rivers proper where canals or breaks in the dikes open into the streams.

It's obvious why such openings are prime locales. The bass concentrate in the deep water at the rice paddy outlets waiting for a meal. They know the bait fish have to leave the shallow flats as the tide falls. Thus the outlets are ready-made chow lines for hungry bigmouths.

If you fish with rice paddy veterans, you soon can learn their hole locating techniques by watching where they anchor, or where they float and fish. Many anchor at particularly profitable holes when the tide is falling extremely fast, and let the fish come to them from the paddies.

As a rule of thumb, rice paddy anglers prefer to fish the outlets through the dikes, but only certain ones. Not every dike outlet is a productive one. Experience teaches which ones are the most productive, and they do change from time to time. Generally it pays to make a few casts at or near any outlet which has water moving from a paddy. Moving water is an important factor in this type of fishing.

Although water movement is preferred, you can catch fish on a dead low tide. Look for sunken logs, undercut banks, and deep holes in the river when fishing this period. However, random fishing success is never as great as when working the old rice field outlets with moving water.

The third important factor is lure selection. Rice paddy bass are as temperamental as any other of their brethren regarding lures they will strike. At one time, they will want top-water lures with propellers. At another, they will prefer shallow-diving minnow-types. Sometimes they angrily attack buzz baits. Then sometimes they want deep-diving crank baits, or heavy spoons and jigs. Usually the time of year is a big factor in their whims. Although lure color is sometimes important, there are times when it does not seem to matter.

Lure handling is an important facet, too. Remember to vary your techniques if fishing is slow. If the normal, slow, and gurgling bass retrieve doesn't work, then shift to crank down baits or spinner baits fished deep and slow. Or perhaps you will have to buzz the bass, either with regular buzz baits or by buzzing spinner baits just under the surface of the water. And, of course, there are times when the plastic worm is the ultimate lure. Whatever you do, don't get married to just one technique or one lure. Try them all.

Don't assume because the bass eagerly hit a lure one day that they will sock it some other time. I first learned this during a fall sampling of the Cooper rice paddies near Moncks Corner. The local experts with whom we were fishing said that only a black Johnson spoon with a skirt would score in the fall. Did it? No, indeed!

Frustrated after repeated casts with nary a strike, I switched to a gold Johnson spoon with a gold, plastic tail, and boated fish. Then I topped the performance by landing another 4-pounder on a gold Cordell Redfin (a shallow-diving minnow-type). Several Moncks Corner anglers soon added gold lures to their tackle boxes for rice paddy fishing.

After fishing with several rice paddy experts it's apparent lures and locations on the Cooper River in general apply to any river having rice paddy bass. There are exceptions, of course, but generally the pattern is this:

During the cold weather of the first quarter of the year, many use bucktail jigs in the one-eighth to three-eighths of an ounce size, or Little George-type tailspinners, or deep-running crank baits.

A white bucktail, particularly a locally made one called Millie's Bucktail, that has a green feather in an otherwise white skirt is very popular. Crawdad and fire red are preferred crank bait colors.

The fishing areas are the rice field breaks and deep banks, where the water will be from 15 to 35 feet deep. The Cooper River, particularly, is deep in many places, and the deep holes are where the bass are found during cold weather. The same rule holds true for other rice paddy streams.

From April through June, one of the prime fishing periods, most anglers fish in the rice fields (where it is legal) using shallow-running crank baits over the grass. Such lures as the Rebel Wee R series, Bomber's Model As, and Bagley's balsa crank baits are effective.

Although the colors vary, the most popular are black and silver, and black and gold, along with Tennessee Shad. The clarity of the water is a big factor in color choice, lighter colors are usually preferred in clear water, and darker hues are preferred in murky water.

You fish in water that's two to three feet deep over grass beds, and also by casting tight against the river banks. The bass during this period are not very deep, for the water temperature is just about perfect.

The hot months of July through September require a change in technique. Early in the day, assuming the tide is right, you can fish the rice field edges and the rivers with top-water lures such as Devils Horse, Tiny Torpedo, Nip-A-Diddee, and similar single and double propeller plugs.

Buzz baits such as the Lunker Lure and Floyd's Bucktail Buzzer are very productive *if* you fish your lure tight against the bank.

You can fish worms deep with three-eighths of an ounce leads, rigged weedless Texas-style. Popular colors are firetail black, purple, and strawberry with worms ranging from six to nine inches in length.

During the October-to-December quarter, deep-running crank baits again are favored such as Rebel's Deep Wee R, Bagley's Diving Killer B and B-II, Model A Bomber, and similar lures. You fish these crank baits along grass beds off the channel banks. The bass are in 3 to 9 feet of water.

Rice paddy anglers find it necessary to use a variety of lines, ranging from ten to twenty-pound test. The clarity of the water governs how heavy a test you can use. Both bait casting and spinning tackle are successful.

There are plenty of launching ramps on South Carolina rivers. You can get a list of them from the South Carolina Wildlife Resources Dept., P.O. Box 167, Columbia, SC, 29202; or from the South Carolina Dept. of Parks, Recreation, and Tourism, E.A. Brown Bldg., 1205 Pendleton St., Columbia, SC 29201.

If you want a different fishing experience, the next time you're in South Carolina try rice paddy angling. It's unusual bass fishing, and the bigmouths are cooperative on the right tides.

# 4

# Surprising Santee-Cooper Bass

I still recall vividly my initial trips on the bass-fishing waters of the Santee-Cooper Lakes in the heart of South Carolina. Joining me were Tom Eanes and Warren Crabtree, a pair of experienced Santee-Cooper guides. They not only surprised me with their choice of fishing terrain, but also with the results.

Tom provided the first surprise. After running down Lake Marion a short distance, he headed his bass boat with the electric trolling motor towards some widely scattered, tiny cypress trees in very shallow water.

"We'll flip our worms at the base of the cypress," Tom explained. "Then, if there's a bass in residence, watch out."

You never argue with a guide in his home waters, but there's no law against doing some thinking. I was doing plenty. Fish a worm with a slip sinker in such shallows late in the spring? Although it did not seem logical, I kept my thoughts to myself and watched.

Eanes demonstrated the technique. He flipped an eight-inch blue worm with a quarter-ounce slip sinker at the base of an isolated cypress, let it fall to the bottom, and then quickly retrieved.

He wasted no time with the usual dawdling, teasing worm retrieve. Six or eight feet from the tree, he began a superfast retrieve, obviously to regain his worm for another cast, not to entice a bass into hitting. Any bass hitting a worm retrieve at that speed would have to turn on all aft burners. A bigmouth could catch it, of course, but it wasn't the usual worm technique.

Being Florida based, I was accustomed to a slow retrieve. This certainly wasn't. Would it pay off? The answer came quickly. Tom hit the trunk of another tree. His worm dropped straight down quickly. After only one turn of his Ambassadeur reel handle, he made an eye-crosser heave with his stiff rod.

The violent boil at the tree's base immediately indicated this was no yearling bass. Tom applied maximum pressure with his 20-pound test line and worm rod, and unwillingly the bass came away from the tree roots.

Objecting frantically, the bigmouth jumped but failed to throw the hook. Despite the steady pressure, the bass jumped again, but again failed to shed the barb. Now the steady pressure of the stiff rod began to show. Slowly, Tom worked the fish along for netting.

The fish weighed 8½ pounds, a bragging size to conquer in close-quarter combat in such shallow water among numerous underwater obstructions. But finding lunkers in the shallows is one of the surprises of fishing Santee-Cooper.

During the spring, you find the lunkers in such shallow water. On this trip, Tom not only boated his wall mount, but we also put several other bass in the boat in the 2 to 3-pound class. Every fish came from the base of an isolated cypress tree, and hit within six feet of the roots. They did not pursue the worm any distance.

While it was surprising to watch Eanes land his trophy, my greatest surprise came fishing with Warren Crabtree. Twice he guided me to trees where I had 17-pound test line broken as if it was sewing thread.

The bass—at least in the 8 to 10-pound class—just picked up my worm and headed back into their lairs breaking line despite my best efforts. I just couldn't turn them. Fishing among the young cypress can be hard on tackle. Either you turn them (as Tom did) or you lose them (as I did). That's one phase of Santee-Cooper fishing.

However, worm fishing isn't the only angling surprise. On another trip, Tom surprised me with his lure recommendation—a black Jitter-bug.

Now a Jitterbug is a famous and productive lure *but* generally it is used at night or at dusk. However, Tom was recommending a black

Jitterbug for early morning, a couple of hours after daybreak. The day was bright and clear with no cloud cover.

I had no Jitterbugs, but did have a black Tiny Torpedo with its white markings. With this lure, I learned Tom was right. The Santee bass wanted a black lure regardless of the clear daylight sky. In quick succession, we boated half a dozen bass, none huge, but scrappers nevertheless.

Not only does casting worms at the base of isolated cypress produce fish, but you can do the same with spinner baits. Tossing spinner baits in such a manner was worth $800 first place money for Danny Whaley one weekend during a tournament.

Using the tree-bumping technique, the South Carolina bassman won with a string of bass weighing 18 pounds, 7 ounces. He culled his winning string from a total catch of twenty-seven bass. Danny was using an underhand flip cast to flip his spinner bait at the base of small cypress trees in three to four feet of water, and the bass were aggressive.

Anglers who have fished Lakes Marion and Moultrie, which comprise the Santee-Cooper impoundment, agree these are two of the finest bass holes in the Southeast, although the bigmouths can be as difficult to catch as any of their clan at times.

Surprisingly, it is only in recent years that bass fishing has achieved general recognition and sufficient stature to challenge the popularity of the landlocked (stripers) rockfish that first brought the impoundment national fishing fame. When it was learned that the rocks (a saltwater fish that comes into fresh water to spawn) were reproducing after being trapped behind the dam, the publicity spotlight centered on the stripers.

Black bass were present all of the time, but did not achieve real recognition until bass fishing skyrocketed into nationwide popularity. Now the rockfish are matched by lunker black bass in the angling publicity.

Often bass fishermen encounter stripers. They will hit bass lures usually with shattered tackle results. The rocks far outweigh the bass. Encounter a rockfish in the 20-pound class with bass tackle, and you need a good rabbit's foot to land the striper.

If you are going to fish Santee-Cooper, you should know something of the history of the twin lakes. The two impoundments—officially named Marion and Moultrie lakes—were formed in the early 1940s when the Santee River was dammed and diverted into the Cooper River.

The huge hydroelectric project created two giant fish ponds. Marion, the upper lake, covers 110,000 acres, while Moultrie, the lower, has 60,400 acres. The two lakes are joined by the seven-mile Diversion Canal, which enables you to fish both "holes." This is a major asset. Wind can be a problem, but usually you can find sheltered waters on one of the lakes.

The size of the twin fish ponds can be both an advantage and a disadvantage. The size provides plenty of room for a big bass population, but it also creates a need for a guide. Unless you plan to fish the lakes for an extended period and have the time to explore the fish holding areas, you waste time exploring alone.

Lakes Marion and Moultrie have 450 miles of shoreline, and some areas are more productive than others. In addition, there are numerous islands, ranging from tiny plots to 300 and 400 acres. The island shorelines are bass holding areas, too. You can fish numerous submerged islands, plus miles of shallow water flats covered with cypress and tupelo trees, willows, horn beam, and button bushes.

You also find areas with grass, lily pads, dead stickups, and fallen and sunken trees. Perhaps eighty percent of the bass are caught in waters no deeper than seven feet. The number caught in 2 to 3 feet of water is astounding. Santee-Cooper is not generally regarded as a deep-water fishing area.

Because the Santee-Cooper is a hydroelectric impoundment, the water level is a major factor. When the lakes are full, the water spreads into the shallows, and the bass have much more territory to roam. Fishing then is more difficult.

Local anglers prefer the level of the lakes to be 74 feet above sea level, or lower. In the shallows, a drop of one foot can eliminate a lot of terrain and force the bass to concentrate in slightly deeper water.

Regardless of the water level, there is a monthly pattern to fishing Marion and Moultrie. Fishing is slow in January. South Carolina gets cold, and the bass are in deep water and sluggish. But in February, the action begins. Then and in March, crank and spinner baits are the primary lures, fished in shallow water, 2 to 6 feet deep, around points and brush. Veterans find that chartreuse, black, and yellow (with silver blades) are the most successful skirt colors.

During the April-to-June period, worms become very popular, but you also can score with crank baits. Tom Thaxton demonstrated the effective use of crank baits to me one May in a narrow run between two islands in lower Lake Marion.

The water was shallow—about 3 or 4 feet—over a grass bed that did not appear to be crank bait terrain. But it was. In two half days of fishing, we caught and released twenty-seven bass ranging to four pounds.

In addition, Tom tangled with two lunkers he couldn't handle. The big fish took him around the boat, and finally shook his lure. Shallow-running Bagley B-IIs, golden shiner color, were the successful lures.

A variety of crank baits can be used including Bagley's, Rebel's Deep Wee Rs, Norman's, and Bomber's. While crawdad color is generally preferred, there are times when others produce such as golden shiner, or Tennessee Shad. If one color doesn't work, try another.

A variety of worm colors will work, including black, purple, black-grape, blue, and watermelon green. Blue was the color Eanes used to land his lunker, and blue was the color I used when the two bass snapped my seventeen-pound test line.

April and May are prime months for fishing among the small cypress trees. However, you also find the bigmouths around the points and drop offs, especially where the old Santee River meanders through Lake Marion.

Top-water lures produce in June. Again there's a slight surprise—

The plastic worm fished with a slip sinker and tossed at the base of small cypress trees in the famous Santee-Cooper lakes in South Carolina is effective. You get a hit within a couple of feet of the trees, or you miss. Here, Tom Eanes hand lands an 8-pound bass that hit his worm as it dropped at the base of a cypress tree.

single propeller lures seem to score more than double prop models. Perhaps, it's a case of too much noise frightening rather than intriguing the fish.

During April and May, the bass often are schooling, and top-water lures should be small, even as small as jigs for crappie. The fish are chasing small bait, and your lure should match. Also now you generally fish deeper water, 6 to 10 feet. Shallow-water angling is confined primarily to early and late.

In the summer months, July through September, the fish are in the same deep water. Lures don't change, nor do the colors.

Cooling water in October marks a change in the fishing pattern. From then until December, you again fish the shallows with worms, crank, and spinner baits, using a variety of colors depending upon the water clarity.

During the fall months, spinner bait anglers find that pork rind and twisting plastic tail trailers are most effective enticers with spinner baits. Some add them to a skirted spinner, while others fish the spinners minus the customary skirts. You have to experiment to discover what the bass prefer.

Whenever planning a Santee-Cooper trip, you should do some advance map studying. There is too much territory to go fishing blindly, and even if you hire a guide, it's nice to know where you've been.

Among the maps that have been available at one time or another are: "Roland Martin's Guide to the Santee-Cooper," published by Ole Guide Publications, P.O. Box 373, Smithville, TN, 37166; "Fishing Guide to Lake Marion," published by 4-D Associates, P.O. Box 11535, Capital Station, Columbia, S.C., 29211; and "A Sportsman's Map to Santee-Cooper," by Fishunt, P.O. Box 11872, Columbia, S.C., 29211. Bass structure fishing maps are available from the Santee-Cooper Commission, P.O. Drawer 40-F, Santee, S.C., 29142. Prices of the maps vary.

The two lakes have numerous accommodations ranging from excellent to barely adequate. We've avoided the latter. During our frequent visits we've based at Goat Island and Bell's Marina on the upper lake; and Black's Camp on a small cove off the Diversion Canal for fishing Lake Moultrie, the lower lake.

Goat Island's mailing address is Route 2, Box 145, Summerton, SC, 29148, telephone (803) 478-2728; Bell's, Route 1, Box 332, Eutawville, SC, 29048, telephone (803) 492-7924; and Black's Cross, S.C., 29436, telephone (803) 753-2231.

For surprising fishing, you can count on the Santee-Cooper bass to provide ample surprises, some of them quite startling.

# 5

# Bass Lakes on a Name-Swapping River

In the mountain foothills, the Catawba River meanders from North Carolina into South Carolina achieving two distinctions. First, it is one of the few rivers in the nation that changes its name downstream. Second, it has two ancient lakes—Lakes Wylie and Wateree—that are overlooked black bass fishing holes.

The river travels under the name of Catawba until it reaches Great Falls, S.C., and there it is called the Wateree, which empties into the famous Santee-Cooper reservoir in the heart of South Carolina.

However, bass fishermen could care less what the river's named. They're interested in the two largest fishing lakes—Wylie and Wateree, some of the oldest bass holes in the nation.

Although these two lakes are known to have good black bass populations, they are not widely publicized for two reasons. One, they're ancient reservoirs. Two, the fishing publicity spotlight always has tended to focus on the newer, more glamorous lakes. Nevertheless, Wylie and Wateree are good bass holes, capable of producing bass weighing up to 10 pounds. In addition, Wylie is capable of harboring big stripers or rockfish.

*43*

Lake Wylie is the smaller of the two lakes, yet it sprawls across 12,455 acres with 325 miles of shoreline. It is named for Dr. W. Gil Wylie, who formed the Catawba Power Company, predecessor of to-day's Duke Power Company, which now controls both lakes.

Wylie is the oldest reservoir on the Catawba River. The lake was first created by a dam near Fort Mill, South Carolina, in 1904, and twenty years later this dam was rebuilt expanding the impoundment to its present size. Generally it's rated number one in popularity with fishermen because of its location near such centers of population as Charlotte, North Carolina, and Rock Hill, South Carolina.

The lake extends upriver into North Carolina. Half of its acreage is in the Tar Heel State, the other half is in South Carolina. As a result, you need both a South Carolina and a North Carolina fishing license if you intend to fish the entire lake. However, if you stay within the boundaries of either state, then you need only one permit.

Lake Wateree, constructed in 1920, is larger than Wylie. Although it spreads over 13,710 acres, its 242 miles of shoreline is less than Wylie's 325. Although Wylie's acreage is slightly smaller than Wateree's its shoreline is longer as a result of its location. Wylie was built in more mountainous terrain with the result that more narrow and steep valleys were flooded providing additional shoreline. The fact that many coves had deep water great distances from the main river channel is an important factor in your fishing success.

Wylie's twisting shoreline is tree covered and studded with homes. Boat docks are numerous, and often are good fish havens. When you fish Wylie, you are fishing a lake surrounded by civilization, but don't let that bother you. The fish don't.

I was fortunate enough to be introduced to these two antique bass holes by a pair of expert anglers, Hank Parker, a young up-and-coming fisherman on the B.A.S.S. pro tournament trail, and Danny Whaley of Abbeville, S.C., a part-time tournament angler when he isn't earning a living as a railroad engineer.

Parker evaluates Wylie thus: "If a bass tournament with 300 entries were held on Wylie during May, I believe fifty percent of the fishermen would catch their limit of eight fish."

In other words, he thinks the tourney would see a total of 1,200 bass hooked. That's a lot of fish on any lake regardless of age. It's also a lot of fish from a lake so heavily used.

Hank's opinion is supported by some of his experiences in May. One May, he caught four fish over 7 pounds with a black and silver Bang-O-Lure in the shallow water of one cove. One fish weighed 8 pounds, another 7 pounds, 8 ounces, and the other two each weighed

7 pounds. That sort of success would make any angler favor May fishing on Lake Wylie.

Although Wylie and Wateree are similar terrain, they offer different angling problems. Both lakes are located in the mountain foothills. You would think that the coves would be similar, but they are not. In the case of Wylie, the coves that were flooded were narrow Vs, with the result that the water is deeper farther back than would be expected. Wateree is different. Its water is shallower because the valleys that were flooded were broad ones with gentle slopes. As a result, the water on Wateree deepens only gradually, and often you must fish less than three feet even though a mighty long cast from shore.

However, the two lakes are also similar in many respects. Since both are ancient impoundments, they lack dead-standing timber usually found in younger impoundments. Most of the submerged trees have long since disappeared in Wylie and Wateree. There is very little if any of this type of fish holding structure in the two lakes.

There are certain natural structures such as old channels, flooded creeks, and rock outcroppings, but no dead, submerged timber. In this situation, where do you look for fish holding areas?

Smart anglers capitalize upon man-made brush piles introduced around private docks for crappie fishing. Crappie are popular in both lakes, and civilization is very apparent around the impoundments in the form of docks of every size and shape. The bass hold around the docks and the brush piles feeding on small crappie and upon the bait fish that gather around such cover.

The key to locating the crappie (speckled perch) brush piles are the lights on the piers. You can be certain the light will be aimed at the brushy locations, for night crappie fishing is a popular sport.

When checking a dock, note where the lights are located. If they're at the end of the pier, the brush pile will be directly off the end. If they are in the middle, they'll be on the side where the lights are aimed. In that case, work your lure along the side of the dock where the brush is submerged.

Spinner baits obviously are very popular on both lakes, being particularly suited to working along docks, and over brush piles. Often you have to spot cast to any submerged snag, or stickup, for the bass hold around whatever little structure they can find, particularly if there are no docks available.

Sloping points are another good bass holding area, often having rocks for cover. Usually these are located at the entrance to coves and along the old river channel.

According to Hank and Danny, Wylie and Wateree are eleven-month fishing lakes. There's very little fishing in January. It just gets too cold for it to be enjoyable in this part of South Carolina.

Angling activity begins to pick up in February and March. In places the Catawba River has 60-foot holes in Wylie, and it probably averages 35 feet in the main channel. The bass naturally hold in the deeper water.

In both lakes you find the bass in deep water from 6 to 16 feet around points running into deeper water. You also find the bass are holding around brush piles and docks, particularly those in deeper water.

For this point fishing, Parker prefers a deep-running crank bait, such as Norman's Big N, or the Deep Little N. Of course, other crank baits will produce, too, such as Rebel Wee Rs, Bomber Model As, and Bagley deep-diving balsas.

This is also the time when spinner baits can be worked slowly along the bottom, or run deep. A slow retrieve is essential because the bass aren't actively chasing food. But if your lure passes under ol' bigmouth's nose, you may be in business.

Around brush piles you should retrieve spinner baits at a snail's pace to score. Spinners that have double copper blades with various skirts are used. Popular skirt colors are chartreuse, white, and blue. Chartreuse and white work best in murky water.

During the best period on the lakes—April through June—a wide variety of lures are effective. Beginning in late March as the water temperature rises, the bass move into shallower water heading for the back of the coves to spawn.

When you are fishing water up to 8 feet deep, the Bomber Speed Shad is recommended. Hank found that Speed Shads with either silver or gold inserts in the clear body are often successful.

Cranked fast, the lure runs at a medium depth. However, sometimes a minimum of cranking to keep the lure just below the surface produces better. The retrieve that succeeds depends upon the reaction of the bass on any given day.

This is the period, too, when floating, shallow-diving lures such as Bagley's Bang-O-Lure, A.C. Shiner, and Rebel minnows work in the back of the coves in the shallows. Black and silver, and black and gold are the preferred color combinations depending upon water conditions. Top-water chuggers work, too. Among the favorites are Pico, Rebel, L & S, and Creek Chub.

The stop-and-go retrieve with a floater-diver is the most successful. This method causes the lure to twitch on the surface like an injured bait fish. However, there are times when it is more effective retrieved fast so that it runs under the surface like a fleeing bait fish.

Late in this period, the plastic worm becomes effective. Most anglers prefer the six-inch worm although some like the seven-inch worm. Most use the Texas weedless rig both with and without a slip sinker depending upon the depth of the water being fished. Popular worm colors are black, purple, and purple-grape.

It is during this period that a special four-inch worm (Dr. Walker or Fish Finder, they're similar) is used. For some reason the bass, at times, want a small worm. These four-inch worms have two hooks rigged on a nylon harness inside the worm. They have open hooks, and are far from weedless, but seldom snag because of the relatively clear bottoms.

Often the four-inch worm is fished with the Carolina rig utilizing a three-way swivel. A twelve-inch monofilament leader with a sinker is attached to the first ring. To the second ring is attached the worm (floating) with an eighteen-inch mono leader. And the third ring is attached to the main line. When the sinker bounces along the bottom, the worm floats some eighteen inches above, and the bass often cannot resist.

A similar technique utilizes a similar system with but one swivel. An egg sinker is attached above the swivel on the main line. The worm is attached to a mono leader, twelve to eighteen inches in length, which is fastened to the other end of the swivel. Again when the sinker is dragged along the bottom, the worm floats twelve to eighteen inches above.

Both systems require constant attention, because when a bass picks up the worm there is only a very slight signal. But at times, this is the only way to use worms effectively, whether they are four or seven inches long.

In the July-to-September period you find the bass retreating from the coves to deeper water. You do best fishing drops and ledges nearer to and on the river channel. The fish are found in water ranging from 5 to 15 feet in depth.

Plastic worms are the primary lure, usually rigged weedless Texas-style with various sinkers depending upon the depths being fished. Favored colors are blue, black, and purple-grape. At times, the four-inch, green worm is needed.

In some instances when fishing deep water you can use Little George-type tailspinners, or Hopkins spoons. The secret is to cast and retrieve these lures rather than letting them drop straight down alongside the boat.

October, the beginning of the last quarter, is the second best fishing period with angling success dropping as cold weather arrives. Spinner and crank baits are the productive lures.

With spinner baits, you cast to any standing sticks you see, or around deep brush piles. As in the spring the bass also are around the sunken trees and stickups. They begin holding near such structure in mid-September, and generally remain there until the middle of November.

In the fall, the bass react differently to the spinner baits, according to Hank. Seldom do you get a bass to hit the spinner as it falls. Instead, they clobber the lure on the retrieve.

"A favorite method," Parker explains, "is to burn the spinner bait near a brush pile, then slow it down, but don't stop it completely. When you speed up again, the bass thinks a meal is escaping, and jumps on the spinner."

Crank baits are particularly popular at this time because often the bass school in the middle of the coves to feed on shad. When you locate a feeding school, you can score quickly with floater-diving crank baits. The favorite crank down colors are shad and baby bass. All of the standard crank baits will score.

Wateree has an abundant population also of white bass, and often the blacks school with the whites. When you cast into such a melee, you are never certain what you are going to hook. The white bass get as large as three pounds.

If you are seeking schooling white bass, you will probably do best with small, silver spoons, Little George tailspinners, and small, white or shad-colored, crank baits.

Wylie not only has black bass, but also has been stocked with striped bass, also known as stripers or rockfish. While the stripers cannot reproduce, they do grow and they can be caught in the 35-pound class. Stripers at times will hit bass lures, and if you hook up with one of the big rocks, you're in for a real fishing brawl.

Wylie and Wateree may be some of the oldest lakes in the nation, but they can produce good strings of fish for thinking anglers. You have to work, but you can score.

# 6

# Challenging Lake Murray

You could hear them hollering half a mile across the broad arm of Lake Murray. Obviously, our fishing partners were very excited.

"I'll bet the 'Preacher' did it!" exclaimed Jim Fulmer, my fishing partner. "I know he has landed a big bass!"

Jim headed our boat for the other shore to see what was causing the Rev. John Koch and Thad Hentz to sound like wild Indians. As we neared their drifting bassboat, the answer was obvious. The "Preacher" was holding up a nice 6½ pound bass. Now that's a good bass in any league.

"Preacher" had flipped a Rebel crank bait—black back with green sides and an orange belly—near a dock, and immediately tangled with this scrappy bass. Fortunately, he was able to survive a pair of jumps, and keep the bigmouth from diving under the dock.

If he hadn't loosened his drag at the right time, the ten-pound test line might have broken. But the "Preacher"—a retired Lutheran minister and an adept angler—did things just right.

Only a few minutes before, another hefty bass hit his lure, but it tore loose before he could gain control. That time, things weren't right.

Such incidents are far from unusual on Lake Murray, one of South Carolina's little publicized bass holes that affords capital fishing almost on the doorstep of Columbia, the state capital. The lake's eastern end is only fifteen miles from Columbia.

Murray is a lake that is known to local bassmen, but one that has been overshadowed by more highly publicized fishing holes. It does not lack fish. It has plenty. It's just that it lacks the drum beaters to extoll its angling virtues. Maybe this is by chance, or maybe it is because the canny South Carolina anglers aren't too anxious to spread the word that you can catch big bass in Lake Murray.

Murray has a good fish population. On one trip, in two days four of us landed a total of thirty-four bass, ranging up to 3 pounds. They provided plenty of action, and if the fishing gods had been smiling, the bass might have been even bigger. Ironically, the day after I left, Thad did land a lunker—a 9-pound, 8-ounce fish.

Only two weeks earlier that May, Thad Hentz boated a 7½ pounder on a natural bass-colored Rebel Deep Wee R. In the first week in April, he put an 8-pounder in the boat, again with a Rebel Deep Wee R, this time crawdad color. His biggest bass to date has been a 9-pound, 8-ounce trophy. He has landed a pair—the first one the day after I left, and the second in 1981. He released both fish because they had not spawned.

However, he knows of fish weighing more than 13 pounds being caught in Murray, and his ambition is to break that mark. His chances are good, because he's a part-time guide—one of the few on the lake—who has time to fish and who is enjoying his retirement from the U.S. Air Force.

Lake Murray is unusual in many aspects. It's one of the oldest reservoirs in the nation having been built between 1927 and 1930 as a hydroelectric project on the Saluda River. The lake covers 50,000 acres, and has 528 miles of shoreline. There's a lot of room for the fish to roam, and roam they do.

But being so ancient, Murray presents unusual problems that anglers accustomed to fishing more modern reservoirs have never encountered. For one thing, most of the underwater cover naturally available when the impoundment was flooded long ago has disappeared. You don't find the submerged, dead trees, sunken logs, and other debris usually associated with an impoundment that just has been flooded recently. As a result, man has to help provide cover for the fish whether they be black bass, crappie, bream, or stripers.

You discover the majority of the lake's fish attractors—usually brush piles—have been placed by anglers who are seeking the abundant crappie or speckled perch. However, the bass also move into the brush piles following the forage fish that gather there. These artificial covers are effective, but their locations aren't as obvious as natural ones.

Locating such fishing holes is tricky. It helps, of course, if you can fish with a local expert, but if you're on your own, you have to do some studying. A depth finder is a big help. However, many of the fish holding areas are relatively small, and shift with the water movement. But if you study your finder intently, pay attention to those who have built docks along the shore, you can locate likely fishing areas. Then you have to test them.

Good fishing areas change from time to time. Hentz has observed this often, and as far as he's been able to observe, there is no telling when a particular area will become a lunker haven.

One year, a point he's always found to be very good became a big bass hole. He landed and released eight bass weighing 7 pounds or more. He never was able to figure out why this particular point drew the big fish, but he certainly didn't mind putting them in the boat. Who would?

There are two other factors that influence the lake's productivity—water level and clarity. Because it's a hydroelectric impoundment, the level fluctuates depending upon the rainfall along the Saluda's watershed, and the amount of water being drawn through the electric generators.

A low lake level usually produces the best fishing because the bigmouths cannot roam at will in unreachable shallows. Also, low water often causes productive brush piles to be only a few inches below the surface, sometimes with stobs showing. It is a lot easier to find them then.

Water clarity, too, is a big factor. When the water is gin clear, as it often is, the largemouths are spooky. They can see you and your boat, and they also can see your lure. Local experts much prefer to fish dingy water, as long as the cover is suitable. Of course, murky water won't overcome fishing where there are no fish.

Water color, of course, is governed by the rainfall along the Saluda. Heavy rains result in a surge of muddy water which can give the lake the proper dingy stain despite its size. If you can plan a trip when the lake is murky, your chances of success are much, much better.

After fishing Lake Murray several times with Hentz, Fulmer, and Bill Smith, all ardent local fishermen, it is apparent there's a pattern to scoring on the lake. You have to change your techniques according to the time of year.

The three experts generally agree that the following is the calendar angling pattern:

They rate the February-to-April period—just prior to spawning

When fishing Lake Murray don't overlook the numerous docks of private residences around this ancient impoundment. Crank baits fished parallel to the docks often produce lunker bass such as this 6½ pounder. You can also fish spinner and buzz baits parallel to the docks successfully.

time—as the best months. During these months, they find that fishing submerged points covered with either rock or brush are productive. Bumping crank baits across the bottom scores. Sometimes deep-, sometimes shallow-running crank baits are used. Colors vary with crawdad and orange being favored in murky water, while lighter colors seem best when the water is clear.

If the water is murky, spinner and buzz baits become very effective because the sound attracts the bass even if they can't see the lure. Rattling crank baits are also effective for the same reason.

The bass move into the shallows to spawn during April, May, and June and then return to deeper water. When the bass are in the shallows, the prime fishing locations are around brush piles and piers. This is the time for top-water lures, usually the balsa-type shallow runners that can be either blurped on top or run just a few inches under the surface.

It was during a May trip that the balsa-type lures really produced. Thad eased our boat up into the shallow end of a brush-infested cove, and we got fish because the fishing gods were smiling.

It was the toughest top-water fishing area I've ever seen. All we could do was make short flip casts, and hope we could handle whatever pounced on our lure. We did because none of the bass were over 2 pounds. Nevertheless, it was ticklish work landing a scrappy fish in the brushy water. But that was where the bass were, and that's where we had to fish.

During the spring period, if the water is murky, top-water propeller lures are effective. These noise makers however, are less effective with gin clear water. Then the noise spooks the fish instead of angering them. They don't charge, they retreat, and fast!

All three anglers rate the summer period—July through September—as the most difficult one. You have to fish the deep drop-offs in 20 to 30 feet of water. Veteran anglers turn to the plastic worm during the hot months, using various weight sinkers, depending upon the water depth, wind, and current. Usually the bass are suspended at whatever depth they find most suitable.

Another method used at this time is to utilize white bucktails—one-half to three-quarters of an ounce—or heavy slab spoons to bump the bottom. Some bassmen troll with deep-running plugs, often with a bucktail trailer treble. This system also results in hookups with big stripers (rockfish) that have been stocked in the lake. Then watch out!

The October-to-December period is another time when fishing is excellent. Early in the fall, the bass again move into shallower water. Hentz and Fulmer like to look for the bigmouths in 3 to 6 feet of water. They use both worms and crank baits.

This is also schooling time, and the blacks are all over the lake, often running with stripers, white bass, and hybrids (which also are regularly stocked). When you cast your lure into surface schooling fish, you're not certain what you'll hook, but you can be certain you'll tie into scrappers.

If you tangle with a huge rockfish, the odds are against your landing, unless you are using heavy line—at least twenty-pound test. Striper anglers prefer twenty-five to thirty-pound test when fishing for big rocks. Stripers weighing more than 30 pounds have been landed. When you play with that weight, you need stout tackle.

It's uncertain just how big the Lake Murray stripers grow. Fish over 30 pounds have been landed. However, dead rocks that apparently died of old age have been found floating that weighed 85 pounds. Now if you ever tie into one of those and land it, you'll have something to brag about.

The record for fresh water stripers is 59 pounds, 12 ounces. The fish was caught in the Colorado River in 1977 by Frank Smith with a seven-inch diving Rebel minnow. The previous record was held by South Carolina when a 55-pound rockfish was caught in the Santee-Cooper reservoir. Who knows? Lake Murray might harbor a new world record striper if anyone can hook and land it.

Stripers, incidentally, often clobber bass lures, hence when you're fishing Murray be ready for a real battle if you hook a rockfish.

Lure colors don't seem too important for bass fishing. Black and silver, and blue and silver tiger stripe paint schemes are very productive with balsa-type shallow runners.

Of course, when the water is murky, you have to change colors. Crawdad becomes the favored hue for crank baits, while yellow seems to rate number one with spinner baits.

You won't find any particularly unusual worm colors. They're pretty standard and include black, purple, firetail, blue firetail, lime green, and sometimes red or strawberry.

For worm fishing, the standard rigs (either the Texas weedless or the weedless hook) are used with a wire guard. At certain times the experts prefer the Carolina rig, consisting of a floating worm rigged Texas-style on a leader which is fastened to a swivel. The swivel is attached to the main line, and the sinker fastened above the swivel.

This enables the lead to rest on the bottom, while the worm floats a foot or so above the bottom. It's effective at times, but requires close attention, for it's difficult to detect when the bass picks up the worm.

You will find limited rental accommodations around the lake. The main ones are at the Top O' the Lake, located as the name indicates at the top of Lake Murray near where the Saluda River enters the impoundment.

There are two motels in nearby Newberry. We have stayed at the Newberry Inn, part of the Best Western chain. The other is Whitaker Motor Lodge, an independent.

There are few guides on the lake. A couple book out of Top O'the Lake, and there's Thad Hentz. You can contact him as follows: Thad Hentz, Route 1, Box 124, Prosperity, SC, 29127, telephone (803) 364-3562.

Lake Murray may not have been making the angling headlines, but the bass are there, and they offer an angling challenge with a good chance of hooking some line stretchers, particularly if you stumble onto stripers. Don't say you weren't warned.

# 7

# Dock Hopping Scores On Lake Greenwood

"There oughta be a bass at that ramp," remarked Danny Whaley from the bow of his bassboat as we eased along the shoreline of Lake Greenwood, one of South Carolina's little-ballyhooed bass lakes.

Danny's remark puzzled me. Now I've caught bass in odd places, but never had a fishing partner calmly declare he was going to find one at the foot of a concrete boat ramp. Was Danny kidding? Fishermen do have an odd sense of humor at times. I made no comment. I just waited to see what would happen.

Danny flipped a double-bladed, all-white spinner bait within inches of the end of the concrete ramp, and began a quick retrieve. His lure didn't travel five feet when he felt contact, snapped up his rod tip, and a bass broke water in a jump.

It was a brief fight, and soon Danny was swinging a 2-pound bass aboard. That scrappy fish had been holding just where Danny had said—at the foot of a private concrete boat ramp, and not in very deep water.

Checking out Lake Greenwood with Danny Whaley proved to be a surprising fishing experience. After two days of fishing the lake with

Danny and Don Dillard, a one-time major league outfielder with Cleveland and the old Milwaukee Braves, it became obvious that Greenwood is one of those sleeper lakes. It's a reservoir with a good bass population that has never been in the fishing spotlight.

Fish biologists have one way of measuring a lake's bass population, and probably are much more accurate with their block netting and chemical sampling. However, ardent anglers, particularly tournament fishermen, have a method of their own, and it, too, gives a rough idea of bigmouth population. This yardstick is the number of pounds needed to win, or at least finish in the money in a tournament.

Lakes with large bass populations always require greater total poundage to win or place. The reason is simple. The more bass, the more the tourney anglers catch, and the larger the winning poundage will be.

By this yardstick, Danny, who likes to fish local and regional tournaments when he isn't engineering on the railroad, rates Greenwood as the the third best lake in South Carolina.

Based on his tournament experiences and years of fishing, he estimates it takes a 20-pound catch (based on a 10-fish limit) to finish in the money in a tourney on Santee-Cooper or Lake Secession.

Greenwood isn't far behind, where he estimates a 17 to 18-pound string will score. But the surprise is that Greenwood requires a larger catch than do such more famous lakes as Hartwell, Clark Hill, or Keowee. On these lakes, a 14 to 15-pound catch will put you in the money.

Don Dillard, who's lived on the lake and owned Dillard's Lake Resort for twenty-five years, agrees with Whaley that Greenwood is a little-known and underrated bass hole. "Greenwood's got a fine bass population, but most of our customers are more interested in the excellent crappie fishing," explains Dillard. "The bass are there, but the bass fishermen, outside of a few locals, are unaware of Greenwood's potential."

Greenwood not only has a good bass population, but also holds some big fish. The biggest Dillard has seen was a 13-pound, 14-ounce bigmouth caught by a local angler living in the little town of Ninety-Six. However, bass in the double-digit class aren't too common, although they are there.

The biggest bass that Dillard has boated weighed 7½ pounds. Whaley's biggest from Greenwood weighed 6 pounds. However, his personal record is much bigger—9 pounds, 14 ounces caught in Lake Secession, another little-known bass hole.

One thing you immediately notice about Greenwood bigmouths is their size. They fool you as to their weight. They are short, chunky, and hefty fish that obviously have ample food, but they fight harder than do some impoundment bass. The hardest fighters are those in the Saluda River and the upper end of the lake.

Greenwood is an old impoundment, one of the two on the Saluda River that twists through South Carolina and eventually joins the Congaree and Broad Rivers near Columbia, the state capital. The other impoundment on the Saluda River is Lake Murray.

Covering 11,400 acres, Greenwood was built as a power reservoir years ago, by the county of Greenwood, and now is owned by Duke Power Co., which still uses it for hydroelectric purposes. The lake is about eighteen miles long, and relatively narrow, being just a bit more than a mile across at its widest point.

Like all ancient impoundments, Greenwood offers special fishing challenges. The lake is so old that there is an absence of deep-structure fishing locales. There are places with 20 to 25-foot water depths, mainly in the old, twisting river channels, but compared to more recent impoundments, Greenwood is classed as a shallow lake. The deepest water is in the lower half of the lake nearest the dam.

There are three general fishing areas, each prime at various times of the year, namely: the Saluda River near the top of the lake; the upper half of the lake above the U.S. 221 bridge; and the lower half near the dam. Each requires a different technique depending upon the time of year.

The Saluda River, which can be fished for some three miles above the lake before becoming too rocky and shallow, is excellent spinner and crank bait water. You also can use plastic worms, but the river's current makes worm fishing more difficult. You have to fish your worm fast, sometimes too fast if the bass are sluggish.

On the river's banks are numerous fallen trees, sunken logs, and frequent rocky outcrops. Each looks like a natural bass holding area. It's obvious this is prime water when conditions are right, when water level is normal with a slight tinge.

When the river is flooding, fishing is difficult, and when it's too low, angling success dwindles. Mud always hampers, and gin-clear water also creates problems.

Where you fish in the lake proper depends upon the time of year. During the spring spawning season, the prime areas are in the back of the coves, which are more numerous in the upper half of the lake. However, the bass spawn wherever they find suitable conditions.

Again in the fall, the bass are found in the shallows near the banks.

However, at this time, you catch more small bass with an occasional lunker.

When the bass aren't in the shallows, the best way to fish Greenwood is to dock or pier hop. Most fishing is done that way. Danny demonstrated the productivity of dock hopping on our second day of exploration. In less than five hours of fishing time, we caught and released eleven bass in the 1 to 2-pound range. All but two were landed with white spinner baits.

However, there obviously are tricks to this dock-hopping angling. If you know some of the quirks, your chances of success are greatly improved, and Greenwood fishing does have quirks. For example, there's a trick to finding the most productive docks. You score most often fishing piers that have brush piles near them, but the brush piles—normally placed to attract speckled perch (crappie)—aren't always where you'd expect.

On some lakes you can automatically assume the piles are at the end of the piers. You can't do this on Greenwood. Instead, in the majority of the cases, the pier owners put their brush piles under their docks. Why? Apparently this seems to be more appealing to the crappie.

Then how do you locate the brush piles? It's not hard. Just check where the pier owner has placed his lights, which not only are used for night crappie fishing, but also for catching the abundant catfish. If the lights are located on the end of the dock, then the brush will be off the end. But if the lights are in the middle of the pier towards the shore, you can be certain the brush has been placed under the middle of the dock.

Danny found that dock fishing gets into high gear as soon as the water temperature reaches sixty degrees. The bass linger around the docks until the heat of the summer when they seek deeper, cooler water.

Like other Greenwood regulars, Danny has developed special techniques for dock hopping. His favorite lures are white spinner baits, either single or double bladed and crank baits, preferably shad or baby bass colors unless the water is dingy. With murky water, he likes crawdad and chartreuse colors.

He also uses plastic worms, the color depending upon the type of day. For bright days, he prefers a blue or red worm, while on dark days, he finds purple-grape or black the best.

Many of the bass, Whaley has observed, are stationary. They won't pursue a meal or wander too far from their sanctuary. If you shove a worm under a bigmouth's nose, he will just inhale it without the normal firm tattletale strike. You don't have time for an eye-crossing, yo-heave setting the hook. Instead, a snap of the wrist does the trick, and either you have an angry bass at the end of your line, or you have missed.

If the brush is located so that flipping isn't needed, Whaley prefers to skip his worm into the area with an underhand cast. For this type of fishing, he uses a 6-inch worm rigged Texas-style with a 2/0 hook, and a 3/16ths of an ounce sinker. Short worms generally are preferred by most Greenwood bass fishermen.

The type of day also influences how you fish, according to Danny. On dark days, the fish are found along the edges of the docks, but on bright ones they concentrate under the middle of the dock in the deepest shade.

Early in the spring and again in the fall, your second choice fishing locations are the numerous points and the ripraps along each point, along the causeways of the two bridges spanning the lake.

In either location, you fish fast. If you don't score with a crank or spinner bait within a hundred feet of each point, Danny says move. You aren't going to find fish there. The action either starts immediately, or there is none.

Positioning your boat is the key to fishing the points and riprap successfully. You should position your boat in such a way that you are retrieving in the same direction the water is moving.

Bass lie facing into the current looking for a bait fish meal. By casting and retrieving with the current, your lure gets the bigmouth's attention, and often a strike. But if you retrieve against the current, your lure comes up behind the bass and usually spooks it rather than provoking a strike.

Danny found that when the fish come from the deep to shallow water to feed, they are found on both sides of the point, or at the corner of riprap. Most fish are found near points and riprap adjacent to 20 to 25 feet of water.

Each dock presents a different problem. If the brush is so abundant that it comes to the edge of the dock, Danny first tries a spinner bait, then a crank bait, and finally resorts to flipping a worm into the brush.

He's found that running a spinner or buzz bait alongside the dock and brush is very effective. Then there are times when a crank bait will do better.

When Whaley's tournament fishing on Greenwood (or on any lake where dock fishing is important), he rigs two rods with specially tuned crank baits. One bait is tuned to run to the left, the other to run to the right so that the lure can be retrieved close to the brush on either side of the dock. Sometimes getting just a few inches closer to the dock is the key to success.

He has found that this crank bait system works well when the fish are loose and not concentrated in one area under a dock. It's especially effective after a weather front has passed.

If these lures don't produce, then he resorts to flipping a worm into the middle of the brush, and letting it drop. If there is an eager bass, the hit usually comes on the fall, and then the brawl begins with the odds in favor of the fish in the brush.

You need a minimum of twelve-pound test line, regardless of the size of fish, because it is impossible to haul a bass out from a dock without dragging line across either the brush or against the pilings. It is easy to weaken a line with such abuse.

During the heat of summer, the best way to fish Greenwood is by trolling. Evidence that trolling is productive is presented by Cecil Tollison of Greenville, South Carolina, who has landed seven bass over 8 pounds while trolling during the heat. He has the patience to troll using Bomber and Waterdog lures.

The secrets of trolling are patience (it sometimes takes hours to score) and the ability to bump the bottom with deep-diving lures. You have to bump the bottom to score because the fish are deep. The best results come from carefully following the old winding river channel. A depth finder helps you to stay where the fish are found in the twisting channel.

The year-round summary of Greenwood goes like this: The January-to-March period can produce good fishing if the winter isn't too severe and the water doesn't get below fifty-two degrees. The successful lures are deep-running crank baits with green or blue backs and with silver sides.

This combination is similar to the threadfin shad which are a major part of the bass diet. Eight to ten-pound test lines are preferred in order to get the lure to run at maximum depth. Deep Wee Rs, Bagley's deep divers, and other deep-diving lures score as long as they resemble shad. You also can use Little George-type tailspinners. Worms are seldom used.

You locate the bass off corners of riprap and off points near 25 feet of water by fishing your lures parallel to the shoreline. Naturally, you position your boat to retrieve with the current or with the wind.

During the April-to-June period, the situation changes. Spinner and buzz baits become the number one lure with plastic worms second, shallow-running crank baits third, and top-water lures fourth. The prime months for top-water plugging are late in May and in June. Such lures as the Devils Horse in various colors and Chugger spooks are popular. You also can use Tiny Torpedoes, Nip-A-Diddee and other single and double propeller plugs. Blipping balsa and plastic minnow-type lures on the surface also is good.

Danny prefers white spinner baits for all types of water, using both one-quarter and one-half ounce lures. He is so fond of white spinner baits that he will vary the blade size before going to a different color.

You find the fish around the boat docks and in the back of coves both before and after spawning. Spring is a time when the lake can quickly get murky, even downright muddy, from the rains. In muddy water, most anglers prefer to use spinner baits with larger than normal blades in order to attract the bass.

With worms, a heavier weight often is needed during April through June. For dock fishing, the ³⁄₁₆th of an ounce lead is preferred, but for fishing elsewhere, most anglers use a quarter ounce.

During July through September, trolling is the best method, with most of the fishing being down in the deepest part of the lake near the dam. In this area, the points have a lot of stumps, and these are potential bass hideouts.

If you don't want to troll, then you can fish deep with worms using the Carolina rig, with Hopkins-type spoons, with Little George-type tailspinners, and with deep-diving crank baits. The crank baits are most effective fished off points early in the morning before the bass return to deep water after dawn feeding.

The last quarter of the year has one of the best months—October. The fish are moving back into the creeks and coves, and are found along the riprap and docks. Crank baits are the primary lures for fishing off points, while spinner baits are tops for fishing around brush. Plastic worms rate third when fishing around docks.

As the water cools, the fishing techniques become the same as during the January-to-March period. Deep-running crank baits and fast-sinking tailspinners are the main lures.

When fishing for black bass, don't be surprised to tangle with white bass or stripers (rockfish). Both have been stocked in Greenwood, and they can surprise you with their sudden strikes.

Danny and I experienced this unexpectedly. We were fishing the riprap near the lake's upper bridge when Danny got a hard hit. We were under the bridge, not the best place to encounter a scrappy fish.

"Get the net!" hollered Danny. "I got a real wall mount this time!"

But when I netted the fish, it wasn't a black bass but a 3-pound white that had fooled Danny with the hard strike. A short time later, I got a smaller white as the school swept through the area.

You can imagine what it would be like to tangle with a 5 to 10-pound striper unexpectedly. It certainly would send your adrenalin soaring.

Greenwood is locally famous for its crappie fishing. During the cooler months—October through April—it is possible to consistently catch crappie (speckled perch) in the 2 to 3-pound range. But in warm weather, you get only small fish.

During the prime season, live minnows and tiny jigs are the favored lures. In the summer, minnows are favored by the crappie experts.

Greenwood may not have any publicity men, but it has black bass. And if you tangle with one of the stripers that have been stocked, hang onto your rod!

# 8

# Bass Hole in the
# South Carolina Mountains

Tucked away in the mountains where the Blue Ridge begin to fade into the northwestern corner of South Carolina is a little-known, young bass hole that is slowly reaching its potential. It is Lake Keowee—800 feet above sea level—and it has already produced a lake record bass weighing 14 pounds, 1 ounce.

Lake Keowee was made in the 1970s by Duke Power Company to be used for its Keowee-Toxaway hydroelectric and nuclear power plant near the town of Seneca. Many expected immediate fishing success. But in the early years, Lake Keowee failed to live up to its expectations and several major bass tournaments held on the lake were disasters. Even the pros couldn't catch fish.

However, the lake's bass population began to develop when an adequate food supply was provided by the South Carolina Wildlife Resources Department. When a sizeable population of threadfin shad finally was established, Keowee bass began to thrive. Now 8 and 9-pound bass are caught, and who knows how much bigger the fish may be that roam the lake.

Lake Keowee is developing as a good bass lake, although not a highly publicized one. According to many of the local anglers who have a choice of fishing either Clark Hill, Lake Hartwell, Keowee, or Lake Secession, Keowee rates second behind Clark Hill, which is generally considered the prime bass lake in the area.

Today, Lake Keowee covers 18,750 acres. It is approximately half a mile wide in places, twenty-three miles long, and it has 225 miles of meandering and forested shoreline with numerous deep coves. It was formed by damming the Keowee and Little Rivers. The name Keowee comes from a Cherokee Indian word meaning the place of the mulberrries, and mulberries still are found growing wild in the surrounding forest.

Keowee is located in one of the most historic regions of South Carolina. The lake now covers the onetime capital of the Lower Cherokee Nation. In the eighteenth century, the area was known as the Pendleton District. Today, the eighteenth century district has been carved into the modern counties of Anderson, Oconee, and Pickens. The little-known town of Pendleton with its picturesque eighteenth-century village green remains as a link with the historic past.

Keowee is a challenging lake. Fed by pure mountain streams, it is a gin-clear pool most of the time, and the bass are spooky, as bass usually are in clear water. Lighter lines are essential. Lines testing more than twelve pounds more often than not scare the fish.

After sampling Keowee with a group of experienced local fishermen including Danny Whaley, Sam and Mike Hanvey, Kent Cole, Eddie Rodelsperger, Ed Drake, and Rodney Morgan, some of the quirks of fishing this mountain pool became obvious.

It is a lake that requires you adjust your fishing techniques to the calendar. During our fall explorations, we depended upon crank and spinner baits and worms to score. The crank downs were the most productive, but that isn't always the case.

Because of the clarity of the water, light-colored lures are favored I've found that an all-white crank bait was effective but that the usually effective crawdad color was useless. Water clarity was the explanation.

As with any lake, success depends upon locating the bass. It is sometimes very difficult in Keowee because of the hydroelectric operations which cause the water level to fluctuate more than in natural lakes. As a result, the fish shift locations more often.

Extensive electric generation can lower the lake rapidly, and the bass change their locations in a hurry. However, moving water is an advantage in certain areas where it causes the bait fish to move more than normal.

The bass are found all over the lake. Sometimes you find them in the narrow coves. Sometimes they are off rocky points, and sometimes they are in deep water. While the time of year is a major factor in where the bass are located, water level is equally important.

After fishing the lake, and numerous discussions with Keowee-wise anglers, the pattern as to how to fish the lake the year around becomes apparent.

The calendar rundown goes like this:

During the cold months of January through March, you can score by fishing the deep water near the dam, locally known as the "Hot Hole." This is where the water returns to the lake after being used in the cooling operations of the electric generating plant. During the cold South Carolina winter, the water in this part of the lake is much warmer than elsewhere. The bass seek the warmest water and gather in the area.

The "Hot Hole" has a maximum depth of about 70 feet, but most of the bass are caught in 40 to 50 feet of water, mainly by yo-yoing your lure up and down below your boat. You don't have to cast. Instead, you merely drop your lure over the side of your boat, and jig the lure up and down. The bass are suspended, and if the lure falls close to them, look out!

You can use a variety of lures for this yo-yo fishing including six-inch worms with heavy sinkers, usually black-grape in color; jigs with Maribou skirts; and Hopkins-type or slab spoons that will sink fast. Lines should be fourteen- or seventeen-pound test because with this deep fishing water clarity is not a great problem. Forty feet down the bass aren't inclined to be spooky.

There are also numerous underwater islands submerged when the lake was filled. These sometimes are good bass-holding waters during the cold weather period. Again most Keowee anglers prefer the yo-yo technique of fishing.

During the April-to-June period, the situation changes. The fish no longer are concentrated in the deep water. Instead, they move back into the shallow coves, and most are caught in water up to 5 feet deep. During the spawning, you find the bigmouths in even shallower water wherever spawning conditions are right.

You begin the spring period by fishing crank baits through the middle of sunken trees, around stickups in deeper water, and off sharp points, particularly where creeks once entered the old river channels.

Sometimes the bass decide to suspend, and then it is necessary to use lighter line to keep your crank baits from running too deep, according to Danny Whaley who specializes in crank baits and spinner

In fishing Lake Keowee in the South Carolina foothills, you need a full tackle box. Shallow-running balsa lures are particularly effective in the back of the coves during the spawning season in the spring. Kent Cole and Ed Drake are shown landing a scrappy Keowee bass.

bait fishing. The most popular crank bait colors are crawdad, frog, Tennessee shad, and white.

Late in April, top-water lures begin to produce. It is profitable to work a top-water floater or a shallow diver around the top of a stickup. Oddly, it's often the lone stickup that holds the bass, not a clump. You also can fish over grass beds in the shallows. The bass are usually found in 5 feet or less water.

During this period, the bass come off the beds and can be particularly aggressive. They are hungry and mean. April and May are the prime months to fish Keowee, and this is when fish in the 8- and 9-pound classes are boated. Among the favored top-water lures are balsa lures such as Bagley and Rapala manufacture; shallow-diving plastic minnows à la Rebel and Norman; top-water propeller plugs including Devils Horse, Tiny Torpedo, Nip-A-Diddee, Bomber, Buck 'N Brawl, and other prop lures; stick baits—Carrott Top and Devils Toothpick, or Bomber—and chuggers such as Heddon Creek Chub and others also produce.

Sometimes the double propeller lures are the most productive, at other times they seem too noisy, and you need to go to single prop lures or stick baits. You have to experiment to discover just what will arouse the bass.

Many use ¼- and ½-ounce spinner baits. Both single and double blade models are popular with white, white and chartreuse, and white and green skirts working best in the normally clear water.

There is also a great deal of use for a special plastic worm called the "Fish Finder." It's only 4-inches long with two exposed hooks, but Keowee anglers find that it is deadly. Since they are fishing comparatively clear water with few snags, they can use open hooks. Green is the most popular color.

The summer—July through September—is the toughest fishing period. The fish are in deep water, and locating them often is difficult. Once you locate the bass, you have to jig for them, either with spoons such as Mr. Champ or Hopkins, or Little George tailspinners, or with worms with heavy leads.

Your worm color depends upon the type of day. On cloudy days, Keowee experts prefer a dark-colored worm—such as black, dark purple, or dark blue. However, on bright days, lighter colors such as ice blue, pale purple, or chartreuse are favored.

Most anglers use the Texas-style weedless rig, and the secret is to cast to the bank and work your worm slowly into the deeper water. You need to feel the bottom as you slowly retrieve your worm.

Worms are either four or six-inch and fished with ⅛-ounce slip sinker. The big worms used on other waters have not proved successful on Keowee as yet, although the time may come when they will score.

In this hot weather period, the cagey anglers often resort to dragging a worm rigged Carolina-style down the middle of deep channels. With this type of trolling, you can cover a lot of territory, and it is an effective way to locate the bass.

The Carolina-rig is particularly effective for this type of fishing. It utilizes a three-way swivel. To one ring is attached a heavy egg sinker on approximately twelve inches of monofilament line. To the other ring is attached a floating plastic worm on eighteen inches of line, and the third is connected to your main line.

With the sinker bumping along the bottom, the worm floats some eighteen inches above, and the bottom prowling bass are intrigued by the offering. However, it takes skill to detect a soft pickup with the sinker bumping bottom. But when a bass really takes the worm you know it, pronto! You also can bottom-bounce by using a heavy egg sinker attached to your main line above a swivel to which a floating worm and hook are attached on an eighteen to twenty-inch mono leader. As the sinker drags bottom the worm floats free.

During the last quarter of the year, the fish begin moving to deeper water and most bass are caught in 20 to 25 feet. Most Keowee regulars regard these months as a prime time for plastic worms. You have to get your worm down to the fish, which means you need a heavy lead.

However, some anglers score with the deepest running crank baits, and a few bump heavy spinner baits along the bottom. You have to have a half-ounce spinner bait to do this successfully, and single blades sink faster than do tandems. The big problem is getting your lure down to the fish. Deep jigging with jigs or Hopkins-type spoons also will work.

Access to Keowee is convenient with 11 paved ramps that are strategically located around the lake. The ramps are Warpath, South Cove, Watergate Marina, Cane Creek, High Falls, Stamp Creek, Keowee Town, Fall Creek, Crowe Creek, Mile Creek, and Gap Hill. A free map of the lake showing the launching sites can be obtained from Duke Power Company, Box 2178, 422 S. Church St., Charlotte, N.C., 29242.

There's little danger of getting lost on the lake despite its length, but you can get misplaced. Each of the hundreds of coves look alike, and caution is advised when exploring the upper end of coves because the water level fluctuates according to the generating requirements.

You have no problem finding accommodations during a trip to Keowee. There are motels in Anderson and Clemson. However, if you are staying in the latter town make certain you have an advance reservation if you're going to be there during a Clemson University home football game. The Clemson Tigers have devoted followers. They swarm into the area from all over the state for football weekends.

If you have a camping rig, or want to rent a cabin, the Oconee State Park is only half an hour drive from Keowee. The Park has rental cabins (each with a fireplace) and ample camping facilities. Reservations can be made c/o Superintendent, Oconee State Park, Star Route, Walhalla, S.C., 29691, telephone (803) 638-5353.

Additional information concerning Lake Keowee can be obtained from the Duke Power Co., P.O. Box 2178, 422 Church St., Charlotte, N.C. 28242; SC Department of Parks, Recreation and Tourism, E.A. Brown Building, 1205 Pendleton St., Columbia, S.C., 29201; S.C. Wild-

life and Marine Resources Dept., P.O. Box 167, Columbia, SC, 29202;
or Pendleton District Historic and Recreation Commission, P.O. Box
234, Pendleton, S.C. 29670.

Lake Keowee is a little-ballyhooed bass hole but the bass are there
and are growing. If you want the challenge of fishing in the mountains,
Keowee offers a stiff one.

# 9

# Lake Secession—Little Known Bass Hole

The answers you get when you ask about fishing possibilities in unfamiliar waters is amazing. Instead of recommending some highly publicized lake or river, local anglers more often than not suggest little-known waters, waters you've never heard about.

This has been my typical experience in roaming South Carolina. If you corner a knowledgeable Palmetto State bassman and ask him where the chances are best of encountering largemouth, black trophy bass, you are almost certain to be surprised at his answer.

More than likely, he won't name such famous waters as Santee-Cooper, Murray, Greenwood, Hartwell, or Clark Hill. Instead, the odds are that he will suggest Lake Secession, a fishing hole definitely lacking in publicity drum beaters.

Although the lake is shown on the state road maps, it is not named on many of them, and strangers naturally assume it's part of Rocky River. Quiz your South Carolina informant a bit more and you learn that Lake Secession is an impoundment, actually the water reservoir for the city of Abbeville in western South Carolina.

Now a sleepy little town, Abbeville's niche in history is linked with the Civil War. It was the site of one of the first meetings calling for secession from the Union prior to the outbreak of the Civil War. It also was the site of the last meeting of the Confederate cabinet on May 2, 1865. The lake's name resulted from the nineteenth-century secession meeting.

If you are fortunate enough to talk and fish with some of the Lake Secession experts, you will quickly learn that the lake can be red hot, or "it sure can humble you," as Dennis Botts, Ed Perry, and Danny Whaley admit. They are recognized as three of the finest bassmen on the lake, and they know the quirks of this little-known bass hole as few anglers do.

Like most good bass holes, Secession can be fickle. But when in a cooperative mood, it can produce some big fish. Study Bott's fishing log and you get a rough idea of the lake's capabilities.

From this stump-filled lake, which wasn't cleared when built, Botts has landed a 10-pound bass. He has also landed nine bass weighing more than 9 pounds, plus twelve bass over 8 pounds, and another fifteen bass between 7 and 8 pounds. He doesn't keep meticulous records on bass weighing less than 8 pounds. Hard to believe, but true. His tally on 6 and 7-pounders could be even larger. A lake has to be an unusual one for an angler to ignore bass weighing less than 8 pounds. In many places, angling headlines are made with 4 and 5-pound bass, but not on Lake Secession.

Of course, Botts is still trying to equal the lunker bass Ralph Simpson landed from the lake. Simpson's bigmouth weighed 12 pounds, 3 ounces. He was fishing with another Secession veteran, Ed Perry, and landed the trophy using one of the original Bagley Balsa B lures.

Perry's biggest fish in this little known lake tipped the scales at 9½ pounds. He caught it with a plastic worm. One of the most spectacular catches was made by Danny Whaley, who landed a 9-pound, 14-ounce bass on eight-pound test line using a crawdad colored Deep Wee R. Eight-pound test is not recommended for Lake Secession because of the over supply of underwater hazards, but the fishing gods were smiling on Whaley that day. Yes, there obviously are big bass in this little known lake.

But any fisherman immediately wonders why such a lunker hole is so little known. There are a number of reasons. Many anglers, knowing that it can be either red hot or frigid, avoid testing their skills in Lake Secession. They opt for easier angling waters, particularly fishing holes with few underwater snags.

If you ever get a chance to see Secession during a radical drawdown as I did, you would be amazed at the number of standing stumps left in the lake. To think about boating over this jungle of snags sends chills up and down my spine. It is not a lake for high-speed boating if the water is the least bit low.

However, probably a more important cause of Secession's relative obscurity is its geographic location. By happenstance, it has highly publicized competition for the fishing spotlight. To the northwest some twenty-five miles lies sprawling Lake Hartwell on the Savannah River, and about the same distance to the southwest is huge Clark Hill, also on the Savannah River.

When these two impoundments were built in the 1950s and 1960s, they quickly outshown little Secession. Today, the majority of local anglers head for Clark Hill, or Hartwell, particularly the residents of nearby Anderson, largest city in the vicinity. Naturally, bassmen from out of state, having never heard of Secession, head for the big, highly promoted impoundments.

Despite the lack of publicity, or perhaps because of it, Secession has a good bass population. Built in 1941, the 3,460-acre impoundment has a very good population of bigmouths in the 6 to 10-pound range.

Why does such a good bass population exist? Again there are several reasons. The lake has a good population of gizzard and threadfin shad, always popular items on a bigmouth's menu. The gizzard shad can't grow too large because the lake was stocked with rockfish (landlocked stripers of the Santee-Cooper strain), and the big stripers can feast on big shad. Thus there is little chance of the shad taking over the lake. Bass eat one size. Stripers eat all sizes.

Equally important is the abundance of cover or structure. The lake was never cleared, and with the exception of the old channel of the Rocky River, there are towering stumps underwater everywhere. Often these dead trees are ten to fifteen feet tall. Obviously, you need to operate carefully particularly when out of the old river channel, which ranges from 15 to 35 feet in depth. Keep your depth finder on at all times when cruising.

There's another factor—the coves are unusual. These fingers off the main channel have sharp drop-offs until you get two-thirds of the way towards the back. The drop-offs are surprisingly abrupt. Within only a couple of feet of the banks, the water changes to six to nine feet in depth. That's a sudden depth increase. You wouldn't logically expect such a rapid depth change in a cove.

Because of this drop-off, bass, even when chasing bait along the banks, are never more than a few feet from deep-water safety. It is easy to understand why deep-running crank baits are one of the top lures in Secession.

However, despite the abundance of deep water, there are ample shallow spawning areas in the backs of the numerous coves. Even there, the bucketmouths have great safety, for the sandy bottom shallows are so infested with floating logs and debris that you cannot possibly reach the bigmouths consistently with a lure. Even flipping works only in a few places. And if you do hook a hefty bass, the odds are the bigmouth will find a snag or other convenient underwater hazard on which to break your line.

Secession has numerous quirks. For example, it does produce big bass during the hot months. Dennis Botts favorite fishing time is during the heat of summer. Fishing large plastic worms in 17 to 30 feet of water, he has had twenty-five-pound test line broken by fish he couldn't turn. Ed Perry, too, succeeds in the summer by fishing the upper end of the reservoir where the Rocky River enters the impoundment.

However, most locals prefer to seek the lake's big bass in April and May, and again in October and early November, how long in November depending upon the weather.

After fishing the lake and discussing its quirks with Whaley, Botts, and Perry, the annual picture of the angling techniques becomes apparent.

During the cold weather—the January-to-March period, these experts prefer to jig spoons in the bends of the old creek channels, and off rocky points in the main lake. Favored lures for this type of fishing are half-ounce Mr. Champ spoons, and Little George-type tailspinners.

If this period is mild, you also can use crank baits off deep rocky points. By early March, crank baits become the prime lure. Initially, they are fished off the deeper rocky points, then gradually into shallower water in the coves as the bass move towards spawning areas.

Light-colored crank baits such as shad and orange are favored if the day is bright, particularly after the passage of a weather front, and the water is clear. If the lake is murky, then crawdad is the most productive color.

The pattern changes in the April-to-June period. The big fish are caught using crank baits along and over old ditches that were flooded when the reservoir was filled. You need to crank your lure down to maximum depth. When you feel contact with the cover, stop cranking. Often a lunker will hit the slowly rising or suspended lure. Then watch out! Ol' Bigmouth has attacked from cover, and intends to head for safety pronto. Sometimes you head him off. Sometimes you can't. If you fail, you have another yarn about the big one that got away.

During these months, you also can use spinner baits and buzzers. The local anglers prefer spinner baits with large blades. The big blades

When you see Lake Secession during a drawdown you realize the abundant cover available in this little known South Carolina lake. The impoundment was not cleared when it was filled. Although you can expect to foul often, crank and spinner baits do a good job of working their way through the maze. Plastic worms fished with slip leads, too, are effective. Danny Whaley is shown pausing to re-rig after working his bass boat into the back of a cove during a drawdown.

turn slowly, and let the lure gradually descend. The bass seem to hit better with a spinner bait moving slowly.

Both single and tandem blades are used either with silver or copper colors, depending upon the type of water, and the reactions of the bigmouths. Usually silver is preferred in clear water, with copper or gold in murky.

A variety of crank bait colors produce. Selection is a personal choice, and a case of using the color in which you have the most confidence. Popular colors are crawdad (generally rated number one), chartreuse, and baby bass. Some prefer Tennessee shad.

Plastic worms become a valuable lure in April, too. Most anglers prefer eight or nine-inch worms. Big worms mean big fish. There are times, however, when the bigmouths are temperamental, and then the cagey Secession anglers resort to six-inch worms, sometimes with the Carolina rig. Normally, most anglers fish their worms rigged weedless, Texas style.

Black is rated the number one all-around worm color. However, if the water is exceptionally clear, blue becomes a prime hue. Green becomes effective when a green algae develops later in the summer.

During the April-to-June period, the bass are still in the creeks and coves. In April, the bigmouths like to spawn around sweet-gum trees, but beginning in May they move from the shallow cove ends to deeper water near the main lake.

The standard pattern then is to begin by fishing the shallow water in the upper end of the coves. If this doesn't produce, you shift to deeper water nearer the lake, moving until you find the water depth in which the bass are holding.

The real test comes during the July-to-September period. During these months, most anglers fish plastic worms deep during the day, but use the plastic enticers in the shallows early and late in the day.

Dawn and dusk are prime times for top-water lures, and big fish will clobber the surface plugs. Botts caught his largest top-water bass— 8 pounds, 14 ounces—with a small Devils Horse with only two sets of gang hooks.

Any double propeller plug, and frog colored Jitterbugs are productive. Experts toss the waddlers past the willows, and hang onto their rods when the gurgler passes the shady spots.

This is the season when the Rocky River just above the reservoir produces. For some reason, the bigmouths like to hide under the overhanging willows and ambush a passing meal, or a noisy, top-water plug.

September is the toughest month of the warm period because the fish suspend. However, frequently you can locate them using a depth finder. Often you pick up a school of shad on your finder, and when you do, the odds are great that there are bass lurking below.

Lake Secession experts use crank baits such as Deep Wee Rs. They crank them through a school of shad and catch big fish as well as good strings.

During the warm months, you can fish plastic worms successfully around the brush piles off the docks on the main lake. While the brush piles are placed as crappie attractors, they also draw bass, and the most effective lure is the plastic worm.

The final three months of the year see the lake veterans returning to the same pattern used during the spring with the same lures and color combinations. If the water level is high, the bass again are found around the sweet-gum trees, otherwise they're not as far back in the coves.

If the weather turns cold early, then the winter pattern becomes the key, again using spoons and weighted tailspinners.

Although there are no lakeside accommodations, there is one small motel in Abbeville. Anderson, S.C., only fifteen miles to the north, has several chain motels. We've stayed in Anderson when fishing Secession, and also at Hickory Knob State Park, thirty-five miles to the south on the South Carolina shore of Clark Hill impoundment. This is a modern resort park, and makes an ideal base if you want to fish both Lake Secession and Clark Hill.

Additional information can be obtained from the Pendleton District Historical and Recreation Commission, P.O. Box 234, Pendleton, SC 29670; S.C. Wildlife and Marine Resources Dept., P.O. Box 167, Columbia, SC 29202; or the Dept. of Parks, Recreation and Tourism, E.A. Brown Bldg., 1205 Pendleton St., Columbia, SC 29201.

Lake Secession may be overshadowed by the huge impoundments nearby, but it does have lunker bass, and a terrain that challenges any fisherman's expertise. It can "humble you" or provide fabulous fishing.

# 10

# Tantalizing Lake Hartwell

If you ask a veteran angler to describe tantalizing Lake Hartwell in the South Carolina mountain foothills, the odds are great he will say "terrific" or "terrible," depending upon what his luck has been on his most recent trip.

That's a good summary of this 55,950-acre impoundment where the Blue Ridge mountains taper slowly to the highlands of the South Carolina upcountry. You either have fantastic success fishing this clear, deep lake, or you wish you had stayed at home. Fishing fortunes here are as fickle as on any of the Southeastern waters.

If you have an experience like Ed Perry and Ron Chistenbury did one night, you would be in anglers' heaven. In two hours, they fought eleven largemouth black bass, weighing up to 4 pounds, plus twelve hybrid bass, the latter weighing from 6 to 8 pounds.

For two hours, they were mighty busy anglers flipping a green and white Devils Horse and a white Striper Swiper into the schooling fish that had hemmed a school of bait fish. There is nothing more exciting in bass fishing than encountering schooling bass that will hit surface lures with abandon.

Or if you hit a bonanza like Bill Hughes and Bud Payne of Anderson did one day, the fishing is fantastic. One April—always a prime month on Hartwell—they caught forty-four largemouths with plastic worms and kept twenty, the South Carolina limit. That is fantastic worm fishing.

However, such fantastic catches are not daily occurences on this big mountain lake. They do occur for anglers who know how, where, and when to fish. It takes more than just general knowledge to score along the 962 miles of shoreline. That's a lot of fishing territory.

Not only can fantastic catches be made, but you also can tangle with hefty bass, often over 10 pounds. Bill Hughes' personal record is 11½ pounds. He caught it one October while fishing a six-inch purple firetail worm in eight feet of water.

As with any fishing water, it helps to know the history. The lake was formed by the Hartwell dam, located seven miles below the junction of the Tugaloo and Seneca rivers, fifteen miles southwest of Anderson, S.C. and five miles east of the town of Hartwell, Ga. The Tugaloo and Seneca join and form the headwaters of the Savannah river, the border between South Carolina and Georgia.

The reservoir extends up the Tugaloo past Toccoa to the Yonah Dam. In these upper reaches, you can have a field day in the spring catching white bass and hybrids during the spawning run. To the north cast, the lake extends up the Seneca River to the city of Clemson and beyond to the headwaters of the Seneca formed by Twelve-Mile Creek and the Keowee River. Major creeks flow into the huge lake from all sides.

The Hartwell Dam is an enormous structure, the concrete portions extending 1,900 feet, and the earthen embankments 13,356 feet, making the total length 17,790 feet. The concrete dam, completed in 1963, is 204 feet above the river bed.

Because it is located in mountain valleys, Hartwell does not have miles and miles of shallows such as are found in some impoundments. This has an important influence on fishing techniques. When the reservoir was filled, the waters backed up into the numerous narrow valleys which had been carved through the centuries by the tumbling mountain streams.

The valleys are deep Vs with steep sides, and where the little mountain creeks still tumble are prime fishing areas at certain times of the year. Bass do like moving water. Knowing which cove is creek fed simplifies locating good fishing waters.

While cove fishing is important at certain times of the year, on the whole Hartwell is classified as a deep-water impoundment, and deep-water fishing techniques apply. Deep-water bass here are like deep-water bass anywhere, and the proven techniques do produce, perhaps with minor local modifications.

After several discussions and fishing trips with such local bass experts as Danny Whaley, Bill Hughes, Ed Perry, and Henry White, several facets of Hartwell fishing become apparent. One factor is their preference for small, plastic worms. They rate the four and six-inch worms as the number one size, with the seven-inch sometimes being used.

Bigger worms are not used. Why? They have no statistical evidence to back their opinions, but from experience they have learned Hartwell bass hit small worms better. They theorize it's because the fish are accustomed to small meals.

Another factor influencing worm size is the lake's clarity. Normally Hartwell is gin clear. The bass don't spook as readily upon sighting or hearing the splash of a small worm as they do when a nine-incher lands.

While most anglers prefer the plastic worm virtually year around, there are others such as Danny Whaley who prefer spinner and crank baits. They score, too. Whaley particularly likes to fish these lures early in the spring and late in the fall, cranking them down off riprapped shorelines and around rocky points, areas the bigmouths frequently haunt.

But moving water is the key to crank downs and spinner baits. When the Hartwell hydroelectric plant is operating, the water flow pulls the plankton and bait fish off the rocks, and the bass are there waiting for a meal.

Another trick that Whaley has learned is that after you catch two or three fish off a section of rocks or a point, action stops. He theorizes that with the water gradually falling during generation, and no cover available, the bass retreat into deeper water. It's logical. Normally, you would think that fishing was over in that particular area, but Danny has learned that if you return to a successful fishing spot a couple of hours later, the bass return to feed again.

The secrets of scoring on sprawling Lake Hartwell are knowing where and when to fish. All of the local anglers agree that if you don't fish the right spots at the right times, you will not score.

An idea of how you have to change your fishing techniques is shown by the local experts' review of the calendar and the type of lures to use at various times. In the January-to-March quarter, when it really gets cold in this part of the country, those anglers who are brave enough to don insulated underwear and winter gear generally prefer to do most of their fishing by vertically jigging Hopkins-type spoons, or Little George-type tailspinners.

On warm sunny days, when the water temporarily warms causing the fish to move up into shallow cover, you can score with crank-down baits such as Rebel's Deep Wee Rs, Bagley's deep divers in balsa, and Big-O types in general. You also can use plastic worms fished deep with heavy sinkers.

Favored lure colors are crawdad and shad. Worm colors vary including purple with red tails, blue with glow tails, purple with white dots, black, and strawberry. Who knows some other oddball color may be the answer on your next trip. Try 'em all, if you don't find the right combination immediately.

Most fishermen use the Texas-style weedless rig, although a few prefer hooks with the wire weed guard. There is also extensive use of the Carolina rig with a ¼ ounce sinker. Bill Hughes finds that he catches more bass with the worm suspended off the bottom. However, others prefer the slip sinker system.

During January, you have to fish deep water, holes 25 to 40 feet deep with various types of structure. Generally, the holes are not near the main river channel. Sometimes they are, and sometimes they are located in coves.

Normally, the fishing pattern begins to change in February. Some fish find their way into the coves. The secret is to look for dingy water. When you find slightly discolored water with the right temperature, you often score.

Although the lake has numerous coves, each has its own characteristics. For example, in Fair Play creek which empties into the Tugaloo River on the Georgia side, the fish begin hitting earlier than in other coves. Some coves are better spawning grounds.

By March, the pattern shifts more. You find the fish in the central river area around rocky points, old road beds with submerged trees and debris, and in up to 15 feet of water.

The April-to-June period, which also is the peak season for hybrids and white bass, is the peak for black bass. Some anglers rate the worm as the number one lure then, while others prefer crank baits. This is also the period when Little-George-type tailspinners, and Doll Flies (jigs) are used. Crank bait colors are shad, crawdad, or chartreuse.

Now the fish are on the banks in up to ten feet of water. You still fish around rocky points, riprap, and close to the shore *if* the water is dingy. Water color is a key to successful fishing at Hartwell. You do best when you can find fishable waters that are not window-glass clear.

In May, the bass are bedding, usually in five to eight feet of water. During this time, they can be particularly aggravating, just knocking the lure away from the beds. They are difficult to hook. This is when a natural bait—spring lizards—is productive. The bass hate the lizards and try to kill them when you fish lizards near the beds. But there's a secret to hooking—don't strike too soon. You have to give the bass time to kill the lizard.

In June, the largemouths begin schooling. This can start as early as the latter part of May depending upon the weather. You find the fish around submerged structures and underwater islands, but close to deep water. During the day, the bass are found in water from 12 to 15 feet deep. Early and late they come into the shallows to feed.

In the upper end of the lake, where the water often is murky in the spring, you can do well with spinner baits and crank downs, while in the lower end, which tends to be much clearer, you often can use top-water lures. Among the popular ones are balsa shallow divers such as Bagleys or Rapalas, or the same type lure in plastic such as Rebel and Norman. Shallow points and brushy creek banks are prime fishing areas for this type of top-water lure. Some have success with propeller plugs such as Tiny Torpedo, Nip-A-Diddee, Bomber, and Devils Horse.

Hartwell veterans regard the July-to-September period as the tough test, although you can catch fish if you work at it. During this period, many troll with deep-diving lures. The lure color depends upon the color of the water. Again dingy water is preferred.

Bigmouths can be best caught at night using dark-colored worms when you can find brush in 10 to 25 feet of water, particularly around sunken islands near creek channels. During the day, your best chances are in the heavy cover in the more stained waters far up the Seneca and Tugaloo rivers. Plastic worms are generally preferred for this type of cover fishing, although you also can use buzz baits, or buzz spinner baits through the brush.

Come mid-September, the fishing pattern alters. The bass begin returning to the rocky points as the water cools. You now find them in 10 to 15 feet of water, and the same holds true during October.

As fall arrives and the trees begin to turn color, you also find the bucketmouths around old road beds, gulleys, and the same rocky points they favored in late September. Fall also is the time for schooling hybrids, and largemouths and white bass also can be found chasing shad. This can be some of the most exciting fishing of the year.

When a harried school is located—you can tell from the frantic surface action—almost any lure will produce when thrown into the melee. But the old standbys such as Hopkins-type jigs, Eppinger and

Cleo-type spoons, and Little George-type tailspinners, as well as Rat-L-Traps and Spot sinking lures will score most often.

The final two months of the year find the bigmouths preferring deep holes, up to 50 feet. Again they want structure around the holes. In December, the producing holes are usually the main channels. This again is the time for vertical fishing. Deep jigging with Hopkins-type spoons, worms with jig heads, and spinner baits allowed to bounce off the bottom produce. There is also some use of worms with heavy slip sinkers.

There is a Hartwell bonus fish that sometimes surprises bass anglers—the scrappy hybrids, now officially labeled by the International Game Fish Association as whiterock bass. The cross of a white bass and a striper (rockfish) is a fighting fool, although it won't jump like a black bass. But underwater it is a rugged fighter, rated by many as a harder battler than a black bass. The whiterocks hit the same lures as do black bass, and they also school with the blacks and the whites.

The hybrids, which are stocked annually in the lake because they cannot reproduce, thrive on the abundant shad population, and grow rapidly. It is not unusual to catch them weighing six to eight pounds, and frequently you encounter whiterocks weighing 15 pounds or more.

During the spring, the whiterocks school and move into the coves fed by the creeks and then return to the big water. Often you find them schooling on the surface just as the rock and white bass do.

During the summer, a popular and effective way to catch the hybrids is to fish under the bridges. Hartwell anglers anchor beneath the bridges and hang a lantern over the side to attract the bait fish. Shad come for the bait fish, and the hybrids and blacks come to feast on the shad.

Most anglers catch shad with nets, and use them for bait. At times, the action can be frantic, with huge catches being made. Often the bridges look like miniature cities because there are so many boats with lighted lanterns anchored around the bridge supports.

The fish attractors which have been placed by the Corps of Engineers and the South Carolina Wildlife and Marine Resources Department further enhance the fishing. A total of twenty fish attractors have been installed, and their locations are shown on the Hartwell map. The map and an informational pamphlet can be obtained by writing Resource Manager, P.O. Box 278, Hartwell Lake, Hartwell, Ga. 30643, telephone (404) 376-4788.

Georgia and South Carolina have a reciprocal license agreement: a license from either state is all you need to fish in Hartwell Lake or its tailwater. Residents of other states may purchase a nonresident fishing license from either Georgia or South Carolina. Fishermen with nonresident Georgia or resident Georgia licenses do need a Georgia trout stamp if they have trout in their possession on the Georgia shore.

Interstate 85 crosses several arms of the lake, and motels are found in Hartwell and Lavonia, Georgia, and in Clemson and Anderson, South Carolina. Make certain you have reservations during fall weekends if you're staying at Clemson. Also, there are eighty-one boat ramps at strategic points around the lake.

If you have a camping rig, you can utilize state parks such as Sadlers Creek in South Carolina and Tugaloo and Hart on the Georgia shore. There are several camping areas under the jurisdiction of the U.S. Corps of Engineers.

Hartwell is a fine bass lake for thinking anglers. The fish are there, but locating and hooking is a real challenge.

# 11

# Cove Hopping Brings
# Clark Hill Success

Danny Whaley flipped his half-ounce spinner bait past the thick brush pile quickly beginning a deliberate below surface retrieve in one of the nameless coves dotting the shoreline of the Clark Hill reservoir on the Savannah River. Shared by South Carolina and Georgia, the massive impoundment is a famous fishing hole which annually produces its share of angling headlines.

Just as the spinner fell after easing over a submerged limb, he felt the strike. Savagely he set the hook. The water was only two and a half feet, and the bass had no choice but to jump, and jump it did! At once, Danny knew he was in trouble. This was no bass to hand land. Also he could see the hook wasn't too firmly embedded. The spinner bait was dangling from the bass' mouth.

"Get the net!" he called to his wife, who was fishing with him that day.

That was easier said than done. His wife wasn't familiar with his new bass boat, and the net was stowed in a hard to reach locker. While she tried to extract the net, Danny had problems battling his fish. Cagily, the bass tried to go around the trolling motor, but Danny got the motor up and out of the way in time. Again the fish jumped. Danny applied maximum pressure hoping his tackle would hold. This wasn't a small bass. The fish continued wallowing, and finally his wife freed the net, as the bigmouth made a third leap.

Just in time, his wife got the net over the side and Danny led his prize into it. Then he sat down to quiet his nerves. He had every reason to be jumpy. The fish weighed 8 pounds. When an 8-pounder starts jumping, you are often in trouble. Fortunately, Danny conquered his trouble.

The incident is typical of what you often encounter while cove hopping in Clark Hill, the 70,000-acre reservoir on the Savannah River, the boundary between South Carolina and Georgia.

The reservoir was built as a hydroelectric impoundment between 1946 and 1954, and since completion, it has been one of the most famous fishing areas in the Southeast. Unlike so many reservoirs that peak in five to seven years after filling, and then decline as fishing areas, Clark Hill has been a consistent fish producer. It is noted for its hefty bass, crappie, and bream.

Its angling menu has been expanded by the stocking of white bass, rainbow trout, and hybrid bass. The latter was developed by South Carolina fish biologists by crossing the striper (striped bass or rockfish) with the white bass.

When you're fishing for black bass, you sometimes have surprising encounters with whites and hybrids, for the three fish often school together. When you encounter a hybrid (or whiterock bass), you meet a hard-fighting fish. The all tackle world record for the whiterock bass is 20 pounds. It was caught at the old city lock and dam above Augusta in the Savannah River. The fish originally was stocked in Clark Hill, or in its tailwaters.

Located twenty-two miles upstream from Augusta, Georgia, Clark Hill is big, one of the largest impoundments east of the Mississippi River. With 1,200 miles of shoreline and a great variation in water depth and bass cover, it requires different fishing techniques at different times of the year.

The sprawling reservoir stretches forty miles up the Savannah River, twenty-nine miles up Georgia's Little River, and seventeen miles up South Carolina's Little River, as well as six and one-half miles up the Broad River. There is ample fishing terrain if you know how to utilize it.

The presence of two Little Rivers can be confusing to a visiting angler seeking local fishing information. If a local tells you the bass are hitting in Little River, make certain you know which river is meant.

In the spring and again in the fall, Clark Hill bass are often found way back in the numerous covers of the reservoir. Although often in shallow water, they're always under thick cover, and you need to work a spinner bait skillfully to score. Danny Whaley is shown with an 8-pounder that hit his spinner bait savagely.

They are several miles apart. Going to the wrong river can be an aggravating boat ride.

During the spring of the year and again in the fall, cove hopping is a very productive bass fishing technique. Several trips with Danny showed this facet of Clark Hill angling to me, but there are tricks to this type of fishing. It's more than just heading for a cove and throwing lures.

Danny prefers to fish the coves during the spring, usually in April and May, and then again in the fall. The latter is usually the October-to-December period, or until they begin lowering the lake. The Corps of Engineers drops the lake five feet in the fall in order to be able to handle the winter's rain and snow. When the reservoir is lowered, the bass naturally head for deeper water in the main lake.

There is a natural reason for the black bass being in the coves. The bait fish head for the shallows as soon as the water begins to warm in the spring, and the bass follow their chow line.

But not all coves are productive, even though they may appear to be. Danny prefers to fish coves which have creeks emptying into them because the supply of oxygen is better. "Wet weather" creeks, those little streams that run after a rain, are his second choice. When running, these, too, provide greater amounts of oxygen and are better holding waters.

Smart fishermen use their depth finders when probing a creek, for in all of them you find a crude channel. However, these twist and turn unpredictably. Often these narrow channels are where the fish stay, but not always.

As a rule, Danny finds during the spring you do best fishing the button bushes way back in the creeks. This is spinner bait territory. Other types of lures are too prone to foul in the brush. A worm is second choice, but doesn't seem to stir up the bass as a whirling spinner bait does.

However, in the fall, your chances are best when fishing the edge of the creek channels. Knowing where the channel edges are is mighty important. Naturally, you fish both brush and channels either in the spring or fall. If the bass aren't in one area, they will be in the other. However, in either case, you are fishing shallow water. Most creeks are only four feet deep in the channels, and become much more shallow in their upper ends.

Your lure selection for cove fishing is limited by the submerged hazards. Number one choice of most anglers is a spinner bait. Some prefer single blades, others tandem, and at times surface buzz baits.

Usually the ⅜th of an ounce lure is preferred for clear water and the ½ ounce for murky.

The second lure choice is the reliable plastic worm, usually the six-inch length, fished with the lightest possible sinker. The preferred colors are purple, black, blue, and sometimes strawberry. Selecting worm colors is a matter of determining what the bass want.

A third lure that sometimes can be used when fishing a channel in a cove is a shallow-running crank bait such as Rebel's Wee R or Bagley's balsa Shad. Again, colors vary depending upon what the bass want. Shad and crawdad colors are particularly popular.

While cove hopping is very productive, it does cover only certain periods of the year, and to fish Clark Hill successfully, you've got to be able to adapt. Whaley points out the obvious fact that the fish aren't always in the coves, and that you have to be able to fish elsewhere depending upon the season.

His run down for fishing the rest of the year goes like this:

During the winter—January through March—most bigmouths are caught around rocky points in up to 25 feet of water. During January, they move very little being sluggish in the cold water. However, beginning in February, the bigmouths become more mobile. Then they are usually around rocky points where creek channels bend or enter the main lake.

Deep-diving crank baits are particularly good during this period with the blue and green backs, the color of the shad at this time of year. Also this is the time to try Little George-type spinners and heavy spoons as well as plastic worms.

The April-to-June quarter—one of the prime periods for cove hopping—sees a change in tactics with spinner baits becoming the number one lure followed by shallow-running crank baits in various colors. This too, is the time for the biggest bass, and for some reason the bigmouths are caught first in the Georgia Little River arm of the lake.

Local anglers theorize that this happens because the water warms faster in Georgia's Little River. Unlike the upper end of the lake, Georgia's Little River does not have any great number of feeder streams introducing cold water in the spring. Hence, the water warms faster and the big bass move in earlier as they prepare to spawn.

In addition to spinner and crank baits, this is the time to use floating worms without weights. Most anglers fish them rigged weedless Texas-style, although hooks with wire weed guards work well, too.

Tactics change again for the hot weather months of July through

September. During this time, you fish the drop-offs near the main river channel, but the depths vary according to your location on the lake. In the upper end, the best depths are from 17 to 25 feet, but in the lower—deeper—end, the fish are often caught in 30 feet of water. The depths at which they suspend depend upon the water's oxygen content.

As fall arrives, you change your tactics again, this time utilizing deep-diving crank baits. You're looking for long sloping rocky points close to deep water. Little George-type lures also produce. Some anglers prefer to use fast sinking spoons.

Deluxe accommodations are not always found on good fishing waters, but they are at Clark Hill. If you want to stay in luxury, then headquarter at Hickory Knob State Park, a resort-destination park of the South Carolina Department of Parks, Recreation, and Tourism. The park has motel rooms, comparable to any major motel chain, as well as deluxe rental cabins.

The park also has docking facilities with fuel and a tackle shop. This is where we generally stay. Hickory Knob is particularly popular during the warm months, and reservations are essential. They can be made by writing Superintendent, Hickory Knob State Park, Rt 1, Box 199-B, McCormick, SC 29835. You also can find accommodations at Clark Hill Marina near Plum Branch, SC; at Little River Sportsmen's Camp, Leah, GA; and Soap Creek Lodge near Lincolnton, GA.

There are other state parks including Baker Creek and Hamilton Branch in South Carolina, and Clark Hill, Keg Creek, Mistletoe, and Bobby Brown state parks in Georgia. All parks have camping facilities. In addition, the Corps of Engineers operates twenty campgrounds.

Georgia and South Carolina have a reciprocal license agreement. A license from either state is all you need to fish in Clark Hill Lake or its tailwaters. Residents of other states may purchase a nonresident fishing license from either Georgia or South Carolina.

Brochures that show the location of recreational facilities such as boat ramps, camping, and picnic areas are available free from the Lake Manager's office. There is a small charge for a navigational map which shows fish attractor locations. A topographic map of Clark Hill which sometime fishermen find useful is also available at a cost of $2.25.

Mailing address for maps and information is: Resource Manager, Clark Hill Lake, *Clarks* Hill, SC 29821, telephone (404) 722-3770.

Clark Hill is a thinking bassman's lake. But if you adjust your technique to the time of year, you can encounter some line-stretching largemouth bass.

# 12

# Lake Eufaula—Still One Of the Southeast's Best

When Lake Eufaula on the Chattahoochee River was completed in the 1960s, it soon developed into the "hottest" largemouth black bass lake in the Southeast and one of the few outside of Florida capable of consistently producing lunker bass. It not only produced big bass, but big strings.

In July, 1972, the lake produced a record that probably never will be surpassed when Tom Mann and David Lockhart brought in a stringer of twenty-five bass weighing just under 155 pounds—an incredible average of over 6 pounds a bass. The largest weighed 13 pounds, 2 ounces. The bass were caught using worms and Little George tailspinners fished over ledges and along river and creek channels.

This bass bonanza was landed in the days when the bag limit was fifteen bass per angler. More than likely, it will stand forever, for it would be almost impossible to match this poundage with the ten-fish limit of today.

Lake Eufaula straddles the Alabama-Georgia border south of Columbus, Georgia, and stretches up the Chattahoochee River for eighty-five miles, sprawling over 45,180 acres with 640 miles of shoreline. Obviously, the bigmouths have ample elbow room.

For years, lunker hunters headed for Lake Eufaula, known officially as Lake Walter F. George, and filled their stringers while compiling fabulous tales of broken tackle. I was fortunate enough to sample Eufaula during these years, landing numerous bass including several in the 6-pound class. I was never able to break into the double-digit status. But I had more than enough action with all types of lures.

Then like all man-made impoundments, Eufaula declined to a point where newer reservoirs grabbed the publicity spotlight. As the lake faded from the angling headlines, fishermen began to forget the sprawling impoundments. Some even bad-mouthed the huge reservoir little realizing how wrong they were.

Like all man-made reservoirs, Lake Eufaula leveled off. Even so, it remains as one of the best bass holes in the Southeast. And judging by the number of double-digit fish—as big as 14 pounds—that have been landed in the last couple of years, Eufaula appears to be on an upswing. The unofficial lake record as far as Alabama is concerned now stands at a little more than 14 pounds. Bass of this size are far from common outside of Florida, and they make headlines in the Sunshine State.

Eufaula is big, and when fishing a lake this size, it is wise to get local information. The fish do move, and by getting the latest information you can save yourself a lot of fruitless cruising to waters where the fish are or are not hitting.

There are twenty-one public launching ramps well spaced around the lake. There are also three marinas affording fuel and necessary supplies. On the Alabama shore, there are Chewalla Creek Marina and Lakepoint State Park, one of Alabama's finest parks. It's a resort park rather than a day-use one, and if you want to have a luxurious fishing base, that's the place to go. It's very popular, and of course, reservations are necessary. On the Georgia side, you can launch at Florence Landing Marina, which is the farthest upriver from the dam site at Fort Gaines. It is the only marina on the Georgia side.

You can fish Eufaula any time of the year, although few do during the really cold weather. But you have to tailor your techniques to the season. Local experts summarize the year around fishing by saying that in January, there are very few who will get away from the fireside because it can get cold in this part of the country then. However, if a few warm days occur, you can catch bass by fishing deep. But on the whole, the weather makes the hot-stove league much more inviting.

Come February, and fishing begins to pickup. You generally find the bass holding along shallow ledges and around the mouths of creeks in five feet or less of water. After two or three warm days, you can catch bigmouths on the shallow points and ledges in even shallower water. The shallow water warms faster, and the bass know this.

During the first quarter, which is the prime time, you can utilize a wide assortment of lures depending upon your exact fishing location. Six-inch plastic worms, generally purple and blue metal flake, have been very effective in recent years. However, don't get married to these colors only. The day you fish, the bass may want some off-beat hue such as watermelon green or strawberry pink.

Then there are times when the old reliable colors such as purple-grape, black, and blue with and without firetails are more effective. While the shorter worms are generally preferred, there are times when you will want to use eight and nine-inch worms, or even plastic lizards.

You also can use crank baits to root along the bottom. It is a case of your personal preference as to which crank bait to use. They all produce. You can use Bomber Model As, Mann's Razorbacks, Rebel's Wee Rs, Cordell's N series, Bagley's balsas, or Hellbenders. Regardless of which manufacturer's you use, the favored colors are chartreuse, pearl, and crawdad. Which color you find the most effective depends upon the color of the water. Crank baits are particularly effective fished along the shallow four to eight-foot ledges in Barbour, Cowikee, and Patula creek areas.

Eufaula is flanked by the rolling hills of the Chattahoochee Valley, and in the spring muddy water can be a problem. A gully washer of a rain during the spring plowing can wash huge quantities of red Georgia clay into the lake and keep the water stained for weeks.

Then wise bassmen head for the south end of the lake to fish the riprap of the dam, and any clear creeks they can find. All of the creeks do not necessarily get muddy simultaneously. As a result, you have to hunt, but usually you can find clearer water. Of course, with stained water, the crawdad and chartreuse colors are favored. Even the brilliant orange produces at times under these conditions.

During the first quarter, spinner baits are also effective. Both single- and double-blade spinner baits are used, generally with silver blades with yellow, chartreuse, and white skirts. For stained waters, sometimes gold or bronze blades are preferred with either yellow or chartreuse skirts.

Late in March, there begins to be action with the shallow-diving minnow-type lure such as those made by Rebel, Bagley, and Rapala. Black and silver or black and gold are the popular colors. Some like the natural finishes that have been introduced in the last few years, but it's hard to beat the old reliable hues. Also, they seem to be easier for the bass to see.

The April-to-June quarter, of course, covers the spawning period, and generally provides the most action. The bass are in shallower water (two to three feet deep) than earlier in the year, but always near some deeper water sanctuary.

This is the time when top-water lures become effective. You can use Tiny Torpedoes, Nip-A-Diddees, Lunker lures, Dalton Specials, Devils Horse, Buck 'N Brawl, and similar top-water lures. However, for some reason the single propeller lures seem to be more productive than the double props. Perhaps, it's a case of the latter creating too much noise, and too much noise spooks rather than intrigues the fish.

The basic top-water lure colors are frog, white with a red head, and silver flash. If you're blipping a Rebel, Bagley, or Rapala minnow-type, either black and silver, or black and gold are scoring colors.

You also can use deep-running crank baits in the deeper water, if you do not get action in the extreme shallows. Again all of the standard crank baits work, and the favored colors again are crawdad, pearl, and chartreuse.

This is a good time to use spinner and buzz baits, racing them across the grass flats. The area north of Cowikee Creek to Florence Landing is studded with grass coves that produce for this top-water buzzing. A few anglers use Johnson-type spoons with pork rinds or plastic skirts, zipping them across the top of the grass.

Also, you can use plastic worms. Again, six-inch worms are preferred, although some go to seven and one-quarter and eight-inch sizes. If the water is not being released for navigation or hydroelectric purposes, you can use one-quarter ounce leads. However, if they are pulling water, then you need a heavier sinker, depending upon how fast the current is.

The hot weather of the summer—July through September—sends the bass deep. You find them in 12 to 20 feet of water along the edges of the main channel.

Surprisingly, many of the creeks have holes in them as deep as 25 feet, so don't hesitate to explore them with your depth finder. The cooler water is found in the lower part of the lake, particularly near the dam, and much of the fishing is down on the lower half of the reservoir for this reason. Some of the better creeks during this period are Barbour, Cowikee, Thomas, Cheneyhatchee, and Pataula.

When looking for good channels and ledges to fish try to find those that have moving water. The reason is obvious—moving water has more oxygen. Local experts recommend fishing the downstream side of the outside river and creek ledges.

Plastic worms fished deep are the primary lures with the same

Plastic worms have always been very effective for luring Lake Eufaula bass into striking. They are fished with slip leads, and without any leads as floaters off points, around brush piles, and other natural bass holding areas. However, don't overlook other lures such as crank-down baits, spinner baits, and even shallow runners. Clarence Moore doesn't wait for help, but hand lands a small Lake Eufaula bass as Jerry Stanley stands by with the net.

colors as used earlier in the year. Most anglers use twelve to seventeen-pound test line and select their sinker's weights after determining whether or not water is being released at the dam.

The fall, or last quarter of the year, finds you again fishing back in the creeks in the shallow water five- and six-feet deep. Top-water lures often produce when fished from shallow to deep around the points. In many creeks, the bass are present all year around, having a sufficient range of water depths to provide the ideal year-round conditions.

While the largemouth black bass have brought publicity to Eufaula, the lake is not just a one-fish impoundment. It has a sizeable population of white bass, and hybrids have been stocked. When you encounter bass that are schooling, you're never certain whether you will hook up with a black or white bass or with a hybrid—the white/striper cross-breed.

The lake is also known for its slab-size crappie or speckled perch. They sometimes grow larger than three pounds. Now that is a hefty crappie. They are aggressive, too, and are known to attack small and not-so-small bass lures with all the vigors of a bigmouth.

On one trip, I had a hefty crappie try to take a white Hellbender bass lure away from me. The spec hit vigorously like a bass, and for a few seconds it was uncertain whether I would land the crappie with eight-pound test line.

There are numerous places to stay in the town of Eufaula. There are several motels, including those on the lakeside that include such places as Chewalla Motel, Lakepoint Resort State Park, and Florence Landing Marina. All have first-class accommodations, as well as docking facilities. Chewalla Motel and Lakepoint Resort also have restaurants. For the angler with the camping rig, there are several camping areas, both improved and unimproved, around the lake. There is a KOA campground in Eufaula.

It helps to have a map of any lake, and Eufaula is no exception. You can obtain a map from the Resources Manager, Walter F. George Lake, U.S. Army Corps of Engineers, P.O. Box 281, Fort Gaines, Ga. 31751.

For additional information concerning the lake and the Chattahoochee Valley, you can write Douglas C. Purcell, Executive Director, Historic Chattahoochee Commission, P.O. Box 33, Eufaula, Ala., 36027, or Eufaula Tourism and Convention Commission, P.O. Box 347, Eufaula, Ala., 36027.

Lake Eufaula is definitely on the upswing. It's a fishing hole that's climbing back into the national spotlight, and well worth investigating whenever your local waters begin to bore you. Don't be surprised if you tear up some tackle.

# 13

## Often Overlooked
## Lake Blackshear

Although thousands of bass fishermen haul their rigs annually along
Interstate Highway 75 in central Georgia, they often overlook Lake
Blackshear, only eleven miles east of the Interstate. Despite being one
of the oldest of Georgia's numerous impoundments, this 8,500-acre
lake (formed by a power dam on the Flint River at Warwick, twenty-
two miles north of Albany) has never grabbed the fishing publicity
spotlight.

It is not that the fish aren't there. They are. What has happened
is that Blackshear has been shoved into the background by much larger
and much more highly publicized fishing waters.

Approximately fifteen miles long and a mile wide, Blackshear was
formed in the 1930s as a privately financed hydroelectric impoundment.
In 1925, the citizens in the area decided to produce their own electricity.
The Crisp County Power Commission was formed, a bond issue floated,
and the Flint River was dammed and generation facilities installed.

Fishing and recreation were not the main goals when the impoundment was formed. They developed as water sports zoomed in public
popularity after World War II. Blackshear was not highly publicized

prior to the 1970s perhaps because it was a dangerous lake. When the impoundment was constructed in the 1930s, it was designed for one purpose—to retain water for the power generating plant. As a result, the area was flooded with no thought of removing trees, stumps, and other objects which became water hazards.

For forty-three years, the underwater hazards posed dangerous threats to fishermen and other water sports devotees. However, by the 1970s it became obvious that something had to be done to improve the safety of the lake. In 1973-74, the lake was lowered and in some areas drained for a period of several months. During this time, stumps and snags were cut and removed from below the U.S. 280 bridge.

Now the lower half of the lake is safe for water sports enthusiasts, although not particularly frequented by fishermen, unless they are fishing some of the creeks that empty into the lower half.

It's in the upper part of the lake, where the stumps and timber were left untouched, that the bass fishermen congregate, naturally handling their boats very carefully. It's no place for hot rodding. The upper half channel is marked with buoys as is the channel below the 280 bridge.

The lengthy drawdown not only made it possible to clear the lower half of the lake, but it also helped rejuvenate the fishing population. As with all older impoundments, Blackshear had leveled off, but the extensive drawdown resulted in an expansion of the fish population both bass and panfish. Blackshear has been stocked by the Georgia Fish Division three times during the 1970s, resulting in an increased population.

The lake has another asset. While its level does not vary over one and a half feet normally, once a year the Power Commission makes an extensive drawdown to enable lakeside property owners to clear debris from the submerged land in front of their cottages. This annual drawdown, naturally, helps the fish population by exposing part of the lake bottom, which affords an expanded food supply when re-flooded.

Although not generally regarded as a "hawg" bass (i.e. 10-pounds or over) lake, Blackshear does produce 8 and 9-pound bigmouths to anglers expert enough to lure them into hitting. There probably are bigger ones waiting to be caught. Blackshear fishermen were startled in 1978, when an Americus angler boated a 14-pound bucketmouth.

With a shoreline of seventy-seven miles, unusually extensive for the small-water acreage, Blackshear has an abundance of coves and hidden sloughs in addition to numerous creeks where fish find favorable surroundings.

Feeder creeks, particularly in the upper end of the lake, are natural bass hangouts. If you listen to local anglers discussing their favorite sites, sooner or later you hear mentioned such names as Swift and Cedar Creeks, Fort Early Branch, Boy Scout Slough, Gum Creek, Parker Slough, Limestone Creek, Cannon Branch, and Collins Branch.

Some of these have clear spring-fed waters, while others have waters covered with an algae locally called "moss." While close examination shows the so-called moss supports small aquatic organisms, which are a food source for smaller game fish, Georgia fish biologists work to control the algae. When it becomes too abundant, fishing becomes exceedingly difficult.

By most impoundment standards, Blackshear is rated a shallow lake, although there are holes with depths of 40 to 50 feet particularly in the old Flint River channel. However, the lake's average depth is approximately 15 feet, depending upon the rainfall at the headwaters of the Flint River.

Visiting anglers should remember that they are fishing a shallow impoundment, and many of the structure fishing techniques of the deep water impoundments are of little use on Blackshear. You have to adapt to local conditions, and you do well to seek the advice of knowledgeable local anglers. They may not tell you the exact locations of their private "glory" holes, but they can clue you as to the types of lures best suited to the various seasons.

After fishing Lake Blackshear and discussing its year-round quirks with such knowledgeable local anglers as Jim Green, Olin Withering Jr., M.W. "Slim" Jordan, and Marvin Smith, it is apparent that Blackshear should be classified as a full-tackle-box lake. At sometime during the year, you can use almost every type of lure on the market. Of course, when and how you use them is the key to fishing success.

Having fished other more famous lakes such as Eufaula on the Chattahoochee River, Lake Jackson near Tallahassee in Florida, and Lake Seminole on the Georgia-Florida state line, Jordan is of the opinion you can catch just as many fish in Blackshear as in these other lakes by fishing hard. You do have to work, but you can score. His biggest Blackshear bass weighed 9 pounds, and hit on a silver-flash-colored Dalton Special, a plug he was using for the first time.

Veteran anglers have learned that success in Blackshear means following the water temperatures even more closely than in many other lakes. Blackshear reacts faster to weather changes because it is shallow.

When the weather is cool, and good catches are made in the winter by those anglers willing to don insulated long johns and ski suits, most of the good strings are caught in the shallows around the grass beds. The shallow waters, naturally, react faster to the warming rays of the sun, and bass like the most comfortable temperature they can find. However, as the weather and water warms, the bass move into deeper, cooler water, and the local experts change their fishing techniques accordingly. The river channel is now the main fishing area.

As with all bass fishing, no rules are infallible, and if the bigmouths aren't where they're supposed to be, or if they aren't hitting the proper lures, don't hesitate to experiment. Also, at any time of the year, floods on the Flint can change fishing conditions radically and abruptly. Hence, the following calendar affords a rule of thumb only, subject to local conditions when you make your fishing trip.

In January and February, the coldest months usually in this part of Georgia, crank baits are preferred fished in five to eight feet of water, usually along the old Flint River channel. Sometimes you can locate deeper holes—a depth finder is especially useful—and fish for bass suspended even deeper using one-half and three-quarter ounce jigs. This yo-yo type of fishing isn't as popular on Blackshear as it is in the larger and deeper impoundments farther north.

What crank bait you use is strictly a matter of personal preference. I found that Blackshear anglers use Big Os, Bomber Models As, Rebel Deep Wee Rs, Bagley Balsa Bs, and fat Rapalas. In clear water, one-quarter-ounce white Rooster Tail spinners are preferred by some. More than likely Mepps, Abu, and other similar spinners would work as long as the color was white.

The color of the water, of course, dictates the color of your crank bait. In clear water, black and silver, white, or pearl are preferred. In stained water, the colors are chartreuse, crawdad, perch, or shad. These colors, naturally, are more visible in murky water conditions.

During March and April, when the bass are going through their family ritual, the lures change as do the fishing locations. The bass are found in shallower water wherever they find suitable conditions for bedding. Look for them in quiet sloughs and coves with plenty of cover.

Before going on the beds, and after coming off, the bigmouths are much more aggressive, and this period is rated the prime one on Blackshear, just as it is in most lakes. Early spring is the time of year when safety pin-type spinner baits are very effective. Also some anglers use Snagless Sallys, and Hawaiian Wiggler lures, basically spinner baits of slightly different designs and actions, but highly effective at times.

Both single- and double-propeller blades are used on the spinner baits. Skirt colors vary according to both the water color and the personal whims of the anglers. Chartreuse, yellow, and yellow and black skirts are the most popular. Both silver, bronze, or gold spinner blades are used, the former for clear water, and the latter two for murky conditions. Johnson-type spoons with and without pork rinds are very effective around the numerous lily pads in the various coves and sloughs.

The months of March and April mark the beginning of serious worm fishing by anglers who prefer these plastic enticers. Seven-inch worms are the most popular, but a few fishermen use eight-inch, and in some cases five and six-inch worms, depending upon how the bass are hitting. Black, black-grape, and blue are the favorite colors. Anglers rig both the weedless, Texas-style, or use hooks with wire weed guards. Both are effective.

Because most of the fish are found in hazard-studded waters, most worm fishermen don't wait long before setting the hook. Wait too long, and your prize probably will have found his way around some sunken log, stump, or other snag.

May and June see another shift in tactics. The bass are still in the shallows—3 to 4 feet—both around the islands in the river, and along the banks. This is a period when top-water lures are effective. This is the time to entice ol' bigmouth into clobbering lures on the surface, and clobber them they do.

Among the most popular top-water lures are Tiny Torpedo, perch color; silver flash Dalton Special; and black and white striped Devils Horse.

Buzz baits also produce. Lures with silver blades and yellow skirts are rated number one, although the color of the water is the governing factor. Frequently in clear water, silver blades and white skirts are combined, while in murky water, yellow skirts and copper blades sometimes work better. There is some worm fishing in the shallows, but most anglers prefer the thrill of a savage top-water strike.

In July and August, fishing is tough. The water is warm and the bass are found in deep water, ranging from 6 to 10 feet in depth. Most anglers fish six to eight-inch worms with a weedless hook, or the Texas weedless rig. The best fishing time is from dawn until about 9:00 A.M. The best locations are found on the shady side of the lake, or the river where it enters the impoundment.

As fall approaches, fishing improves, and from September through November fishing is best upriver in swift water. Single-blade spinner baits are very effective early in the morning, while crank baits, such as crawdad-colored Bomber Model A, Rebel's Deep Wee R, and Bagley's various balsa deep divers are effective later in the day.

During December you return to fishing in the lake rather than in the river, and use the same crank baits as during the January-February period. Fishing success depends upon the weather, and a mild winter means much greater action.

Not only do you encounter largemouth black bass, but Blackshear is one of the few places in the South where you encounter the shoal bass, often called the "Flint River smallmouth." Actually the fish is not a smallmouth bass, although it does resemble this famous fighter somewhat. It's a fish that prefers swift water and rocky bottom, and usually is caught in the upper end of the lake where the river enters, and in the Flint itself.

You score with this scrapper by using small lures, primarily one-quarter-ounce sizes. Small crank baits fished along rock banks are deadly, as are Spot and Rat-L-Trap sinking lures. You also can score with small, top-water lures such as Tiny Torpedoes, or tiny, floating Mirrolures.

Shoal bass do not grow as large as their bigmouth brethren. A three-pound shoalie is a trophy fish. Georgia's state record is a little better than 8 pounds. However, the shoal bass are strong fighters, primarily because they live in swift water.

Don't be surprised if you encounter some hefty crappie—speckled perch—too. Crappie will hit small and not so small bass lures at times, and Blackshear has an excellent crappie population. However, if you want to load the boat with specs, then use either tiny jigs or live minnows fished either with a float or freelined.

There are ample launching sites around the lake, mostly no charge, including Georgia Veterans State Park, Campers Haven, Smoak Bridge, Cedar Creek, Lake Shore Marina (fee), Fisherman's Headquarters, and Swift Creek.

It's no problem to find a bed for the night with the abundance of motels along Interstate 75 at such towns as Vienna, Cordele, and Arabi. You also could stay at motels in Albany, which is only twenty-two miles away. Lakeside accommodations are limited to rental cabins at Georgia Veterans State Park. The marinas and fish camps provide only camping space in a few instances.

Blackshear may be overlooked, but the bass are there, if you're an expert enough fisherman to lure them to your bait.

# 14

# Lake Seminole—Big Water Big Stumps, and Big Bass

First-time anglers invariably neatly describe Lake Seminole on the Florida-Georgia state line as a lake with big water, big stumps, and big bass. The first two items are immediately obvious. It sometimes takes a little longer to contact the bass, but the lunkers are there. In fact, Seminole is one of the top bass lakes in the Southeast.

Like fine wine, the lake seems to get better with age, and as impoundments go, it is ancient having been completed in 1957. Today, Ol' Sem sprawls over fifty-eight square miles and its waters extend forty-seven miles up the Flint and Chattahoochee Rivers. As a result, the lake has 250 miles of shoreline. Just above the Jim Woodruff dam, the two rivers merge and become known as the Apalachicola River across Florida to the Gulf of Mexico.

Although the lake has 250 miles of shoreline, the Flint River arm seems to rate highest with most anglers. There's a reason. It's along the Flint that the impounded waters overwhelmed other streams such as Spring Creek (one of the top fishing areas), Fish Pond Drain, Silver Lake Run, and those without names as well as a number of springs.

Here, too, considerable second growth timber, along with some respectable oaks and cypress, were flooded and, today, the stark skeletons of the ex-woodlands create modernistic sculpture against the sky.

Although the tree skeletons towering from the water are the most impressive (don't get too near or bump them solidly because they might tumble down) the underwater stumps, snags, and fallen trees are the most important. First because they provide unseen boating hazards, and, second, because this abundant cover plus numerous grass beds provides Lake Seminole bass ample hiding places. It also guarantees that heavier lines are essential, if you intend to argue with lunker bass with the odds so loaded in their favor.

Like many other anglers, I've found Seminole can be as frustrating as a midnight backlash, yet so fantastic at times that you need a washtub to carry your catch. But to make Seminole fantastic instead of fickle, you have to know how to fish the lake. If you know some of Seminole's quirks, you can tangle with some line stretchers. The largest bass that has been weighed at Wingate's Lunker Lodge docks tipped the scales at 16 pounds, 4 ounces. Now that is a wall mount!

One thing that always has impressed me is the lake's all around productivity. It's not just a hot lake for a short period. It can and does produce all year-round. I've caught bass in the winter when fishing for chain pickerel, and encountered the splendid splinters in the spring when fishing for bass. And I've caught bass when I was fishing for them.

There are several keys to success. The first is knowledge of the underwater terrain. Although it's a man-made impoundment, it's different, and this can upset visiting anglers' plans.

The lake is an excellent bass hole because of special circumstances. While most impoundments are located on a single river, Seminole isn't. It has two main rivers flowing into it—the Flint and Chattahoochee. Also, it is fed by a number of creeks, some of them quite large such as Spring and Fishpond Drain. Springs either feeding the river or creeks are still another water source. In addition, having varied underwater terrain, more diversified than some impoundments, Seminole has abundant spawning grounds, essential to sustain a good bass population.

The lake offers the normal large impoundment-type fishing utilizing sand bars, channels, and old creek beds in 18 to 20 feet of water. But it also has 12,000 acres of standing stumps, because only the channels were cleared when the lake was formed. You don't go hot rodding off through the stump fields.

Ol' Sem also has 5,000 acres of weed beds, and a couple of thousand acres of lily pads and similar cover. Also, the lake is suited to wade fishing. There are areas where you can wade fish a mile from

Lake Seminole is a full-tackle-box lake. You never can be certain what lure will be needed. When fishing around the dead, standing timber, you often score with crank-down baits, or with plastic worms. Jack Wingate nets an 8-pound bass for Kit Hunn. The fish hit a deep-diving lure.

shore in any direction. It's also great fly rod water for bass and bream using inner-tube floats.

There are 250-odd islands in the lake with shallows surrounding them, as well as twenty miles of channels on the Flint and Chattahoochee Rivers, providing slow-moving water with up to 20 foot depths along the banks. With such a variety of fishing waters, it's obvious you have to select where you want to fish, and it's easy to make mistakes.

The quickest way to learn some of Ol' Sem's quirks is to corner Jack Wingate, widely known as Mr. Seminole from his long association with the huge lake, and ferret out some of the lake's oddities. Jack will gladly tell you, although it's sometimes like conducting an interview on the run because he's so busy. He's a gold mine of information— firsthand and practical.

Jack was born only a few miles from Hutchinson Ferry Landing where his Lunker Lodge is located. He started fishing from his daddy's lap using a tiny pole, and he has never lost the angling fever. He fished the Flint and Chattahoochee Rivers before the impounding. He knows where the old creeks and dropoffs are, and he has watched the new fishing areas develop as the lake filled. Also, he's a thinking angler.

According to Jack, the most common mistake made by first-time anglers is heading for the standing timber. "It looks good, but it ain't top fishing most of the time," he explains. "Nine out of ten newcomers head for the dead trees which are standing in 20 to 25 feet of water in a mud bottom. Seminole bass don't like such water.

"What you should look for are sand and rock bottom in 8 to 15 feet of water. Worms, deep divers, and sinking lures produce there, and sometimes the bass are on top."

In addition to knowing where to fish, you also need to know the monthly track records. Seminole produces the year around, but, naturally, varies from month to month. Knowing the monthly probabilities is the second key to success.

The normal yearly cycle goes like this, according to Jack. Starting in February, the bass begin thinking about spawning, and the biggest are caught then. February is noted for its individual size, although not necessarily for the largest strings.

Come March, and your bag will increase in numbers and still contain lunkers. This excellent fishing is illustrated by the results of one March professional bass tournament when 1,603 pounds of fish were weighed in.

May and June are highly productive with good heavy strings. During June, you can tangle with white bass and hybrids, both schooling then, after the whites have spawned upriver.

July and August, too, produce good strings with lunkers stretching lines frequently, but like all summer fishing the bass are deep. September is a hit or miss month, depending upon the hurricane season. If there are no storms, the bassing can be excellent, and during the latter part of the month, top-water action begins to increase peaking in October and November.

Successful bass fishing in December and January depends upon the weather. If it's a mild winter, bass fishing can be above average. If it gets cold, the fishing success drops, mainly because most anglers prefer to toast their shins by the fire rather than get frost-bitten tootsies in a bass boat.

However, knowing only the terrain and the monthly track record is not enough. The third thing that you need to know is what to use, when and where. You've got to put it all together, and if you don't tailor your angling thinking to the bass, Ol' Sem can be frustrating.

Again, here's the calendar breakdown for lures. For the lunkers in February and March, spinner baits fished slow, Spots and Rat-L-Traps are prime lures. Oddly, the most popular worms are not too widely used.

However, the April-to-June period requires a new approach. Plastic worms become highly successful along with some spinner baits early in the period. Also deep-diving crank baits such as Rebel Wee Rs, Bagley Killer B-II, Hellbenders, and Bombers produce.

Also, early and late in the day, top-water lures become most effective. This is one of the prime periods for top-water plugging with either single or double propeller lures. Among the popular ones are Spin-A-Diddee, Dalton Special, Rebel Top Prop, and Devils Horse. This is also the time to use shallow-running lipped lures such as Rebel's Minnow and Bagley Bang-O-Lures. These can be blipped across the surface, or retrieved just below. Both systems score when the bass are on the prod. Top waters are particularly effective over the grass beds.

Grass beds, too, can be fished with Johnson, Weed-Wing, and similar spoons retrieved fast to skip over the surface. Lake Seminole veterans use the spoons with plastic skirts of various colors, sometimes short plastic tails, and frequently with pork strips and chunks. Some buzz baits are successful during this period.

In July and August, you have to work a deep pattern primarily near sand bars and banks along the river channels. The fish are in 15 to 20 feet of water, and you have to get your lure down to them. Worms with weights, of course, are effective as are lead-spinners such as Mann's Little George. In addition, the deepest running crank baits are used, as are sinking Spots and Rat-L-Traps.

Crank baits are particularly effective in the Spring Creek area of Lake Seminole. Marty Butler is shown displaying a hefty Lake Seminole bass that hit a Bagley balsa crank-down bait in the creek. Because the lake is normally gin clear, light-colored lures are the most effective.

The navigation channel is maintained at nine feet, but there are many deep holes. A depth finder is a useful tool for locating the holes and deep dropoffs.

Although the primary fishing is deep during this period, there's still some top-water angling very early and very late in the day. You can count on scoring during the hour after sunrise and the hour just before the sun sets. Otherwise, top waters aren't too productive.

Hit and miss September is a month for top-water lures early and late in the shallows, and for spoons bounced off the bottom. The deeper working lures are the most productive. Many use deep-diving crank baits.

Top-water fishing peaks in October and November when you can cast all day with little problem with bright sun. Late in November, the spinner baits come out of temporary retirement and take over for December and January. The flashy baits—most effectively fished slow—produce during the cold months along with Spots, Rat-L-Traps, deep-diving crank baits, Little George, and Hopkins-type spoons. Bottom jigging with spoons is productive, and a comparatively new system on Seminole.

There are several other little quirks that can be helpful in fishing Ol' Sem. For example, you can almost estimate your chances of success by the color of the water. When the lake gets gin clear, especially Spring Creek, you have to work harder and make longer casts because the bass are spooky. It's different when there's too much rain upriver. The lake can get dirty, and fishing slows unless you can find some water that hasn't become too discolored. The perfect condition is slightly murky water. Then hang on to your rod!

Here is another tip. Fishing is best Tuesday through Friday. The impoundment was built for hydroelectric and navigational purposes. The generators normally are shut down on Friday and started again Monday morning. The starting upsets the water stability. However, by Tuesday the water stabilizes, and the fish are much more cooperative.

Seminole has another fishing bonus—hybrids and stripers (rockfish). The hybrids have been stocked successfully and are thriving on the abundant shad population. Hybrids—the cross of white bass and rockfish—are scrappers, and they grow fast. When they hit a lure, they mean business. You often find them schooling with white bass.

Stripers obviously are spawning, just as the landlocked stripers (rockfish) do in the Santee-Cooper impoundment in South Carolina, and the stripers grow big. Some have been landed in the 25 to 40-pound range. These are real line stretchers and tackle wreckers.

Prior to the closing of the Jim Woodruff dam, stripers annually came up the Apalachicola River, and then up the Flint and Chatta-hoochee to spawn. The dam stopped this, but in recent years evidence of spawning—i.e. baby stripers—have been discovered. It is believed the reduction of pollution in the two rivers is enabling the rocks to spawn successfully once more in the Flint River above Bainbridge. The Flint here has the necessary rocky bottom and turbulence to permit the striper eggs to mature.

Overnight accommodations aren't too numerous around the lake. We've found Wingate's Lunker Lodge at Hutchinson Ferry Landing to be an excellent base. It's the only resort on the lake with a restaurant, and it's famous locally for its food, always a good sign. The address is: Jack Wingate's Lunker Lodge, Rt 1, Box 851, Highway 97 South, Bainbridge, Ga., 31717, telephone (912) 246-0658.

You also can stay at Reynolds, Dunn's and Snead's Landings. If you can't find accommodations lakeside, then you have to utilize motels either in Bainbridge or in Chattahoochee, Fla.

Fishermen with camping rigs can utilize two state parks—Seminole in Georgia and Three Rivers in Florida. There's also Bass Island Camp-ground adjacent to Lunker Lodge, privately operated and open to the public for a fee, as well as several public Corps of Engineers' camping areas.

Ol' Sem is big, and it's a good idea to have a guide on your first few trips. A number of guides book through Lunker Lodge. We've enjoyed fishing with such experts as Jack Wingate (when he's available and not tied up with Lodge business), Marty Butler, Lou Hart, Ron Bobrow, and Jerry Sims. They are not blarney artists, but real fish-ermen.

It's also a practical idea to study available maps. You can do so by utilizing the Corps of Engineers' map, which can be obtained free by writing the Reservoir Manager, P.O. Box 96, Chattahoochee, Fla. 32324. Or you can use two, privately printed maps. One is the Lake Seminole map published by Southern Guide Fishing Maps, 500 Gulf Shore Drive, P.O. Box 1326, Destin, Fla., 32541. The other is published by Ole Guide Publications, Smithville, Tn., 37166. The latter contains more detailed fishing information about Seminole than any other map I've seen.

Ol' Sem can be fickle, frustrating, or fantastic, and if you under-stand these foibles, your chances of having a fantastic fishing trip are greatly improved. Of course, you have to hook 'em and land 'em. The bass are there.

# 15

# Elusive Flint River Bass

The Rebel quarter-back plug dropped within inches of the huge rock behind which the Flint River was eddying above Bainbridge, Georgia. Two turns of the reel handle, and I felt a solid strike. Snapping my rod vertically, it was obvious from the rod's bend that the fish had hooked itself. It was not a typical lake or impoundment bass strike. But then this wasn't typical impoundment fishing.

The fish darted away from its lair into the swift current of the Flint. Then it took to the air in a violent leap, realizing it was in serious trouble. However, the maneuver failed to shake the lure. The aerial acrobatics revealed it wasn't a big fish, but it was a scrapper, far stronger than its size indicated.

Then the fish headed downstream seeking another refuge. Momentarily, the combination of the downstream charge, and the swift current gave me qualms about my eight-pound test line. The gin-clear water demanded you use light line, but the abundant rocks posed serious threats if the line brushed the boulders.

Fortunately, we were floating. The drift of our boat neutralized the fish's advantage. As our boat overhauled the scrapper, the fish headed towards shore taking advantage of a current eddy.

*111*

But this maneuver failed, too. As we drifted into the calm of a big eddy, the rod pressure began to show. Shortly I brought the fish alongside for the net. Coming alongside in the other boat, Jerry Powell, an ardent angler from Bainbridge, took one look and exclaimed: "You did it! You got yourself a Flint River 'smallmouth.'"

Then I really felt elated. In the first hour of fishing on the river, I had achieved my goal—landed a Flint River smallmouth, the local name for what was really a shoal bass. There are no true smallmouth bass in South Georgia, but this shoal was more akin to the "smallies" than to the regular largemouth bass of the South.

The fish weighed 3 pounds, but it fought like a 6-pounder or larger. Its fighting ability, of course, was aided by the fast water. Swift-water fish always fight harder than do their lake brethren.

Little did I realize that I had landed a trophy fish. Being based in Florida where a 3-pound fish is hardly considered a trophy, I was slow to realize what I'd caught.

It was a trophy fish because the Flint River smallmouths weighing 3 pounds or more are considered trophy fish for two reasons. First, they aren't numerous. To catch one of any size is an unusual angling experience. But the second and more important reason is that they don't get huge. The biggest I've seen boated is a 4-pounder Jack Wingate landed one trip using a chrome Mud Bug lure. The fish gave him a very stubborn argument.

The Georgia state record is 8 pounds, 3 ounces caught in the Flint River in 1977. What a battle that must have been—an 8-pound fish in fast water. Whew!

As our boats drifted down river, I continued to study my prize. The fish was beautifully marked with greenish tan, vertical stripes on a faintly bluish green body. However, it lacked the blue cheek stripes typical of the redeye bass of the upland Southern streams. Too, it had a more streamlined body than that of a regular largemouth black bass.

This rare fish has more aliases than a con man. Although locally called the Flint River smallmouth, it's also known as Coosa bass, Flint redeye, and shoal bass. Its correct name is shoal bass. However, it was not named officially until in recent years after it was identified positively as a separate species from the redeye bass, known as the Coosa bass, scientifically named *Micropterus coosae*. It took Dr. John S. Ramsey of Auburn University and other fish biologists several years to make the positive identification.

The shoal bass is restricted both in numbers and in habitat. Apparently, this scrapper prefers rocky, fast-moving waters, and is found only in the tributaries and main channels of the Chattahoochee and

Flint Rivers in Georgia, and the Apalachicola and Chipola Rivers in Florida.

My introduction to these challenging fish came about by accident several years ago. During a visit to Jack Wingate's Lunker Lodge to fish famous Lake Seminole, Jack suggested a float on the Flint. His description of the river intrigued me. As a result, he arranged for Jerry Powell, one of the most knowledgeable river anglers of Bainbridge to take me fishing.

The Flint shoal bass now are found in a very limited section of the river. Although the Flint rises in northeast Georgia and flows 200 miles southward to eventually empty into Lake Seminole, the range of the river's shoal bass has been reduced radically by man.

Originally the Flint bass were found over a wide range, but they do not like impoundments, hence dams forming Lakes Seminole, Blackshear, and Worth have reduced the waters where the fish can survive. They prefer fast water and rocky bottoms.

Today, you can seek these Flint scrappers from Thomaston on the north to Bainbridge on the south. Much of this terrain is suited only to john-boat-type float fishing, or even to canoes.

However, the river above Bainbridge to above Ichawaynochaway Creek can be fished from conventional bass boats, how far upstream depending upon the river's height. Low water makes big-boat fishing almost impossible because of the rocks.

Seeking the Flint shoal bass is a fascinating experience regardless of fishing success because the terrain is so different. It's a startling change from normal impoundment flat-water fishing.

The Flint above Bainbridge to Albany is bordered by steep banks. The river has a very rocky bottom, and with normal water has a swift current. You find the river usually is so fast that electric trolling motors are useful only for controlling your boat's position from the shore. Whenever you need to run upstream, you have to utilize your big motor.

Years ago, steamboats operated up the river as far as Albany. During the years of the great depression, a WPA project built rock islands to direct the current's flow to help maintain the channel.

The steamboat days are long gone, but the rock islands are still there, some plainly visible above the water, some partially or entirely submerged. Naturally, you have to be mighty careful cruising upstream. If you have a depth finder, keep it operating continually and watch it closely!

Fishing for the Flint River shoal bass is a different type of angling. There are unexpected quirks to this float fishing, but these add to the challenge of seeking a rare and elusive fish.

When seeking the shoal bass of the Flint River above Bainbridge, Georgia, small lures are most effective. The shoal bass like to lie in eddies behind rocks, and ambush passing bait fish. While they live in fast water, they don't want to spend all of their lives fighting a stiff current, hence never overlook a riffle behind a rock, stump, or some other object in the river.

After fishing the Flint several times with Jack Wingate, Lou Hart, Jerry Powell, and Buck Bray, I've learned some of the tricks of this river fishing.

If you're a top-water lure enthusiast, you will be surprised at the little use of the floating rumpus makers. Rarely do you succeed with propeller-equipped lures. As Wingate says: "You can throw 'em, but nine out of ten times you're just practice casting. You gotta get your lure down to their lairs."

To reach their lairs, the Flint River experts favor diving plugs (crank baits), spinner baits, and worms. Also reaching the fish requires expert casting.

The shoalies lurk around the rocks, seldom in the middle of the river, unless there happens to be a decaying rock pile there. You find these bass love to lie in the eddies behind the rocks, and you have to knock on their front door with your lure. They're not inclined to chase a lure very far.

Not only does this fishing require pinpoint casting, but you also cast from a moving boat with constantly changing ranges. Fishing the Flint River is no place for wild casters. It gets awfully discouraging wasting time retrieving lures from snags because of inaccurate casting. Often it's impossible to check your boat in time to go back and retrieve your lure. The fast current makes boat handling difficult.

Your choice of casting targets is all important. You can cast to obvious no-bass hideouts, but if you're smart you cast where the bass should or could be. You look for quiet pockets behind rocks, old stumps, brush piles, cypress and tupelo trees standing in shallow water. You have to place your lure within inches of your target.

Sheer rock walls, too, are likely targets. There are always cracks and crevices where the bass can hide. But getting your lure to them requires extreme accuracy. The perfect cast, landing within inches of the rocks, requires a quick retrieve. Even moving your lure quickly won't always prevent hang ups, but it's all part of the game. Also you have to crank your lures rapidly to make them dive deep. Crank-down baits such as Rebel's Wee R series, Bomber's Model A, Bagley's Killer B-II and Small Fry, as well as Hellbenders and similar lipped lures are effective.

You also can use shallow divers such as the minnow types made by Bagley (balsa) and Rebel (plastic). Sinking lures such as Lewis Rat-L-Trap and Cordell's Spots retrieved fast are very effective. Usually if you haven't gotten a strike in the first ten feet of retrieve, forget that cast and make another. Long retrieves seldom pay off.

Small lures are preferred. Flint River experts claim the shoal bass spit out big lures much quicker than small ones. It's logical, for most river food fish are small, and the shoalies aren't bucketmouths, either.

Lure color is also important. Black and silver is generally the best combination when the river is clear, but there are times when others work better. Sometimes all silver or chromes will produce as happened on one trip with Jack. We got only two bass, but one was a 4-pound shoalie that hit Jack's silver Mud Bug. At other times, particularly if the river is murky, crawdad, black and gold, and orange colors are productive.

Worm fishing is more difficult, not that the Flint River bass ignore the plastic enticers. The problem is that you have to use heavy leads to get the worm down because of the current, which often makes it hard to feel the pickup of the worm by the bass.

Also the river's current is so fast that your worm can't stay on the bass' doorstep. Nine out of ten times the pickup comes while the worm is falling. You have to watch your line constantly to detect the contact. Shoal bass hit quickly, or not at all. You can't delay attempting to set the hook. If you feel a tap, rare back, and pray.

Jack pointed out another factor in fishing this area of the Flint— choice of banks. You'd assume either bank would be a fish haven, but this isn't true. The best fishing is on the east bank. Why? There are several reasons. For much of the day, the east is the shadow side of the river, and shoal bass prefer shade. Because of the high banks, the east side remains in the shade until well after noon.

Also, there is a physical difference in the banks. The eastern is the most rugged, has the most rock walls, the most tupelo and cypress, and shows the least influence of man. The west bank has more sand bars, fewer trees, more signs of man, and in general fewer hideouts for the shoal bass. Remember this, and fish accordingly, and you will do better challenging the Flint.

The easiest way to fish the lowest section of the Flint is to trailer your boat to the County Line landing above Bainbridge off Georgia highway 311. The launching ramp is paved, and normally offers no problems unless the river is exceptionally low.

Then cruise cautiously upriver for two to two-and-a-half hours to Nochaway Creek or Hells Gate, and then begin floating back. It takes the remainder of the day to fish back to the launching ramp.

You also can float downstream towards Bainbridge. However, there are few shoal bass in these waters, but more largemouths, as big as 9 pounds. The river isn't as rocky, broadens, and the current isn't as swift.

Unless you are fishing with a local river expert, it's advisable to have a guide on your initial trip. Guides at Wingate's Lunker Lodge on Hutchinson Ferry Landing on Lake Seminole trailer their boats to the Flint and provide float services.

You can make reservations in care of Jack Wingate, Route 1, Box 851, Highway 97 South, Bainbridge, Ga., 31717, telephone (912) 246-0658.

Lunker Lodge is a good base. It has motel rooms, a stag lodge and restaurant, or if you're using a camping rig, you can utilize nearby Bass Island campground (private). There are also state parks in both Florida and Georgia, as well as Corps of Engineers camping areas on Lake Seminole.

For a different type of fishing challenge consider a Flint River float seeking the elusive, scrappy shoal bass.

# 16

# Georgia's Little Known Lunker Country

Most bass anglers zipping along the 140-mile stretch of Interstate 75 south of Perry, Georgia, are unaware that they are passing through the Peach State's little-known big-bass country, but they are.

It's not surprising, for the area lacks the kind of press agents such as those that helped spread the word about the big bass of Florida a few miles farther south. This Georgia area is still primarily agriculturally oriented. Peaches, peanuts, sweet 'taters, and cotton outrank bass fishermen in the general public's mind.

But by fishing some of the ninety ponds and lakes ranging in size from one to 12,000 acres, you can wet your lines in beautiful cypress-studded waters with a good chance of breaking them, and not on snags.

Bass up to 16 pounds have been landed, and bigmouths over 10 pounds are common, although most of the natives prefer to fish for the table rather than trophies. But the lunker bass are there.

Yet to seek these little publicized trophy bass, you have to step backwards in fishing time to an era when the techniques were different.

It's a type of angling most people have forgotten. With the exception of a few of the larger lakes, this is paddle-boat country. If you don't paddle, you don't go. This is not big motor country.

You don't need big boats nor big motors because the distances are not great. Also, broad-beamed boats have difficulty maneuvering among the cypress, and you fish among the cypress most of the time.

It's the type of bass fishing you don't encounter very often in this sophisticated, late twentieth century, yet it's just as challenging now as it was years ago. Possibly, it's more so, because many of today's anglers have to learn new techniques to overcome their dependence upon sophisticated gear. After all, there is an art to paddling or sculling a boat without sounding like a boiler factory.

Most out-of-state anglers discover the fishing holes by accident, usually picking up a brochure issued by South Georgia Area Planning and Development Commission in Valdosta. The brochures usually are available in Georgia Welcome Stations.

The brochure lists ninety ponds, although a 12,000-acre body of water seems deserving of a different name. Banks Lake, for example, near Lakeland, Georgia, sprawls across 12,000 acres, and there are several others covering 100-odd acres, just a wee bit big for pond designation.

These are private fishing lakes, now open to the public for fees ranging from one to five dollars. In some cases where you also can bank fish, the fee is a modest fifty cents.

Most of the ponds have rental boats—twelve to fourteen-foot wooden ones that you paddle. If you are allergic to paddling, don't try this fishing, for this is angling as it was before the development of outboard and electric trolling motors. Muscle power is all important in this fishing.

There are a few ponds where you can use small motors—three or four horsepower—but you have to bring your own. Rental motors are not available. Many of the local anglers use a small motor to reach their fishing area—even a 100-acre pond is a lot of water to paddle across—then pull the motor, place it in the center of the boat, and paddle while actually fishing. It's amazing how adept the stern man becomes at both sculling and casting. You can cover a lot of territory with this system.

In some cases, such as Banks, Nichols, and a few other lakes, you can launch regular bass boats, but on most of these ponds there isn't room for beamy craft. You are fishing dense cypress, around cypress knees, old logs, stumps, and deadfalls.

Many are single ponds, although one operation is really large—Patrick's. Here you find sixty-three ponds, ranging from one to 100 acres that are stocked with bream and catfish as well as black bass.

Patrick's Ponds have big fish. One trip we were there during a pond draining, as part of the regular management schedule. Whew! Some of the bass netted to be removed to another pond were in the 9 and 10-pound class.

The biggest bass I've landed from these beautiful mini-lakes weighed 7½ pounds. Don't think that size bass can't give you problems among the cypress knees and stumps on eight-pound test, spinning line. The fish hit a gold, Johnson-type spoon with a gold, plastic worm tail instead of the usual pork rind.

Of course, the 7½-pounder really was puny compared to some of the lunkers that have been landed. Nip Purvis, of Lakeland, Georgia, an ardent fisherman, can boast of a 13¾-pounder landed with a Creek Chub Darter, frog-back color. This trophy came from Ray's Mill Pond.

Jim White, another angling acquaintance, also of Lakeland, still talks about the 11¾-pound black bass he caught one dark night on Banks Lake. His wife wanted a mess of fish to eat. He launched, went about 200 yards, tossed a black Jitterbug, and bang! After a rugged fight, he landed his record bass. Needless to say, he did no more fishing that night.

Of course, the best evidence I've seen is the 17-pounder mounted on the wall of the little restaurant and tackle shop at Ray's Mill Pond. Now that is a real trophy fish. J.C. Skinner caught the lunker using a big shiner.

Sometimes the number of bass you can catch is fantastic. Nip still recalls the day he and his fishing buddy landed and released fifty-two bass while fishing Banks Lake. The bass were hitting any lure with reckless abandon. And then again there are days when you have to work to land a bass.

These mini-lakes are located on both sides of Interstate 75, between Ashburn on the north, and the Florida-Georgia state line on the south. I-75 slices the length of Georgia, and, of course, is one of the major tourist routes into Florida.

The lakes all have similar characteristics. None are really deep, averaging perhaps eight feet. This, of course, means you have to change your fishing techniques, especially if you are a deep impoundment angler. There are no deep drop-offs, rock ledges, riprapped banks or the other features of big, deep water impoundment angling.

These mini-lakes were created by dams—many of them a hundred years or older—built in the early nineteenth century to form mill ponds for water operated grist mills or cotton gins. Most of the ponds were formed by daming creeks that snaked through cypress swamps and strands.

The secret of the mini-lakes is that usually they have been drained regularly every five to ten years, man-made drawdowns that achieve the same results as do natural ones.

Thus when the ponds refill, their bottoms have dried out, a new supply of grass develops affording a new food supply for bait fish, and the remaining bass have a banquet, and normally there's a population explosion.

These South Georgia ponds are challenging fishing waters. At times, it is fantastically easy, and again there are times when you have to work to score. But always there is the possibility of hooking a big fish. The day I landed the 7½-pounder, Kit, my wife, fought and lost another that seemed to be in the same weight range. Yet oddly, those were the only two strikes we had that morning. But that's bass fishing.

Many local anglers believe that the next world's record bigmouth may be roaming some of the little-known ponds. The idea isn't too absurd. After all, the present world mark of 22 pounds, 4 ounces came from South Georgia.

Of course, it also may never be broken for it has stood since George Perry made that memorable landing in 1932. But the odds are great if the record is broken, the fish will come from isolated waters free of pollution, and probably not subjected to heavy fishing pressure.

After fishing these lakes several times with such local experts as Nip Purvis, Roy McQuaid, Jim White, and Jim Nix, it's obvious you have to be able to adjust to varying conditions. Different techniques are required for different ponds, and the situation changes during the year.

However, there's one common characteristic—all have an abundance of coontail moss. Because of this, Johnson-type spoons are widely used. Such weedless lures are mandatory most of the year.

The moss dies back during the cold months, but revives rapidly in warm weather. The result is you generally fish a weedless spoon by skipping it across the top of the moss. You have to retrieve rapidly and keep your lure on top of the water, or the moss will foul it.

The bass are beneath the moss or grass, but, while they do charge hard, often they don't connect solidly. You get ulcers watching the huge boils of near misses. It's all part of the game, however.

On bigger lakes such as Banks at Lakeland, different techniques are used. Generally, you don't work the grass flats, but fish around the trees. Banks is regarded primarily as a plastic worm or lizard lake, or good waters for top-water lures with single or double propellers.

How you fish this 12,000-acre lake depends upon the time of year. Early—February through March—you use plastic worms around cypress trees and stickups. You fish fairly deep water. But as the waters warm, the bass move nearer the surface, and by June you can use top-water lures, or spinner baits, the latter being run just under the surface.

There's a trick to fishing Banks during the warm months. Instead of fishing the shoreline, which is a hit or miss proposition during the heat, you seek isolated cypress trees. Your target is the base of the tree.

For some reason, probably because of the shade, and coolness, the bass lurk among the cypress roots. Toss a noisy top-water lure at their doorstep, and you are almost guaranteed violent action. But the secret is that you have to cast to isolated trees. For some reason, you don't find the bass among the cypress roots when the trees are in clumps.

Based upon lengthy discussions with local experts, plus my own observations, the calendar fishing routine is roughly as follows.

During the January-to-March period, black, Johnson-type spoons are the prime lure. Local anglers fish them with either plastic skirts or Twister-type, plastic tails. In clear water, black skirts and tails are preferred.

However, if you find a pond with tannic acid water (clear but black), a white skirt is preferred with a black spoon. Of course, there are always exceptions such as the 7½-pounder that hit my gold spoon with a gold tail.

Beginning in February, depending upon how soon the mini-lakes' waters warm, you can start using plastic worms. By mid-March, top-water lures become effective, both the shallow-diving plugs such as Rebel's or Bagley's minnow-types, or floating, propeller-types such as Tiny Torpedo, Devils Horse, Spin and Nip-A-Diddee.

As the bass go on the beds, plastic worms, or lizards with slip sinkers become productive. The plastic lizard (or a live one) is particularly effective. Bass hate spring lizards around their beds, and hit them hard.

From April through September, the main lure is the plastic worm, but fished without sinkers. The heavy growth of grass makes a lead weight a nuisance rather than an asset. A weighted worm drops into the grass too often. A floating worm without a sinker produces when skittered along the surface.

On those ponds, which are not loaded with grass or moss, during the warm months you also can use top-water lures, generally early and late in the day.

During the latter part of the year—October through December—the weedless spoon again becomes the preferred lure. These produce best when fished near the edge of the grass. Early and late in the day, surface lures of all types are effective. Plastic worms now rate third in popularity and productivity.

Although none of the ponds have overnight facilities, finding a room is no problem. The area is well supplied with modern motels. Along Interstate 75, you find all of the big motel chains with restaurants, and many lower-priced independents.

The best way to sample this off-beat fishing is to base at an interstate motel and make individual sorties to the mini-lakes that interest you. All are within a few miles of I-75 reachable by well-paved highways. It's doubtful if you'll find more luxurious fishing accommodations except at a few, highly publicized resorts on big impoundments.

For complete information and details on Southern Georgia lunker country, you can contact the South Georgia Area Planning and Development Commission, P.O. Box 1223, Valdosta, Ga., 31601, telephone (912) 247-3454.

If you're looking for a different type of fishing, and you don't mind paddling, then schedule a trip to lunker country in southern Georgia. The trophy bass are there if you can land 'em, but remember to paddle quietly.

# 17

# Lake Holley—Lunkers From the Bank

What would you say your chances are of landing a 10-pound, large-mouth black bass casting from the shore? What would you say your chances are of landing a 16-pounder? Ask any angler, and he will quickly tell you the chances are slim, and he may add that you're crazy for even asking.

Undoubtedly, the majority of bass are caught from boats, although they often are lurking near the shore. But to fish from the bank for wall mounts is not usually a successful technique, and there are very few places where you even have a chance of getting such a lunker.

However, you have an excellent chance of tangling with a hefty bass, and possibly landing it, if you are fortunate enough to know and to fish little Lake Holley in the Florida Panhandle.

This 750-acre man-made lake on the outskirts of the little town of DeFuniak Springs continually amazes anglers with hefty bigmouths that are landed from the shore. For example, the lake's record is 16 pounds, 2 ounces. It was landed by a bank angler, Wayne Roscoe of Robertsville, Alabama, in March, 1979. He was casting a plastic worm. Now that's a big fish, especially from the bank.

The previous record was 14 pounds, 2 ounces, held by Harry Clenny of DeFuniak Springs, Florida. His record stood for just one year—1978. There's a special twist to the story of Clenny's feat. The irony of his success is that he connected with the fish on his third cast to the chagrin of another angler who twice had hooked the big bass, but each time lost it in the grass along the shore. Such is angling luck.

Ferrell Ship is another angler who landed a trophy mount. He caught his 10-pounder while casting from the earthen dam that separates the two parts of the lake for water control purposes. Again a plastic worm was the lure.

But possibly the most unusual bank lunker landing was by Louise Brown of DeFuniak Springs, who wasn't even fishing for bass but for bream. After a furious struggle, she successfully landed an 8-pound, 4-ounce bigmouth while fishing with a cane pole and a cricket. Big lures and baits obviously do not necessarily mean big bass in Holley, not when a bigmouth will grab a cricket.

Many anglers believe that someday the lake may yield a bass in the 20-pound class, or perhaps a new world's record, for the catch records seem to indicate the Holley largemouths are growing faster than the Florida average of a pound a year.

I discovered Holley's bank fishing on my first visit. A fierce wind was blowing, ruling out any chance of boat fishing. We had to fish from shore. When I saw the water, which wasn't much over 18 inches deep, I couldn't believe we could catch fish, *but* I landed a 4-pound bass on a chartreuse, plastic lizard, and Ben Holley did likewise with a black lizard. We also lost several other fish, not hard to do when you lack maneuverability.

It was oddball fishing. There were bass-fanning beds within easy casting range, but you either fished for them from the shore, or you didn't fish. No boat could possibly maneuver along the shore among the stickups. No wonder there's a well worn path along the lake's edge.

This unusual lake is not widely publicized. Only local anglers are really aware of it, which, of course, is understandable because there are so many Florida lakes that have reams of publicity written about them. But the word is slowly spreading.

Holley is located four miles north of DeFuniak Springs on U.S. 331 in the Florida Panhandle. This part of the state never has received the freshwater fishing publicity the peninsular part of Florida has, but there's excellent angling if you learn about it.

Lake Holley is man-made and covers 750 acres. It was formed by damming a small creek running through a titi swamp. It was stocked with largemouth black bass, bream, and shellcrackers in 1969, and opened to the public in 1971. It's spring fed, not being entirely dependent upon rainfall.

Learning the lake's history, it seems obvious that it has very favorable bass waters. There were very few big bass in the little titi swamp that was dammed. The big ones now being caught apparently are the result of stocking. Much of the lake is a natural bass sanctuary.

The titi swamp that was flooded is the cause of the sanctuary. A titi swamp is different from most swamps. It's far more dense. The titi is a small tree that thrives in shallow, swampy areas, usually with a small crooked trunk that divides into numerous branches at heights of ten to fifteen feet.

The titi trees long since died, but their skeletons create an underwater jungle that makes boating impossible, provides a perfect bass lair, and guarantees problems of landing anything larger than a 2-pound fish. You may lose a 2-pounder just as easily as a 10-pounder.

Fortunately, the perimeter of the lake was cleared before the impoundment was filled, and boats can operate easily in this area thus enabling you to fish the shoreline and the edge of the stickups.

But there is no way to fish the center of the lake. This sanctuary will play a prominent role in developing lunker bass in the future. They are safe from continuous pressure, and unless the bigmouths choose to feed on the edges of the stickups, you have little chance of reaching them. Fortunately, they do come out at times, especially during the spawning season.

Holley's bank-fishing success results from the fact that the lake is essentially a shallow saucer with an average depth of six to seven feet. Because of this, bass are found just as often near the shore as in the center.

With average casts, it's possible for bank anglers to reach water three and four feet deep, where the bass roam regularly. Of course, landing them among the lily pads, grass, stickups, and sunken logs is a fishing challenge, but it can be done.

Holley's topography contributes to the bank-fishing success. Because of the numerous shallow coves infested with stickups, there are many areas that can only be fished from the bank. This provides shore fishermen with virtually a private angling area, because the boat anglers can't get near. However, you have to be willing to walk, fight more than a few brambles, and perhaps get wet feet, as well as be resigned to losing lures you can't recover. There are some local fishing regulars who wade fish the shallows, and they score.

After fishing this lunker hole with Ben and Gerald Holley, two of the three brothers who originally established the lake, and Gene Wil-

In Lake Holley, you can be just as successful from the bank as from a boat. In fact, there are areas that can only be fished from the bank as Ben Holley and Max Hunn are doing. Plastic worms and plastic lizards rigged either Texas-weedless-style or fished with weedless hooks are the only lures you can use effectively because of the hazards.

liams, another local expert, I obtained a good idea of the year-round methods for this "hawg" hole.

It's obvious that eighty percent of the bass are caught with plastic worms or lizards. However, I know you also can score with crank baits, and shallow-running top-water plugs.

On another trip, I boated a 5-pounder with a Bagley balsa crank bait, lost one equally large, and watched Gerald Holley have the same misfortune. This time, we were boat fishing, casting towards and slightly into the titi jungle in the center of the lake. The bass were feeding near the edge. It's tricky fishing, but it can produce. You also can lose lures in a hurry, if you don't turn your bass before he gets back into the sanctuary. You can be certain they lose no time in heading for the brush pile.

Like most Florida fishing waters, lures used vary with the time of year, although the variety that can be used is rather limited on this lake. For the January-to-March period, the plastic worm or lizard, either black or black-grape colors, is preferred. But don't get married to these colors only. The 4-pounder that hit my chartreuse plastic lizard is a tip-off that sometimes other colors produce. Holley bass are like bass anywhere. They do get moody and color conscious. Then you have to experiment.

March is the prime month for big bass, and with any type of luck, and with favorable weather, which can be tricky in the Panhandle in the spring, you have a good chance of encountering bigmouths ranging from 7 to 16 pounds, or maybe even larger. The odds during the spawning season are good that you will hook up with a real wall mount.

During the April-to-June quarter, you can use a wider assortment of lures, including shallow divers, both Rebel and Bagley types, either with black and silver, or black and gold colors. The tiger stripe is very effective with both of these color combinations.

Snagless Sallys, too, are effective if you are fishing with a green pork chunk and yellow skirts. Spinner baits with white or yellow skirts are used, and, of course, the old reliable plastic worm in a variety of colors.

Crank baits, too, are effective if you are fishing the edge of the central sanctuary. They are not as effective when casting to the shoreline because of the numerous tiny stickups that cause them to foul too often. Too, they are not really designed for shallow-water fishing. Buzz baits work better in this situation.

From July through September, top-water lures such as Devils Horse, Lucky 13, Rebel poppers, and various injured minnow-types are effective as well as worms. Worms are fished both with and without weights, depending upon the water depth and the bass reactions. Again you have to cast accurately to avoid snags, whether you are fishing the shore or casting towards the center of the sanctuary. The favored colors are red and yellow, chartreuse, orange, and solid white for plugs. Worm colors are black and black-grape.

The October-to-December quarter sees renewed use of shallow-running lipped plugs (Rebels and Bagleys), and more use of crank baits (both plastic and balsa), especially the latter as the bass now are holding in slightly deeper water. Worms, too, are used. Colors are the same as before. There doesn't seem to be any radical color change in the lake.

Because of the lake's depth, the year-round fishing location pattern doesn't change very much. It can't. The bass don't have much choice as to water depth. Naturally, cold weather finds the fish in the deepest holes, but they are shallow by most impoundment standards.

In the spring, your greatest success is fishing the shoreline and shallows, and this is the prime time for bank anglers.

During the summer, it's a toss-up where you'll find the bass, as they move continually. You fish for them from the shallows to the deep water, depending upon the time of day. Early you fish in the shallows, and fish progressively deeper as the heat increases. The bass are looking for the most comfortable water temperature.

Fall fishing is best around the snags in the deepest water. However, early and late you can score in the shallows until the water gets too cold. Then the dawn or dusk patrol fades. With continued cold, you look for the largemouths in the deepest holes.

This is one lunker hole when you can fish from your doorstep if you have a camping rig by utilizing the Lake Holley Campgrounds. The campsites are located on a shady hillside near the earthen dam. There are 100 sites with water and electrical hookups, as well as a swimming pool. There is a central dumping station. Special family rates are available whether you're tent camping, or have your own motor home or camping trailer. The fee includes free swimming and fishing privileges.

If you just want to seek the Lake Holley lunker bass, the charge is two dollars a day per person, either to fish from your boat, or from a rental boat, or from the bank.

A small store provides camping essentials, fishing tackle and live bait—used mainly for panfish. The mailing address is Lake Holley Campgrounds, P.O. Box 841, DeFuniak Springs, Fla., 32433, telephone (904) 892-5915.

Nearest motels and restaurants are in DeFuniak Springs, four miles to the south on U.S. 331 highway. DeFuniak Springs is located on U.S. 90 and Interstate 10 highways. Both roads run from Jacksonville on the east to Pensacola on the west across the northern part of the state.

For additional information you can write the Walton County Chamber of Commerce, P.O. Box 29, DeFuniak Springs, Fl., 32433, or the regional office of the Florida Game and Fish Commission, Rt 4, Box 759, Panama City, Fl. 32405.

Lake Holley is one honey hole where you can hook lunkers from the bank as well as from the boat. Of course, landing them is another matter. It's up to you. Better have a lucky rabbit's foot along.

# 18

# Juniper Lake— Lumber Pile On End

*How can I land lunker, largemouth, black bass in a jungle of stickups, both above and below water? How do I even get a lure near a fish hideout?*

Such reactions are typical of many fishermen upon their first sight of Juniper Lake which is located in the Florida Panhandle near De-Funiak Springs. The challenge is huge. But, to a typical dyed-in-the-wool bassman, the greater the challenge, the more interesting the fishing.

Tiny Juniper Lake provides all the challenge you can handle. It's a challenge to even navigate the oversize pond. It is even more of a challenge to get your lure to a bass. And, buddy, it's a challenge to land a lunker of any size after you've hooked up.

Many call this man-made lake of approximately 650 acres a "lumber pile on end." That's a good description. When you realize how the lake was formed, you shudder at the thought of the underwater hazards facing you. What a hideout for bass!

This little lake produces bigmouth bass in the 11 to 13-pound range. The lake's record is 17 pounds, 8 ounces, although Florida Game and

Fish Wildlife officers have seen two catches that went better than 18 pounds.

So fantastic has the fishing been at times that the Game and Fish Commission one year issued a press release *denying* that a new world's record largemouth bass had been seined, tagged, and then released in Juniper. Regardless of the false report, Juniper *does* harbor lunker bass.

An unusual facet of this lunker hole is its location. It's in the Sandhills of the Florida Panhandle instead of the famous Florida lake country. Yet its fishing has been so good at times that rumors concerning the world's record fish were believed along the angling grapevine in north Florida, south Alabama, and south Georgia.

It's understandable why the rumors would be believed. Geographically Juniper could qualify. It's south of the site in south Georgia where the world's record bass was caught in 1932 by George Perry. His mark of 22 pounds, 4 ounces has stood since.

However, Juniper bass live in the same sort of climate and growing conditions as do south Georgia bass. Juniper bass have lacked the fishing pressure of bigger and better known bass holes. A new world's record fish may well be swimming in Juniper, but to date the lake's biggest fall shy of the mark. But if some of Juniper's bass can grow to more than 18 pounds, someday one of them just might keep on growing to a new world's mark.

To understand why such a small body of water is capable of producing lunker bass consistently, you have to understand the lake's construction. Juniper was formed by damming a small creek twisting through a titi swamp. As a result, there is a virtually unreachable sanctuary in the middle where a world record bass could die of old age without ever seeing a fishing lure. Why the sanctuary? It's caused by the "lumber pile on end."

In the 1960s, the Walton County Soil Conservation Service and the Walton County Commission built a dam across a small creek and drained a tiny, natural pond. Surrounding the pond was a titi swamp. The dam was completed in 1962, and all fish life was poisoned. In the fall of 1962, restocking began when bluegills and shellcrackers were placed in the slowly filling lake.

Channel catfish were added during the winter of 1962-63, and bass fingerlings stocked in 1963. The lake was opened to the public in May, 1964, and since has been managed by the Florida Game and Fish Commission.

During the construction of the lake, there was a minimum of vegetation clearing. A narrow stretch was cleared around the shoreline by hand, and in a few places by a bulldozer. Otherwise, everything was left untouched, resulting in the "lumber pile on end" in the middle where the dense titi swamp was originally.

A titi swamp is different from other swamps. It's far more dense. The titi is a small tree that thrives in shallow swamps, usually with a small, crooked trunk that divides into numerous branches 10 to 12 feet above the ground.

The trees are now dead, but their skeletons create an underwater jungle that makes boating impossible, provides a perfect bass hideout, and guarantees broken lines if you do hook a large fish in the maze. It's no wonder that veteran anglers prefer twenty-five to thirty-pound test lines.

That's the background of this half-pint lake where big fish are common if you put all the necessary ingredients together—time of year, fishing techniques, and lures.

Spring—during the spawning season—undoubtedly is the prime time to look for wall-mount bass. Of this period, March is the top month. One March day, Billy Allen of DeFuniak Springs landed two bass on eight-inch plastic worms. One weighed 11 pounds, 14 ounces, and the other 13 pounds, 8 ounces.

Such one-day catches aren't too unusual. Allen Rhodes, another DeFuniak Springs angler, too, had fantastic luck. One March day, he landed three bass, only slightly smaller than Allen's. Rhodes boated bigmouths weighing 8½, 9½, and 10½ pounds. He had three fish totaling 29 pounds or an average of 9.6 pounds.

The lake's monthly records are fairly well established, as a result of a collection of pictures of big catches taken by Grady Clark when he ran a small store called Clark's Landing for several years.

The January-to-April period is the most consistent producer of big fish. The monthly marks during this period range from 12 to 13 pounds. Oddly, even bigger fish have been caught in the hot weather. The biggest landed in August weighed 13 pounds, 10 ounces, while usually slow September has produced a 13-pound, 12-ounce lunker. Such catches are really outstanding.

The lake's record is considered to be 17 pounds, 8 ounces. Grady Clark, when operating Clark's Landing years ago, weighed that fish for a beaming angler. It's a hard mark to beat. Bass that grow larger than 15 pounds are far from common.

Another interesting facet of this oddball lake is you have just as good a chance of landing a big bass at high noon as you do early or late in the day. On one trip to Juniper, I learned of three big bass being landed during the high-noon period. One fish weighed 8 pounds, 5 ounces; another 9 pounds; and Ralph Noble, with whom I was fishing

This 6-pound bass hit a plastic worm in Juniper Lake, the "lumber pile on end." Plastic worms are essential for fishing Juniper because of the overabundance of underwater hazards. Surface lures work sometimes if you can find enough clear water.

along with Grady Clark, boated a 6½-pound bass. Any time you are on the lake, you run the risk of encountering a real heavyweight, which, of course, just makes the challenge of fishing Juniper just that much more interesting.

With this evidence, it is obvious that Juniper can be fished successfully despite its unusual waters. But how do you do so? After fishing the lake several times with Clark, Noble, and Jim Canaday of Freeport, who fishes the little lake frequently, the pattern became apparent.

Your fishing area is restricted, but you can still catch lunkers. You can only operate a boat on the perimeter of the lake and on the edges of the "lumber pile." Even then you must watch out for floating logs and stickups only inches below the water's surface. If you have a very big bass boat, you need to be extra cautious. The ideal Juniper boat is a small skiff in the twelve to fourteen-foot range. You don't need a lot of power or speed, because there is only eight miles of shoreline.

The best lure is the plastic worm, fished in various ways depending upon the time of year. During the January-to-March period, Juniper veterans generally use a worm without a weight. Much of the fishing is in very shallow water, particularly when the bass are beginning to move in to spawn. The preferred colors are black, dark blue, dark green, deep purple, and purple-grape. These colors, too, are good all year around.

While the majority of the lake's anglers prefer worms, there are some who favor top-water lures. The best time for fishing on top, and for deep-diving crank baits if you can find water sufficiently clear of snags to use them, is the April-to-June period. During this time, top-waters with single and double propellers produce, as well as shallow-running lipped plugs. Spinner baits, too, are effective because of their ability to run over and through underwater snags. But no lure is 100 percent free from fouling. Veteran anglers make certain they have extra lures in their tackle boxes.

Color for surface and subsurface lures usually is black and silver, although a few anglers prefer the frog-back combination. Juniper normally is a gin-clear lake, hence black and gold, and crawdad colors aren't too popular. But, as with any statement about bass fishing, there are days when such colors are the keys to success.

During the hot months of July through September, ninety-nine percent of the anglers use plastic worms. These are fished deep with a slip sinker. Of course, Juniper's average depth is only 10 feet.

Early and late in the day, the bass are in the shallows, and top-water lures can be used. The rest of the time, the bigmouths are seeking the shade of the lumber pile. Then, it's a case of tossing a weighted worm to the edges and into the underwater jungle.

In the fall—October through November—again the plastic worm is the best lure, both with and without a slip sinker. At this time of year, the bass are widely scattered, sometimes along the shore, sometimes around the few grass beds, and sometimes along the outer edges of the "lumber pile." You have to keep searching for them, but fortunately there isn't really a lot of water to search.

Juniper virtually has a level bottom, and as a result, the fish roam everywhere. Therefore, you don't have to hunt for specific areas such as drop-offs and structures as you do on big impoundments.

There are a few grassy points that produce more often than others, but your chances of connecting are good anywhere in the pond *if* the bass are in a hitting mood. Juniper bass, like all members of their tribe, can be temperamental and moody.

As most bass fishermen are aware, many of the really big bass in Florida are caught with shiners so big that northern anglers would consider them prize catches. However, Juniper is different. Shiners are not particularly effective. Apparently shiners are not part of the Juniper bass food chain.

For those who prefer live bait fishing, the most effective are spring lizards fished over bass beds in the spring. Anglers from Georgia and South Carolina have brought lizards to the lake and scored big. But you must take your own because spring lizards are not sold locally.

Tackle for fishing this unusual lake is standard. Most anglers prefer twenty to thirty-pound test lines with stiff rods for horsing the bass out of the underwater hazards. Most use bait-casting reels, although there is no reason to overlook spinning tackle if that's your specialty. However, spin fishermen usually prefer heavier than normal lines—seventeen to twenty-pound test. The lures are the standard bass ones used all over the nation.

If you're unfamiliar with the location of DeFuniak Springs, it's not hard to find. The little town is on U.S. 90 and Interstate 10, which run from Pensacola on the west to Jacksonville on the east.

Juniper Lake is located three miles north of DeFuniak Springs between State Road 83 and U.S. 331. The easiest route to follow is Florida 83.

DeFuniak Springs is a small town with very limited accommodations. There are four motels, one of which is at the I-10 interchange, and four campgrounds.

For additional information contact the Walton County Chamber of Commerce, P.O. Box 29, DeFuniak Springs, Fl., 32433, or the regional office of the Florida Game and Fish Commission, Route 4, Box 759, Panama City, Fl., 32405.

While you don't need a map to navigate on this pond, one can help you get oriented, and note the slight variations in the modest depths. The map is published by Southern Guide Fishing Maps, P.O. Box 1326, 500 Gulfshore Drive, Destin, Fl., 32541.

Don't think you're going to land a "hawg" every time you fish Juniper. You won't. But this "lumber pile on end" offers more concentrated chances to score than do many more famous Florida fishing waters.

# 19

# Florida's Forgotten Oklawaha River

It was a short cast, tight against the bank of the fast flowing stream with a shallow-diving crank bait. Two turns of my reel handle, and I felt the solid strike. Immediately a scrappy, largemouth black bass came out of the water like a miniature missile.

Failing to shake the hooks with these aerial antics, he powered off momentarily aided by the current but my rod's spring halted the charge. Then he gamely resisted, as I slowly forced him alongside for Buck Bray to dip the net. The little scrapper was barely 2 pounds, but he had put up a good fight aided by the river's current. And against eight-pound test line and light rod, it was an even match.

The size of the bass wasn't so important as the location. The scrapper came from a portion of the Oklawaha River which has been defiled by the U.S. Corps of Engineers' ill-advised attempt to build the Cross State Barge Canal.

For centuries, Florida's Oklawaha River has meandered northward through the center of the state from its headwaters in Lake Griffin to eventually empty into the also northward flowing St. Johns River. Until the early 1960s, the Oklawaha was a beautiful, primitive stream twisting

*137*

along the western edge of the Ocala National Forest. At one time, small steamboats crossed the lower portion of the river from the St. Johns to Silver Springs, even as far back as when U.S. Grant was president.

But, in the 1960s, man intervened and attemped to build a barge canal across the Florida peninsula. The boondoggle waterway was to utilize the St. Johns River and the Oklawaha River via a series of pools and locks (Rodman and Eureka) after which the canal was to be dug west across the state to join the Withlacoochee River near Dunnellon, and eventually to enter the Gulf of Mexico. Aroused Florida citizens put up a long fight and stopped the pork-barrel project by proving the economics false. Nevertheless, the Rodman dam and pool were completed.

Filling of the Rodman reservoir did two things. First, it momentarily created a super fishing hole until the hydrilla, hyacinths, and other Florida weeds became major problems. And, second, by happenstance it created the "forgotten Oklawaha."

Today, there's a thirty-eight-mile stretch of the Oklawaha River from its Lake Griffin headwaters to the vicinity of the incompleted Eureka lock and dam that's all but forgotten by anglers.

It's a fishing area that can be very productive, and at the same time is vastly different from normal Florida lake fishing. It's also an area where there are only two fish camps. It is do-it-yourself fishing country, which offers no problems because there are ample paved ramps for launching along the river.

After fishing the "forgotten river" several times with Lon Maas, Dick Hale, and Buck Bray, professional guides always eager to take a busman's holiday, it became very apparent you have to explore and learn this thirty-eight-mile stretch of the "forgotten Oklawaha."

Lures that produce in one area flop in another. Undoubtedly, the key to fishing the river is understanding the peculiar topography of the river itself. By happenstance, the thirty-eight miles divides naturally into three sections because of launching sites from highways. The river also is part of the St. Johns water management district, which has a lock and dam located at Moss Bluff where Florida highway 464 crosses the Oklawaha.

There are paved ramps on both sides of the lock and dam, and most anglers launch on the side of the river they intend to fish. However, it's no problem to transit the lock between 8 A.M. and 5 P.M.

You can fish one or all of three sections of the forgotten Oklawaha. Each section has its own peculiarities. The upper third is from the Lake Griffin headwaters to Moss Bluff Lock. The middle section is from the Lock to Florida 40, just below where Silver Springs' run pours millions of gallons of gin-clear water into the river. And the lower third is from Florida 40 to the site of the now abandoned Eureka lock and dam.

It's surprising how different the various sections are. The upper third is a sluggish, slow-moving stream unless water is being released through the Moss Bluff dam spillway. Then the current is much swifter, depending upon how much water is being released. But normally, this is slow-water fishing, according to Lon Maas, who frequently guides on this section. Both banks have heavy cover such as overhanging brush, tall reeds, cat tails, fallen trees, as well as submerged brush. There're also patches of lily pads. Where you choose to fish governs your success.

During the first quarter of the year, Maas recommends fishing tight against the bank because the bass are bedding in the shallow water. Naturally, wild shiners are the number one bait, but he's also had good luck with his parties using six-inch, black worms with pearl blue tails.

During the April-to-June quarter, you modify your technique, according to Maas. You begin to toss your worm around stumps and stickups. In June, you begin to fish more crank baits, such as Model A Bomber Fire Tiger, crawdad color Deep Wee R, Bagley's deep-diving Small Fry, and Killer B-II in either baby bass, or Tennessee Shad colors.

Because the upper third of the river usually is dingy to extremely murky for some unknown reason, your lure colors have to be the ones that are most visible under such conditions. Maas also changes his worm color, now preferring violet and grape rather than black. Some anglers prefer firetail worms if the water is particularly murky.

In the July-to-September period, you find the bass either in extremely heavy cover or in deeper water, in either case trying to find a comfortable temperature. You can use deep-running crank baits fished off the edge of heavy cover, or eight-inch worms. Lure colors remain unchanged, although at times ice blue becomes an effective hue.

During the fall quarter, Maas depends almost exclusively upon worms, sometimes using crank baits. The lure colors are the same.

Lon's biggest fish from the river weighed 7 pounds, 14 ounces, but he knows that there are bigger ones in the Oklawaha. The biggest he has seen weighed from this section was a 14-pounder. The bass was caught with a wild shiner.

Below Moss Bluff lock and dam, the character of the river changes. The water tends to be clearer, but remains discolored to a degree. There's good cover in this section of the river, but it's a different type, consisting of lily pads, and water hyacinths. Whereas the section above Moss Bluff has basically a black, muddy bottom, the middle section has more sand. Too, the river narrows, which increases the current. Moving water, which means more oxygen, is another of the secrets of fishing success in the Oklawaha.

There are several areas where small springs empty into the river, and these usually are fishing holding areas. The moving spring water provides additional oxygen, and also is cooler, particularly during the warm months. You have to be alert to spot the springs, for they're not violent bubblers. In many cases, they are merely indicated by wet rocks or wet banks.

Your choice of lures remains basically the same in this section, and because the river narrows, you're fishing tight against the shore regardless of the time of year.

We found the lower third of the river by far the most interesting. You can launch at a modern, double ramp in a little park alongside Florida 40 where it crosses the Oklawaha east of Ocala and Silver Springs.

By cruising two or three miles upstream, you can begin a downstream float through primitive wilderness beauty that's difficult to find today. The current is swifter than farther up the river, and the forest is dense on both shores. In places, the Oklawaha is a narrow tunnel through a canopy of dense foilage.

This area is the one used most often by Dick Hale when guiding parties on the river, and he is familiar with the quirks of this fast-water fishing.

As the river narrows, the current increases and after passing the point where Silver Springs Run joins the Oklawaha, you are always fishing fast-moving water.

This section offers a different challenge—gin-clear water most of the time. With Silver Springs—the largest in Florida—pouring millions of gallons daily into the Oklawaha, seldom is the river anything but clear. It takes a hard rain to discolor the water, and such discoloration doesn't last long. Hence, you're forced to use lighter lines. Dick Hale, when guiding or tournament fishing, often resorts to four and six-pound test lines and matching lures.

If you want strikes, you have to match your line and lures to the extremely clear water. You may tangle with a fish you can't handle, but that's better than not tangling at all.

Also the Oklawaha isn't a particularly deep river. Our depth finders consistently showed a range of 5 to 10 feet in midstream, but this was the area where we had the most action.

On one trip, we had some thirty strikes—not all landings, of course.

The fish hit a variety of lures: a Smithwick small crank bait, Tennessee shad color; a Fire Tiger Model A Bomber; an all-white Skimmer-Head spinner bait; and five different-colored plastic worms—black with blue tail, brown and orange, motor oil, shad, and grape.

Although we scored with a variety of lures, there was only one place to catch fish—tight against the bank. The banks are lined with deadfalls, overhanging trees, willows, lily pads, a few water hyacinths, rock ledges, and underwater snags.

The current is swift, and it requires pinpoint casting to reach the banks. The fish hug the shoreline cover because of the cool shade, and, oddly, are along the shore in the winter because the water is warmer. Of course, the outpouring from Silver Springs is the moderating influence. An important rule for success in the river is fish the bank *tight!*

Hale, who has lived and fished in the Ocala area since he was eight years old, generally agrees with Maas as to how to fish the river during the year. Like Lon, Dick advises his parties to use shiners if they want big bass during the January-to-March period. For artificials, he prefers small minnow-type shallow-diving crank baits fished tight against the bank. He also sometimes uses a top-water Tiny Torpedo.

"The old timers," he explains, "had a simple system for fishing the Oklawaha. They tossed Tiny Torpedo lures tight against the banks, twitched them once or twice, and then made a speedy retrieve to cast again.

"If the bass were there, they'd sock the Tiny Torpedoes hard. With a good current, the old timers could cover a lot of territory, and put fish in the boat.

"The system still will work," he adds, "but today's basser seems to have forgotten about top-water lures. But I've scored when I went to the system. It's a fast one, and you can cover a lot of territory."

In the April-to-June period, Hale rates plastic worms as the number one lure followed by crank baits. He prefers six-inch fire tail worms if the water is murky, and the standard single color if the water is clear. He uses black, purple, purple-grape, motor oil, and shad. He also will experiment with oddball colors. His favorite crank baits are little Bagley balsa lures in either Tennessee Shad or Baby Bass colors; Model A Bombers, both Shad and Fire Tiger colors.

During the July-to-September period, Dick sticks to worms as his first choice, and he also finds that a yellow Snagless Sally with a pork chunk to be effective around lily pads.

In the fall, he prefers to fish the lakes but does spend some time on the Oklawaha. He uses crank baits and sometimes spinner baits.

Hale's biggest fish from the Oklawaha weighed 8 pounds. However, he's seen a 10-pounder that came from the "forgotten" area, and he knows there are bigger fish just waiting to be caught.

While the forgotten Oklawaha does harbor big fish, it's better known for its action and numbers. When you hook a 3 or 4-pound fish in swift water studded with underwater hazards, you know you're in for a scrap.

While there are a few fish camps on the river you have no trouble finding overnight accommodations, particularly to fish the lower third of the forgotten river. There are numerous motels in Silver Springs, the community on the doorstep of the famous attraction, and of course, Ocala has a great number of motels that are heavily tourist oriented because of Silver Springs. It's a case of taking your choice. The Florida 40 launching ramp is only a short distance from Silver Springs and Ocala.

It's simpler to hire a guide for your first trip, because a professional knows where the fish are at the moment After that you can explore on your own. If you want to contact either Maas or Hale, you can do so as follows: Dick Hale, Route 2, Box 16A, Silver Springs, Fl., 32688, telephone (904)625-2984; and Lon Maas, 5137 S.W. 107th St., Belleview, Fl., 32620, telephone (904) 245-5010.

The bass of the "forgotten Oklawaha" are hard fighters, and subjected to far less pressure than many of the largemouths in other Florida waters. For a different fishing experience, sample the "forgotten Oklawaha." The odds are great you won't quickly forget the experience.

# 20

# Deer Point Lake—Fishing Hole for Sneaky Anglers

Austin Tharp and Chuck Hall are sneaky anglers. They are not dishonest. They catch their fish legally with hook and line, and with artificial lures. But I regard anglers who catch big bass with special lures as very sneaky, especially when I don't own that particular lure.

They've both pulled sneak plays on me on various trips on Deer Point Lake near Panama City in the Florida Panhandle. As a result, they have won a permanent reputation with me as being sneaky fishermen. Whenever I fish with them, I keep one eye on my line, and the other on their line to see what oddball lure they are using. They don't tell you. They just put fish in the boat.

Austin showed his true nature the first time I sampled Deer Point. He joined our party late, first having to get someone to tend his little Camp Cedar while he took a day off to go fishing. He knows the lake like few do. Not only is he an excellent fisherman, but he has fished Deer Point Lake ever since it was formed.

We had been having scant luck in Econfina Creek—one of the main feeders of the lake—when Austin arrived. After finding us, he eased his boat back down the creek around a bend. Ten minutes later, he came roaring back proudly hollering that we ought to learn how to fish.

He had boated a 6-pound largemouth black bass on a sinking Dillinger plug, a type not too often seen nowadays, but a longtime favorite of his. The bass had hit the plug on his third cast near a sunken log.

Of course, he had the only lure of that type. We claimed he had the bass staked out, and maybe he did know the bass lurked there. But knowing where bass are and getting them to hit are two different things. Anyway, we envied his oddball plug.

Now consider Chuck Hall. He, too, is sneaky. Austin and I were fishing with him one day. The grass was near the surface forcing us to use top-water lures. Austin and I threw every lure in our tackle box with nary a roll. But what did Chuck do? He scored, and in a very sneaky way. He had a Bagley Bang-O-Lure with a single propeller. This lure barely runs under the surface during retrieve, and won't dive as deep as the regular Bang-O-Lure with a lip but having no propeller.

By casting his lure across the grass beds, Chuck was able to tease the bass into striking. It appeared they were angered by the propeller buzzing as well as the balsa's tantalizing movements. Regular propeller plugs didn't produce, nor did the regular Bang-O-Lure without a propeller. So Austin and I moaned as he landed a pair of 4-pounders, while all we got was zero.

Maybe you have to be a sneaky fisherman to score on Deer Point. At least, you have to be versatile and not set in your fishing habits. Such incidents as these indicate the versatility that is needed to fish this lake where many local anglers think a world-class bass might be lurking.

Logically, Florida is a leading candidate to produce the next record fish. Growing conditions are ideal for lunker bigmouths. Of course, the present world record of 22 pounds, 4 ounces is held by Georgia. However, that fish came from the southern third of the Peach State, much the same type of country that north Florida has, and bass do not pay any attention to state lines when they are growing.

One visit to beautiful Deer Point Lake and a few queries into its background, and you would probably be inclined to agree with the locals who believe that a new world record bass might be in the cypress-studded waters. Deer Point possibly could be the place. It has the necessary assets.

Undoubtedly conditions will have to be almost perfect for a new record bass to grow. Deer Point has the conditions. Pollution will have to be nonexistent, and it is in Deer Point because the lake—actually

Beautiful Deer Point Lake was never cleared, and you fish among standing cypress and dead pine trees. Worms are effective around the cypress, while shallow-running top-water lures are effective worked over the grass beds that develop late in the summer. Top-water prop plugs are essential when the grass becomes extremely thick.

an impoundment—is a 5,860 acre water reservoir serving the Lynhaven and Panama City area. Also the lake has ample water from Bear, Cedar, and Econfina creeks so much that by design it overflows the dam regularly, the excess water emptying into salty North Bay.

The lake was formed by a dam across the upper part of North Bay, which joins salty West and St. Andrews Bay, which in turn open into the Gulf of Mexico.

A dam was erected across the upper part of North Bay into which the freshwater creeks empty. After the water turned from salt to fresh, all fish were poisoned, and the lake re-stocked. It was opened to the public in 1964, and since has been a steady bass producer despite its tremendously clear water.

As a result of the dam, you can fish for black bass, bream, and shellcrackers above the barrier, and for such saltwater fish as speckled sea trout and channel bass (redfish) below the dam. The saltwater fishing is best early in the fall following the first cold snap. There are fishing catwalks on the saltwater side of the dam.

Too, unlike many artificial impoundments, the lake was not cleared after or before flooding. Today, there is ample fish cover, ranging from tall cypress and underwater snags to shallow grass flats studded with skeletons of dead pine trees. Also there are deep holes, some 18 to 20 feet, in the old creek channels.

Although never cleared, Deer Point offers no great navigational problems to wary boatmen. Obviously, you don't go hot rodding among the dead, fallen, and standing timber, but there are no problems in the old creek channels.

It's also a lake that doesn't require big-bomb motors. Many fishermen use nine and one-half HP motors, while a twenty-HP motor is regarded as ideal as long as your boat isn't too heavy. Anglers with heavy boats generally need bigger motors.

The biggest fish that Austin has seen caught weighed 16 pounds, 2 ounces. He calls it a $150 bass, and with good reason. Austin located the lunker's hangout. Every time he went past the location, he made a few casts. "I hung him seven times," he recalls, "and lost seven plugs on fifteen and twenty-pound test lines. He'd always run back into the brush and pop my line. After losing my seven lures, I quit. That old bass was getting too expensive for me.

"Then I told five other good bassmen where they could find this big fish. They did. They didn't do any good either. Altogether they figure they lost $150 worth of lures fooling with that fish. Then the payoff! A twelve-year-old boy landed the fish!"

Pausing to reflect on the irony of the situation, Austin continues:

"This youngster was fishing with his Dad. They were near the big-mouth's hang out, but they didn't know it. The boy tossed a Rebel top-water lure near the stump. The ol' mossback socked it.

"It's funny how things work out," reflects Austin. "The boy was using a closed-face reel with 8-pound test line. Luckily the bass headed for open water, and the boy's Daddy cranked up their three-horsepower motor, and they started after the bass.

"The line held. They kept up with the bass, and the boy did a good job of rod handling. Finally they tired the lunker, and boated him.

"And to think, six of us donated more than $150 worth of plugs and couldn't land the fish with heavier line."

Austin's biggest fish is a 11-pound, 15-ounce lunker landed on a top-water plug (Lucky 13) on a cold February day in 1972. Hall's biggest is a 12-pounder he landed fishing one July. The bucketmouth swallowed a Muskie Jitterbug. That calls for a big mouth, indeed.

A fascinating aspect of Deer Point fishing is the success at landing big fish with top-water lures. The number of big bass caught with shallow-running lipped plugs is intriguing, particularly during the first months of the year.

Possibly 1976 was an unusual year, and maybe not, but the first four months produced a surprising number of big bass on top-water lures. In January, Johnny Walker landed a 13½-pound bass with a broken-back Rebel. In March, Rory Smith, also of Panama City, boated a 13¼-pounder on a gold Rebel. The same month, Tom Lox of Youngstown, Florida, landed a 14-pound bass on a gold Rapala. And in April, Reuben Lowery landed a 10½-pound bass, also on a Rapala. This doesn't mean you can't catch big bass with other types of artificial lures. You can, but shallow-running top-waters seem to have the edge.

Among the other bigmouths landed early in 1976 were a 13-pound, 4-ounce fish caught by Larry Carroll of Panama City; and a 12¼-pounder boated by Bill Pitts of Lynhaven in February. Both fish were landed with plastic worms.

Another oddity about Deer Point is the importance of gold coloring on lures. Normally, the black and silver color scheme is preferred by most anglers using shallow-running lipped plugs in clear water, although it is not number one on Deer Point, according to Tharp.

Even though the water is usually gin clear, the old rule of silver for clear water, and gold or yellow for murky does not seem to apply too well to Deer Point as witness the hefty bass caught with gold-colored lures.

Even plastic worm fishing has its quirks on the lake. This shows in the color choice. If you are fishing near Bear Creek, the preferred worm color is watermelon green. But a red-colored worm is the best producer in Cedar Creek. Elsewhere purple and black are the prime colors. It doesn't make sense, but that's bass fishing on Deer Point.

It's obvious from the records that the fishing is best in Deer Point during the cooler months, and Austin confirms this. Year after year, he's seen the biggest fish landed during these months. The prime time spans the last two weeks in February and the first two weeks in March. The weather is the governing factor, and the Panhandle's weather is far different from farther south in the state.

Austin knows that the best overall fishing months are November through March. There's a reason. This is the low grass period. The grass partially dies during the cold weather, and is farther below the surface. During this period, you find the fish in the lily pads, around stickups and stobs in water from three to six feet deep.

You have to change your fishing tactics in the spring. Then you fish top-water lures in shallow water, around fallen and standing dead trees, old logs, and various debris. Deer Point has plenty of such cover.

From May through September, you fish deeper water. Late in the summer, most fish are found in Econfina and Bear Creeks near their entrances into Deer Point, and a short distance up the creeks.

In October, with the grass and weeds at maximum height, you have to fish top-water lures over grass beds in eight to ten feet of water with the grass only inches below the surface.

Bass fishing, however, isn't Deer Point's only asset. It's also a fabulous panfish lake. After the dam was completed, the reservoir was re-stocked with bass, shellcrackers, bluegills, channel and blue catfish. There was a basic stock of crappie in the creeks.

The shellcrackers, particularly, have multiplied, and when they are bedding, the fishing can be fabulous. The biggest shellcracker weighed at Camp Cedar so far is 3¼ pounds. Crappie, both black and white, average three-quarters of a pound, although a 2-pound, 4-ounce papermouth has been landed.

Bream fishing is excellent for the cane pole brigade. As many as 330 bream have been taken off a single bed. Thirty-three boats fished the bed for six days to compile this fantastic total. The six days before the full moon in April, May, and June are the top fishing periods for both bream and shellcrackers.

Deer Point is big enough and tricky enough to warrant a guide for initial trips. If you want to fish with Chuck Hall, who guides on the lake, his address is; Chuck Hall, 2622 E. 40th Court, Panama City, Fl., 32401, telephone (904) 763-1871. He guides from a modern bass boat with trolling motor.

With its clear water and abundance of cover, Deer Point is a bassing challenge. Catching a lunker requires angling skill and no little luck, but the big fish are there if you're expert enough to land them. If not, the panfishing is great.

# 21

# Scrappy Choctawhatchee River Bass

Florida's Choctawhatchee River with the jaw breaking Indian name originates in southern Alabama and wends a tortuous course some 110 miles across the Panhandle of Florida to empty into the Gulf of Mexico. First as a small stream, and finally as a respectable river ranging from 100 to 500 feet in width as it snakes across Florida, the Choctaw is a rare outdoors jewel.

It is one of the few rivers in Florida that has escaped damage by man. No nine-foot barge channels are maintained. No reservoirs impede its twisting route, and waterfront real estate projects are almost unknown. It's a stream that's largely unchanged from the nineteenth century, unchanged even from centuries before that when white man first began blundering around the continent of North America.

It's a river with dead heads in unusual places. Sandbars are plentiful, and often unexpected. Don't cruise too close to shore on the many bends, or you may go aground. The deeper water generally is on outer edge of the often deceptive sandbars.

Where the river bank is comparatively high, or when the water is unusually low, exposed tree roots are visible as the untamed river gnaws relentlessly and the trees struggle for life. Often the river wins, and another fish haven drops into the stream.

How long it will remain an untamed river is unknown, but until it does become another Corps of Engineers' nightmare, it is a stream offering all of the thrills of primitive river fishing. It not only produces hefty largemouth black bass, but also stripers (rockfish) in the 20-pound class that can tear up bass tackle, and rare Kentucky spotted bass found only in Florida waters west of the Apalachicola River.

Fishing the Choctaw falls into four divisions, and each is a bit different, although they all provide superb river fishing. The lower section includes the river's delta consisting of Nancy's Cut, Mitchell River, lower part of Black Creek, Williams Lake, Indian River, Duck Lake, Cypress River, Reedy Branch, Sisters River, and upstream to the brackish water line, which varies according to the rain on the Choctaw's watershed.

Moving upriver, the next section is from the brackish water line to where Florida highway 20 crosses the river near the little hamlet of Ebro.

Section three is from Florida 20 to where Interstate 10 and U.S. 90 highways cross the Choctaw near Caryville. And the final section is from I-10 into Alabama where the river begins to dwindle as it nears its headwaters.

From the delta to the Florida-Alabama line, the Choctaw has numerous sloughs, cutoffs, oxbow lakes, and vast swamps. The Choctaw is bordered by primitive land, and the twisting nature of the river makes it far different than fishing huge flat bodies of waters of reservoirs. This is a different situation, indeed. The water and the fishing techniques are different.

As you float downstream backwards because your electric trolling motor handles your boat best while pointed upstream, you encounter a variety of river banks. These vary in height from 5 feet near the bay to 30 feet and more along the Upper Choctaw.

As reservoir bass fishermen quickly learn, river fishing is a different ball game, particularly on an untamed river like the Choctawhatchee. But there's a fascination, a different type of challenge to fishing an untamed stream that hasn't changed much in the last century.

As Chuck Hall, who guides on the river, explains: "I get many reservoir anglers who really enjoy fishing the wild Choctaw 'cause they discover in a hurry, it's a different ball game. That adds to the fun. And a good bassman has no problem adjusting to this river fishing, although some take a little longer than others."

There are several factors vital to success in fishing the Choctaw.

The first, of course, is the obvious question when is the best time to fish? The answer surprises some. You have to fish the Choctaw when conditions are right, and these don't necessarily coincide with the recommended best bassing times by calendar. You can fish the Choctaw any time the water level is right, and this can occur at any time of the year.

For prime fishing, you want the Choctaw to be well within its banks, even on the low side, although too low water can cause problems for big bass boats. These prime conditions can occur any time, depending upon the rainfall on the river's watershed, mainly in the south of Alabama. The Choctaw is subject to constant and often rapid changes in water level, and fluctuations of six to nine feet are common at any time during the year.

As the Choctawhatchee veterans say: "When the river's rising, high, or flooding, forget it! Bass fishing will be horrible!"

They know from experience. Once you've seen the numerous sloughs and overflow swamps that become fish sanctuaries during flood or high-water stages, it's plain why the local experts head elsewhere to fish then. The fish can get way back in the swamps where you can't reach them.

Some of the finest Choctaw fishing is in the river's delta just above the saltwater line. It's in the lowest reaches of the river that you frequently encounter stripers feeding wildly on shad during the spring months. These saltwater stripers aren't too plentiful, but some of them are real line stretchers.

Rockfish in the 20-pound class often hit small black bass lures, particularly top-water plugs and shallow divers in silver flash or shad colors, or even white as long as the lure might be mistaken for a shad.

If you doubt that stripers tear up bass tackle, your opinion will quickly change when you hear of the experiences of Johnny Pate, a local angler who fishes regularly from Black Creek Lodge on Black Creek which empties into the Choctaw near the little community of Freeport.

One April day, Pate was plugging the shore methodically with top-water lures for bass when he found schooling fish chasing shad in Black Creek. It was a mixed school of largemouths and stripers. He hooked five fish on five successive casts, *but* he landed only one, a 6-pound bass. The other fish, all larger and obviously stripers, broke his line or tossed his lure. He got too many thrills and too few fish, but that's common sometimes near the Choctaw's delta.

Some of the tales Jim Canaday, a veteran Choctaw angler with whom I've fished several times, tells sound like fish yarns, but they aren't. It's startling how "hot" fishing can get when the river's within its banks. One July morning with the river low, Jim caught twenty-five bass in the mouth of a slough near East River in the Delta. Then he moved his boat to the back of the slough, and caught seven more from one small area. He caught and released a total of thirty-two bass, all caught with a deep-diving lure (Deep Wee R). The bass ranged from 1½ to 3 pounds, with the biggest weighing 6 pounds.

Only three days later, Jim fished with Johnny Pate near the Ebro bridge. They caught and released over 100 bass. Wow! Thirty percent of them were under a pound, and the rest from 1½ to 4 pounds. What fun!

After numerous trips with Jim, Chuck Hall of Panama City, who guides on the river, and with such other experts as Duncan McQuade, Whymon Willis, Gene Marshall, and Jerry Meyers, some of the tricks of Choctaw angling have become apparent.

One thing these experts emphasize is that the fish change locations in the river. You find them in widely different areas at various times of the year. Knowing this is a big help.

The calendar changes of locations are these. Starting in February and continuing through April, the prime bass areas are in the still water in the numerous sloughs, and the Choctaw is well supplied. The fish are there because the still water is ideal for spawning.

But during May and June, you have to search for the bigmouths. You then find them in both still and running water of various depths. Oddly, ten miles upstream from the delta branches, the bigmouths are still spawning, while those in the lowest reaches of the river have completed their family chores.

It's a different situation in the heat of summer from July through September. It's hot, and the fish are scattered and very temperamental. You find bass all the way to the edge of Choctaw Bay.

You find them even in water that in the fall harbors saltwater speckled sea trout. The period is when the saltwater shrimp make their periodic migration into brackish water. The mouth of the river and the edges of the bay are very productive, and black bass do like a shrimp cocktail.

The location script changes in the fall. By October, the fish begin moving back into the river proper in the delta, and farther upstream into the main channel seeking deeper and warmer water.

During the cold months, the bigmouths are found mainly in the deeper holes in the river, which you can locate with your depth finder.

The holes are scattered, and often you have to spend considerable time searching. Choctaw bass are sluggish as the temperature drops, and you have to put your lures under their nose.

The following is a rule-of-thumb summarization of Choctawhatchee fishing. In the spring, you should fish upriver as far as possible from the delta gradually moving down as the weather warms. The rest of the year you concentrate on fishing the deep bends in the river's channel, and at times in the sloughs and cutoffs depending upon rainfall.

It's surprising how little a change of water can impair fishing. During one trip on the Upper Choctaw we caught fish but Chuck Hall was disappointed. None of the twenty-odd fish were over 3 pounds. Yet only ten days before that October, Chuck had put a 7-pound, 2-ounce bigmouth in the boat.

He was puzzled at the change in fishing until we floated over a sandbar where he had gone aground the day he landed the 7-pounder. Then he knew the answer. The river had gradually risen 18 inches in the intervening time, and that was enough to change the feeding habits of the Choctaw bass.

Water level, however, isn't the only key factor to successfully fishing the Choctawhatchee. You also have to be able to cast accurately. Unless you've fished a wild river before, you have no idea of the amount of debris, ideal fish cover, that collects naturally along the banks. You have to cast close to or into such cover if you want to score.

If you can't consistently cast accurately, you're fated to spend a lot of time retrieving fouled lures. As it is, even expert casters expect to foul for if you don't, you aren't putting your lure where the bass are hiding. Your ability to cast into tight pockets, under overhanging branches and limbs, and work a lure through sunken brush is important in this Choctaw fishing.

Adding to the casting challenge is the current of the river. You're casting from a constantly moving boat, and while you can maintain your range off shore, you can't stop your lure from being carried downstream by the current.

This same current is an important influence on your choice of lures. Because of the current, and the numerous snags and brush, veteran Choctaw anglers depend mainly upon four types of lures: crank baits; spinner baits; plastic worms; and top-water lures.

In each case, a fast retrieve generally is used to avoid having the current carry the lure into some snag. Sometimes the fast retrieve may be too fast, but more often it is the answer, because river bass are

The primitive Choctawhatchee River affords excellent shore cover for largemouth black bass. You have to be able to cast within inches of the shore, and lure the bass into hitting. Spinner baits are very effective because they can be thrown into close quarters with a minimum of fouling.

more accustomed to chasing a speedy meal than are reservoir fish that seldom are hampered by fast water.

The Choctaw is a chameleon with its ability to change hue. It ranges from almost gin clear to soupy clay in color, depending upon the rainfall along its watershed. When rainfall is minimal, the river tends to be very clear from the springs which feed several tributary creeks draining into the main stream. A full tackle box with a variety of lure colors is essential as a result of the water changes.

The Choctaw, like most rivers, isn't noted for huge bass—ten pounds probably is as large as they grow. But there's apparently a good population of bigmouths in the 8 to 9-pound class.

Hall's biggest to date weighed 8 pounds, 2 ounces after spawning. Had the fish been caught earlier in the spring, it would easily have been in the 9-pound range. He caught his trophy with a naturalized crawdad Rebel crank bait.

Where you cast is a personal choice. Take one look at the water eddying around fallen trees, ancient water-soaked logs, brush piles, and sandbars along the bank, and each appears to be logical target. Each is, and you never lack for casting targets floating down the river.

Another logical area to check are the mouths of sloughs and creeks draining into the main river, especially when there's deep water—three to four feet—and some current. But be prepared to tangle with big chain pickerel in such areas, as well as rough and ready bowfin (mudfish).

The Choctaw is one of the few Florida rivers harboring spotted or Kentucky bass, and while these scrappers never grow as big as largemouth, they are fighters. They love gravel-bottom streams and fast-moving water.

Probably many anglers fail to recognize the spotted bass, for they're found in the same waters as largemouths, and hit the same type of lures. The spotted differs from the bigmouth in having a mouth that does not extend beyond the eye, and has spots below the lateral line. Their maximum size is 4 to 5 pounds.

With a river so influenced by rainfall along its watershed all year long, it's difficult to pinpoint fishing methods and locations by the calendar. There isn't really that much change in Choctaw fishing methods, yet there are subtle ones that can have an important bearing on your success.

On a year-round basis with water at the proper height, veteran Choctaw anglers fish like this. During the January-to-March period, they use spinner baits—both the safetypin and Snagless Sally types. Single blade spinners are preferred because they drop deeper and faster in the moving water. Too, a single blade can be retrieved deeper, and during these months the bass are deep.

Skirt colors change according to conditions of the water. In murky waters, yellow, yellow and black, and chartreuse are favored. For clear water, green and white, and all white skirts produce.

Worm colors are purple-grape, blue, and black. Because of the speed of the current, you usually have to swim your worm even if you're using a lead. It's seldom that you are able to get your worm down deep in the speedy current. Six and seven-inch worms are preferred.

During the first quarter, there is some use of deep-diving crank baits, although they aren't considered quite as effective as spinners. Shad and crawfish colors are preferred for the crank downs.

You change your technique during the April-to-June period. You begin adjusting early in April when the bass begin to move into the shallows preparatory to spawning.

Fishing shallower water, you find shallow-diving lures such as Bagley's balsas, or Rebel's plastic minnows most effective. You can work these either to run a few inches below the surface, or blip them on top like injured bait fish. Black and silver, and black and gold are the generally preferred color combinations. Perch also is a good color.

Come June, the Choctaw anglers turn to noise making, strictly top-water lures such as Devils Horse, Dalton Specials, Nip-A-Diddee, and other single and double propeller plugs. The preferred color is perch. Of course, if no action results on top, you can always resort to spinner and crank baits fished deep. Crawdad, chartreuse, and shad are the favored crank bait colors.

The old reliable plastic worms also produce. They can be fished with or without a weight depending upon the river's current. Usually some sort of a weight is needed. Black, purple, and black-grape are favored colors.

During the hot July-to-September period, there is very little change in lures. The top-water period is very short during the first hour after dawn, and then just at dusk. Otherwise, you fish deep with crank or spinner baits, or with worms. The same color combinations as earlier in the year produce.

In the last quarter of the year, the lures remain the same, except green joins the other worm colors. Should the weather be warm in October and November, top-water lures remain effective. But if the mercury slides, you have to go to deep-diving lures as the fish move into the deeper holes.

Although the Choctaw is an untamed river, it offers no launching problems as a result of the Florida Game and Fish Commission's ramp program. You find both paved and unpaved ramps at strategic points along the river. Drive-on trailers have no problems with paved ramps under normal conditions. However, if you're considering launching on unpaved ones, check carefully before doing so.

The Choctaw is a primitive river with limited accommodations. On the lower river you can stay at Black Creek Lodge, Rt. 1, Freeport, Fl., 32439, telephone (904) 835-2541, or in a small motel near U.S. 331 bridge across Choctawhatchee Bay.

However, the limited accommodations are not important. The lower Choctaw fishing is only about fifteen miles north of U.S. 98, the coastal highway via, U.S. 331 highway. There are a number of beachfront motels on U.S. 98. The nearest large towns are Destin and Fort Walton

Beach on U.S. 98. Both are tourist oriented, and have accommodations of all types and prices.

For the upper sections of the river you have a number of choices. There are motels in DeFuniak Springs and Ponce de Leon, both on U.S. 90, and in Panama City and Panama City Beach. Basing at these requires you drive some distance to the river, but it's really no great problem.

Chuck Hall is the only guide on the river. Although living in Panama City, he trailers his boat and parties to the Choctaw whenever fishing conditions are right. Hall can be reached at 2622 E. 40th Court, Panama City, Fl., 32401, telephone (904) 763-1871.

If you have a hankering for a change of pace in your angling and want to sample an untamed river, then schedule a trip to the Choctawhatchee. It offers a type of elbow room fishing in the wilds that's becoming very, very rare.

# 22

# Apalachicola River Delta— A Bassing Frontier

Fishing the twisting waters comprising the delta of the Apalachicola River in the Florida Panhandle often can be a new and surprising experience for bass anglers.

It's not a heavily fished area, although local bassmen find it a fascinating and productive one. However, the Apalach Delta has not received the publicity of other Florida bass holes. As a result, most anglers who come to the little town at the mouth of the river are saltwater oriented, and there's plenty of saltwater angling.

To understand the river's delta fishing, it's necessary to know something about the entire Apalachicola. The river, now Florida's last major undefiled stream with no concrete dams, originates on the Florida-Georgia state line where the Chattahoochee and Flint Rivers of Georgia meet behind the Jim Woodruff dam that forms Lake Seminole.

The Apalach was an important nineteenth-century waterway. Smoke-belching paddle wheelers plied the river taking out the cotton and other products of the upriver plantations, and bringing in goods from the outside world.

Currently, this little-damaged river is threatened by another Corps

159

of Engineers' pork-barrel boondoggle that seeks to turn the present primitive river into a straight gut canal for the barges of the special interests who profit at the public's expense.

The state of Florida is violently opposed to the proposed plans, but it's a political football, with the special interests in Georgia and Alabama pressing hard. The proposed channelization project is shaping up as a real donnybrook, perhaps as long lasting and as heated as the defeat of another Corps' boondoggle—the ill-advised Cross-State Barge Canal. Time alone holds the final answer as to whether the Apalachicola Delta continues to be a bass hole.

Presently, the delta is really a fishing frontier with aspects anglers familiar with reservoir fishing never encounter. It's a far different type of fishing.

As the Apalachicola nears the Gulf of Mexico north of the little town of the same name, it changes from a single channel into a maze of waterways and bays comprising its delta. Here you find such waterways as St. Marks, Little St. Marks, East, Jackson, and Brothers Rivers, Lake Wimico, Chipley, Double Bayou, Huckleberry, Saul's, Johnson, Cedar, and Grassy Creeks. They are all frequently mentioned by knowledgeable local anglers. There are others, too, some with no names, but all harboring black bass. There are hundreds of miles of fishable waterways, some that seldom see an angler.

Today, the Apalach Delta has an estimated 1,100 miles of shoreline offering anglers plenty of elbow room where you can fish all day and never see more than a couple of boats, and more often than not these are locals seeking "meat for the table" in the form of the abundant panfish found in the waters.

You can get an idea of the abundant bass population at Bay City Lodge docks—one of the two fish resorts in Apalachicola—when the guide boats return. It's seldom the guides return empty handed, and they count it a poor day when their parties don't catch their limits.

The biggest share of the guide fishing is with live bait, and it's surprising what you can do with live saltwater shrimp and shiners.

We've fished the delta both ways and have scored. The first time, Kit and I and our guide landed twenty-one black bass in the 1 to 3-pound range in less than two hours, at the same time tangling with flounder, channel bass (redfish), and jack crevalle in the same brackish waters.

Another time, my guide and I were just as successful with live shiners, although this time the biggest fish was a 4-pounder. Don't think landing a 4-pound bass on a willowy bream pole isn't exciting. It is!

The delta isn't lunker country. The heaviest bass you can expect to catch is in the 9 to 10-pound range, but there's plenty of bass, and if you match your tackle to them, they will test your angling skill.

While the emphasis with the guides is upon fishing with live bait, you can catch bigmouths with artificial lures. But there are quirks to this delta fishing that may surprise you unless you're familiar with brackish water angling.

It's always surprising how close to saltwater you find the bass. In the fall, it's common to fish within sight of the causeway and bridge across Apalachicola The bay and the western side of the causeway is really salty. It's so salty that you can catch such saltwater species as speckled sea trout, redfish (channel bass), Spanish mackerel, sheepshead, and even tarpon at times.

One factor that is not found in impoundment fishing and is often overlooked by first-time anglers, particularly when fishing near salt water, is the impact of the tides. You succeed most often when the tide is falling. With the water falling in the grass, the edge of which you fish, the bait fish have to retreat to the deeper channels. The bass know this, and they lie in ambush waiting a passing meal. Flip your lure into the mouth of a likely exit from the grass and hang on! The odds are good a bigmouth will take a fancy to it, confusing it with a bait fish meal.

Even farther inland, the tide is a factor. The best fishing usually occurs when the tide is falling. While the salt water doesn't come inland, an incoming tide does back up and retard the flow of fresh water, flooding the numerous swamps.

Naturally, the bait fish head for the protected shallows for food, and as far as possible the bass follow. On a high rising—and until the tide has fallen for several hours—it's difficult to reach the bass in the brush with your lures. When the tide turns, the inland swamps begin to drain, and the bait and bass return to deeper water where you can reach them with your lures. By studying the shoreline you can discover these natural fish passages.

To really learn these waters, you should first fish the delta on a falling or low tide. Then you get a picture of where the fish routes are, and you can tell where the bass logically should be. Whether they hit, of course, depends upon how hungry or short tempered they are.

First-time bass anglers are always amazed by the limited number of lures recommended by the pro guides. You don't need a big tackle box to follow their suggestions. They prefer a Snagless Sally with a yellow skirt with a pork frog, or a black and yellow Devils Horse for top-water fishing, and black or purple plastic worms. That's all.

Of course, there're reasons for these recommendations. The first is safety, for they much prefer to fish with cane poles, especially with inexperienced anglers, which is understandable in the too chummy sixteen-foot plywood guide boats. The second reason is the fishing terrain which has so much grass in many places that a weedless lure is a necessity. The third reason is due to a lack of experimentation. They are satisfied with fishing the way it has been done for the last fifty years.

However, other lures will work. After experimenting, I've found you can score with several other types, depending upon the type of water you're fishing. The balsa-type shallow divers are very good, and there are places with deep, sharp banks where you can use crank baits successfully. Also you can use single and double propeller, surface lures, and stick baits.

The most interesting experience with stick baits came one day when I was fishing with Bill Brown, a local angling expert. We got to discussing baits at lunch, and I showed him a Smithwick Carrot Top, a stick lure. He was intrigued and borrowed it. Did it work? Definitely! Of the six bass he caught, three were on the Carrot Top. He probably would have caught more if he had used it all day. Just the day before Bill and his wife had landed two limits (total of twenty) of bass using a blue-back Rebel. Obviously, other lures will work if you experiment, and use them in suitable waters.

Another factor in this delta fishing is the height of the river. You do best when the river is 8 to 10 feet at Blountstown, more than forty miles upstream. When the Apalach is at this stage, it's within its banks, and the fish don't have the room to roam that they do when the water is high.

When the Blountstown reading is over 16 feet—approaching flood stage—fishing usually is much more difficult. You have to fish the creeks and not the main river or main waterways of the delta then.

High water usually also means muddy water, which can retard fishing and force you to change your lure colors radically. Crawfish, orange, and yellow are the best colors for murky waters.

The time of year governs where you fish, and with so much fishing territory, the locales naturally change with the seasons. As a rule of thumb, this is where you find the bass at various times of the year, subject, of course, to weather conditions. A front changes all signals, and the Panhandle is noted for its fast-moving weather fronts at certain times of the year.

In the January-to-March period, the largemouths are in the rivers and creeks far inland from truly brackish water. There's some salt in the water anyway, depending upon the flow of the Apalachicola. If the river is low, the brackish water intrudes farther inland, but it doesn't seem to bother the bass too much, although they do retreat farther inland.

This is the period when the plastic worm is the number one lure. Most anglers prefer the seven to nine-inch worms, and the favored colors are black, blue, and purple, with or without a firetail.

In March and April, the guides prefer to fish live shiners—four to five inches in length—either with brim poles or with rods and reels. You fish the shiners with a float to keep them out of the grass, usually with a 2/0 hook (Eagle Claw). Most of the fishing is in the rivers and creeks. This period, too, sometimes finds the Snagless Sally useful as well as the ever popular plastic worms. Much depends upon the weather.

Late in April and during May, the bass are on the flats and in the weeds, closer to the brackish water line. Again medium-size shiners are preferred both with or without a float. Yellow and black Devils Horse and other top-water propeller plugs also are used. A few anglers continue to use plastic worms, often without weights. This, too, is a good time for the Snagless Sally, always with the green pork chunk. The choice is an obvious one because you are fishing around and over grass beds.

In the May-to-July period, you again are fishing the main river using weighted, plastic worms; top-water plugs with or without propellers; Snagless Sallys; and, of course, the guides' favorite—shiners.

The August-to-December period finds most of the fishing continuing in the brackish water on the flats with very little river and creek angling. This is the guides' opinion, and may be as much tradition as fact. I'm not certain the advice is entirely correct.

I have caught fish back in the creeks with artificials, which makes me suspect the guides may be just habit fishing, not experimenting. Undoubtedly, for live bait (shrimp), the brackish water is the best locale, but bass are fickle, and there are good possibilities in other areas that apparently are not fished at this time of the year.

Lures during the August-to-December period are the same as before, although the six-inch worm seems to produce better than the bigger ones during these months. If the water is exceptionally clear, which frequently happens when the river is low and not carrying a load of Georgia clay, you can sometimes score with such small spinners as a yellow Shyster or Abu Reflex.

Standard bass tackle can be used. Although twenty-pound test is the most popular locally, I prefer eight to ten-pound test line, being a confirmed spinning angler. Also, there are times when even lighter line is mandatory if you want to score in gin-clear waters, particularly back in some of the black water creeks. Sometimes six-pound test is needed.

Your rod can range from medium to heavy action, depending upon whether you are worm or plug fishing. Reels, of course, should match your rods.

We've based at the biggest Apalachicola fish camp—Bay City Lodge. Reservations are advised, particularly in the spring and again in the fall. You can obtain them by contacting Jimmy Mosconis, Bay City Lodge, P.O. Box 172, Apalachicola, Fl., 32320, telephone (904) 653-9294. There are two other smaller camps and three motels.

A guide is advisable for the first trips into the delta. You could get misplaced in the winding waterways, although you can always fish the main river which offers no problems, but other waterways do. Also, a guide knows the fishing holes and the tides, and this information can make a trip much more productive. Bay City Lodge books for a number of guides. They don't use modern bass boats, and most of them scull instead of using an electric trolling motor.

You can orient yourself for the Delta by studying the map of the Apalachicola from the Dead Lakes to Apalach, which is published by Southern Guide Fishing Maps, P.O. Box 1326, 500 Gulfshore Drive, Destin, Fl., 32541.

In case you're unfamiliar with the location of the town of Apalachicola, it's on the Gulf of Mexico astride U.S. 98 highway, about seventy miles east of Panama City, the famous Florida Gulf beach resort.

For a different fishing experience, sample the Apalachicola Delta bassing some time. It's different and it can be exciting.

# 23

# Capital Bassing on the Doorstep of Florida's Capital

How often do you find largemouth black bass fishing virtually on the doorstep of a state capital? And how often is this fishing little publicized? Not often. But that's the situation with Lake Talquin near Tallahassee, Florida's capital located in the Peninsular State's Panhandle.

Only twenty miles from the state government offices lies Lake Talquin, well supplied with lunker bass, but its fishing potential has received scant publicity beyond local angling circles.

Talquin is a real sleeper in the black bass fishing league, although its angling possibilities have leaked to a few out-of-state fishermen via the angling grapevine. No fishing hole can ever be kept completely secret. However, to date, there has never been any stampede to seek the big bass of Talquin. The lake yields fish weighing as much as 13 pounds. Any fish that size is a real wall mount. Some veteran local anglers insist that even bigger bass are available, but they haven't been landed yet.

With such impressive fishing credentials, why then is Talquin relatively unknown? The answer is in its geographic location, and its past history.

Talquin is not only located near the state capital, but also is a neighbor of Lake Jackson, which is even closer to Tallahassee. Jackson, in the late 1960s and early 1970s before pollution problems developed, produced astounding catches of big bass, which were widely ballyhooed. Talquin was overlooked in the publicity barrage.

Too, in its fifty-odd years (the lake was formed in 1928) Talquin's has had its problems. In the late 1940s, the lake became infested with water hyacinths. The situation became so bad that something had to be done, and during the 1949-50 period, a massive aerial spraying program with 2-4-D Amine was begun. The program worked, hyacinths were reduced, and many unreachable areas were opened again to fishermen. Then in 1957, the dam broke, and it was 1959 before the lake was back to its normal level. Repairs to the dam took a year.

These events, of course, did not boost Talquin as a fishing mecca, and fishermen have long memories. Then the lake sank to an all-time low in the early 1960s when gizzard and threadfin shad populations reached problem proportions.

To return the lake to a proper balance, a program of selective chemical treatment for shad was begun in 1961. Fish biologists found it was effective, and the gamefish began to reproduce and catches improved. Another selective treatment was carried out in 1964.

With still an abundant shad population, another management tool was utilized in 1968, as the Florida Game and Fish Commission began stocking striped bass (rockfish). Stripers feed almost exclusively on such fish as gizzard and threadfin shad, and they went to work on the Talquin population.

Today, it's obvious the stripers are helping keep the shad population within manageable limits. Stripers in the 10 to 20-pound range are often caught, although for some reason most Talquin anglers don't pay much attention to the stripers.

Twice in recent years, it has been necessary to draw Talquin down to repair the water control structures, and during these drawdowns fishing has been superb. The fishing success, especially during the 1973-74 drawdown, was phenomenal and shows just how good the bass population is. The fish were there, but the anglers were not.

The drawdowns also have had long-term effects by temporarily exposing and drying part of the lake bottom, thus improving the water quality and vegetation. As a result, Talquin's bass population has grown.

Talquin is a graybeard among impoundments, being more than fifty years old and one of the oldest in Florida. The lake was formed in 1928, when the predecessor of the Florida Power Company built a dam and reservoir on the Ochlocknee River, which starts in Georgia and wends its way across the Florida Peninsula to empty into the Gulf of Mexico. The dam formed a 9,412-acre lake which was not cleared of standing timber.

The generating facilities became obsolete in 1970, and the generators were removed. Eventually Florida Power donated 12,922 acres of land, 9,412 acres of lake, and 7,689 acres of flood easements to the state of Florida. This property has been designated a state area for recreation, and the division of parks of the Department of Natural Resources manages the dam site and the water control structure regulating the lake.

The site of the dam is twenty-three miles from Tallahassee, while the upper end of the lake is even closer via Florida Highway 20, which runs along the reservoir's south shore.

You find ample launching facilities—ten public ramps plus those at a number of fish camps. But despite this easy access, the lake never has been overrun with fishermen and boatmen. There's an obvious explanation. It's no place for hot rodding, unless you want to run the risk of needing a new, lower unit on your motor. Hit a submerged log or stump, and you need a trip to the repair shop.

You can run the old river channel, but it's so crooked a snake would have trouble following it. Too, since this is not a Corps of Engineers' lake, there are no channel markers. If you miss the channel at high speed, you're in real danger.

It has happened. One angler made the mistake of running his high performance bass boat at full throttle in waters he didn't know. He hit a submerged stump or log, and garnered a $2,700 repair bill. He was lucky to avoid injury.

The rule on Talquin is *don't* cruise with maximum throttle unless you know the waters, and then there's always the danger of a floating log! Obviously, you need to have your motor's kill switch hooked up whenever running.

However, this underwater jungle doesn't preclude boating and fishing. Instead, these obstructions merely require common sense boat handling. You have to expect to bump a few logs when fishing. After all, the bigmouths do like cover, and the lake has plenty. If you don't find underwater obstructions, you probably won't find the bass. But these underwater obstacles are no real boating problem. Just take it easy when cruising, and watch your depth finder to locate them for fishing as well as for safety.

Talquin isn't a deep lake, averaging 15 feet, with the deepest water near the dam. However, the lake probably is as close as Florida can come to deep impoundment structure fishing. It is not a typical, shallow

Florida saucer. Instead you fish in water ranging from a few inches to 50 feet at various times of the year.

Undoubtedly, the proximity of large, shallow flats adjacent to deep water is one reason for Talquin's excellent bass population. Bass do prefer to feed in the shallows located near deep-water sanctuaries. Talquin is tailor made for the bigmouths.

One oddity about Talquin bass is that they seem to prefer blue coloring of lures at times. At one time, blue was regarded as the primary color, and it still is very popular, although the bigmouths also will hit other colors.

However, to me the most unusual application of blue was with the lures not worms. I've never used blue a great deal when fishing shallow divers, such as Bagley or Rebel minnow-types. However, one trip with Tony Cox convinced me there are certain times on Talquin when blue is the key to success.

He showed me how a blue-back, silver-sided, balsa lure could produce in a rather unusual area. We were fishing the Little River arm in what appeared to be open water, a long distance from shore.

By normal standards, we were too far from shore for a shallow-running lure. It seemed more logical to me to use a deeper diving crank bait. Also, Tony advised using a blue-back, shallow diver, balsa minnow-type.

I watched as Tony flipped his blue-back plug in the general direction of the shore. His lure barely landed when I saw a violent swirl, indicating a hefty bass. Tony skillfully set the hooks, and a barroom brawl developed. The fish elected to fight under water. No tail dancing, just a stubborn, subsurface scrap trying to dive under the boat when the drag refused to yield line.

Soon, Tony got complete control and I slipped the net under his prize. No wonder the bigmouth had been able to argue. It weighed just a shade under 6 pounds. Later I asked him why he elected to fish a shallow runner so far from shore. He explained there was a shallow bar that ran a great distance from shore. He had located it with his depth finder. From experience, he found that bass often roam the shallow water of the bar, hence his choice of a shallow-running lure— just another quirk of fishing Lake Talquin. Like any other lake, the more you know about the bottom, the easier it is to find the bass.

While blue sometimes has been a very good color for Lake Talquin, don't overlook other hues, particularly those that resemble shad—a major bait fish in the lake. As Les Wachter says: "We've had good luck with any lure that seems to resemble a shad in coloring. That applies to surface lures as well as deep divers."

After fishing Talquin several times and having hot stove discussions with various local anglers, it is apparent you have to adjust your fishing to the time of year here just as you do on any lake. During January, one of the coldest months, you fish the deep holes, particularly along the old river channel with fast-sinking spoons or heavily weighted plastic worms. Bottom bouncing is the successful technique.

The bass are deep, sluggish, and often suspend at various depths. You have to retrieve slowly. The bigmouths aren't about to turn on the aft burner in hot pursuit of a meal. But put your lure under their nose, and you probably will get some action.

In February, the bucketmouths start moving onto the flats getting ready to spawn. They are now shifting erratically back and forth from deep water to the shallows. You have the greatest success casting or trolling such deep-running lures as Rebel Deep Wee Rs, Bomber Models As, Bagley's balsa divers, Rat-L-Traps and Hellbenders. Trolling or casting to deep points is particularly productive.

March is a top month. The bass are now in the shallows where you can use shallow divers such as Rebel's and Bagley's, shallow-running crank baits, and spinner and buzz baits. Blue is a popular plastic worm color along with black and black-grape.

The fishing in April is similar to that of March, but sometimes more spectacular when the bass come off the beds. The same type of lure produce, the hues depending upon the color of the lake, which can get dingy with spring rains. Then crawdad is a good lure color, and yellow and chartreuse skirts are excellent for spinners and buzzers.

With spawning completed in May and June, you find the bass in different areas. Now you fish around the stickups, brush piles, sunken logs, and other hideouts, usually in deeper water. Of course, the bigmouths do come into the shallows early and late to feed.

You have a wide choice of lures during these months. However, most Talquin regulars rate the plastic worm as the number one enticer. You also can use crank baits, shallow divers, and sometimes sinking crank baits such as Rat-L-Traps and Spots.

The July-to-September period is the most difficult fishing time on the lake. It's hot. Now you find bass are in the deeper, cooler waters, and a weighted plastic worm is the most popular lure. Of course, very early and very late they come into the shallows to feed.

Many Talquin anglers prefer to fish at night using waddling lures, or top-water, double propeller plugs. Others use nine-inch black worms, rigged weedless Texas-style without a weight, swimming the worm on the surface. Black or not, the bass can find it. Then hang onto your rod!

During the winter months, deep-spoon jigging with Hopkins-type spoons along the old river channel produces bass when other methods fail on Lake Talquin. The most effective method is to locate deep holes in the old channel with a depth finder, then drop your spoon vertically to the bottom and bounce it up and down. Les Wachter caught this 4-pound bass one cold February day by deep jigging.

With the water temperature returning to normal as the weather cools, fishing picks up in the fall. October and November are top months, and sometimes December, depending upon when Jack Frost zips in from the North. During this period, the fish are shifting to winter quarters. If you can find a migration route, you can tangle with lunkers as they leave the shallows. Most of the fishing is in 8 to 10 feet of water with crank baits and worms being very productive. Colors vary according to water conditions. Don't be afraid to experiment.

Recently Talquin anglers have had good success with Hopkins-type and similar heavy spoons by casting them to the edge of the river channels, and then bottom bouncing them over ledges into deep water. During the cool weather, the bass suspend at various depths from 15 to 35 feet. Stripers also are found in these depths. By bouncing the spoons off the bottom, the experts are able to entice the bass into hitting.

Accommodations on the lake are rather limited. The largest camp, where I stay, is Lake Talquin Lodge, Route 3, Box 193A, Quincy, Fl., 32351, telephone (904) 627-3822. Reservations are advised, especially during the spring season.

On strange waters, particularly one as stump infested as Talquin, hiring a guide is a sensible idea for the first few visits. You can book guides through Lake Talquin Lodge. I've fished from the Lodge with Les Wachter (the owner and guide), Bob Albritton, and Tony Cox. They're all expert fishermen.

It's also a good idea to be able to orient yourself on the lake, and fortunately there is a Lake Talquin map, published by Southern Guide Fishing Maps, P.O. Box 1326, 500 Gulfshore Drive, Destin, Fl., 32541.

The hefty bass of Lake Talquin may not be as widely known as other Florida bigmouths, but they're available if you are expert enough to hook and land them.

# 24

# Fishing in the
# Ocala National Forest

If you are thrilled by the sight of a startled deer bouncing unexpectedly across a sandy, wood road miles from nowhere, or by the raucous cries of herons and ospreys resenting your presence, then you are the type of angler who can enjoy fishing the ponds and lakes of Florida's Ocala National Forest.

At one time, the forest lakes seldom saw an angler. Today, the situation is changing. As the angling pressures grow on the widely publicized reservoirs and lakes, fishermen are seeking to get away from it all. The Ocala is a natural for such getting away, for here you can still fish in wilderness solitude that's becoming increasingly difficult to find.

The Big Scrub, as the Ocala is often called, sprawling across some 362,000 acres—more than 565 square miles—of sandy hills in central Florida has some 500 named and unnamed lakes and ponds. The fishing pressure is minimal in many cases, but the fish are there.

There are some lunker fish lurking in these little-known ponds, and if you tangle with one, you might have the fishing thrill of a lifetime. Rocky Morgan, for example, was wade fishing the edges of shallow

Grasshopper Lake in June, one of the prime months to be probing the little-known, hard-to-reach lakes and ponds. He was flipping an eight-inch purple worm near and over the abundant grass bed. Action had been slow, but you don't want to be in a hurry fishing the Big Scrub. Rocky wasn't. He was persistent.

Again and again he flipped his worms and worked it across the surface of the grass beds. This time his worm landed just beyond a patch of grass that was clearly visible in the crystal-clear water. Carefully, he began making the worm slither just a few inches below the surface past a potential bass hideout in the grass.

As his worm dropped to the top of the grass, he felt it hesitate. It could be the worm brushing the grass, or it could be a pickup of a small bass, the tap was so light. He took no chances, and set the hook hard. Immediately there was a 'gator wallow that only a big fish can make. A moment later, a huge bass came tail walking out of the water, and Rock's adrenalin soared. He had visions of a 10-pound bass.

Rocky's heart had reason to go triple time. The hefty bass jumped again, and then bulldogged off in a power run, managing to twist Rocky's twelve-pound test line around a bunch of grass. Holding his rod high while keeping a tight line, Rocky slowly waded to the fish, unwound his line, only to have the largemouth charge off again. Again the bass jumped, and failing to shake the hook, dove for the grassy bottom.

"It began acting like a grouper then," recalls Rocky. "If you've ever fished salt water, you know a grouper dives to the bottom, squats and then tugs, tugs, and tugs at your line. This bass must have had some distant grouper kin. It sure was tugging hard."

Five minutes passed. Then ten, and finally Rocky began regaining line as he slowly waded towards where the bass was making its last stand. The rod pressure was wearing down the bigmouth's strength. The tugs became less violent and less frequent. At last, he reached the exhausted fish and grabbed the lunker's lower jaw.

As he lifted the fish, he realized his first estimate was wrong. The bass was far heavier than 10 pounds. When finally weighed, the bigmouth tipped the scales at an even 14 pounds. Had he caught the huge female during the spawning season, she would have weighed 15 pounds or more.

There're incidents of fish as big as 17 pounds coming from some of these little-known "honey holes," and a new world's record bass might be hiding in some nameless hard-to-reach pond. The Ocala forest is in Florida's big bass belt. However, you can expect to encounter more bass in the 2 to 6-pound range, and these forest bass are scrappers. They can and do provide plenty of action.

Some of the forest lakes such as Bryant, Half Moon, Kerr, and Mill Dam show signs of civilization, and fortunately have modern concrete ramps where you can launch big bass boats. However, you don't really need big boats to fish the forest. You do as well, often better, with small, light boats.

But there are other numerous lakes such as Sellers, Farles Prairie, Eaton, Jumper, and Dorr to mention only a few that have launching facilities of various types, some mighty crude, some merely hard-packed sand capable of holding heavy bass rigs. And there are nameless ponds where you can launch only if you don't mind wading a bit while carrying a light johnboat into the water. Such ponds are fished by only the hardiest anglers, but they encounter fighting bass.

Having been fortunate enough to have explored some of these little ponds and lakes, I know the fascination of this type of fishing. It's far different than fishing a huge reservoir or a winding river. It's a type of fishing that's becoming harder and harder to find in this frenetic age.

Buck Bray, my longtime fishing partner who guides on the Withlacoochee River, and I have been fortunate enough to have explored some of the little-publicized fishing holes with such forest-wise anglers as Rocky Morgan, who sometimes guides from Silver Glen Springs; Dick Hale, of Ocala, who actually lives in the forest; and Lon Maas of Belleview, who spends as much time as he can wetting lines in the forest.

Forest-line wetting is far different than most of today's angling. These fishing holes are difficult to reach. To fish many of these little "honey holes," you need a pickup truck (four-wheel drive is ideal, although not absolutely necessary); a johnboat (twelve or fourteen-foot in length and light enough to be handled by a couple of anglers); and a pint-size outboard motor. Some even use canoes, either rigged to handle a very small motor or paddled. If you want to be ultra-modern, you also can take along a small electric trolling motor. However, more often than not, you also will have to paddle and pole because of the thick vegetation.

Most of these fishing holes can be reached by graded and ungraded sand and clay roads that can be tricky to drive when extremely soggy. Some are reachable only with four-wheel drive vehicles. If you're inexperienced in driving such wood roads, stick to the best maintained roads. Otherwise, you can get in trouble.

Also, there are nameless ponds you can reach only by walking, but you better be an experienced woodsman with sturdy legs, and either know the forest or have a guide who does. It's mighty easy to get misplaced in the Ocala as it is in any major forest.

The estimated 500 ponds in the Big Scrub are a mixture. Some go dry regularly. Some are nothing more than deep holes in vast prairies, and some are tree-lined beauty spots with surprisingly deep water and expanse. Undoubtedly, there are bass in these waters that never have seen a lure, and probably never will.

The angling challenge of these little-known lakes is not only their remoteness, but also their special angling quirks. They're generally extremely clear. These are bass holes where you have to make long casts to avoid spooking the fish and use light lines. Twelve-pound test is the heaviest that you can use. Heavier lines only spook the fish. Six and eight-pound test are even better suited to gin clear conditions. You may lose a few bass with such lines, but going light is essential if you want action.

Rocky Morgan is a certified scuba diver, and he has used his diving ability to improve his bass fishing knowledge by exploring some of his favorite ponds underwater. Surprisingly, he's found each pond varies when studied from beneath the surface, although they look very similar when viewed from the shore. Wildcat, for example, one of his favorites, has unsuspected limestone rocks that you would probably never discover boat fishing. The rocks, of course, are a natural bass holding area. Other lakes have deep grass Vs, and the bigmouths concentrate around the edges of these grass valleys, the Big Scrub's version of fish holding structures.

Local anglers have learned that the bass are usually in the center of the lakes, and not around the edges except perhaps early and late in the day when they come into the shallows to feed. It's wise then to fish the center of the lakes particularly over deep grass beds.

The Big Scrub lakes fall into two general categories. One, the prairie ponds which sometimes almost go dry depending upon the rainfall, but which have sufficient deep holes for brood stock to survive. The others are the sinks—often deep limestone holes that never go dry.

There's another quirk to the forest lakes—the best time for big bass. It varies. The biggest bass are caught during the summer in the prairie lakes, while the sink holes produce their biggest during the early spring spawning period. Morgan theorizes that the big fish are caught in the shallower prairie lakes during the summer because they're driven into the ponds from the surrounding swamps by the falling waters.

When the water is high and the prairies flood at the end of the rainy season, the bucketmouths prefer to roam the swamps. But when the warm weather arrives late in the spring before the normal rainy season begins, the lunkers have to move back into the deeper holes in the prairies. They become more available. It's not the calendar but the water level that triggers the big bass catches in the prairie lakes.

You don't need a lot of tackle to fish these ponds. They are ideal for light lines from four to ten-pound test with matching rods and reels. Six-inch worms are favored with black-grape, purple firetail, and black being the preferred colors. However, don't hesitate to experiment if the bass are reluctant to hit. The forest bigmouths can be as temperamental as any of the brethren.

In some lakes shallow-diving lures such as Rebel and Bagley minnow-types are successful, or very shallow-running crank baits. At times, top-water propeller and stick baits are prime lures. Black and silver, and black and gold are the preferred plug colors, although sometimes Tennessee shad and white produce. Each lake is a bit different as to productive colors, and they all change from time to time.

Of course, as with most Florida waters, the best bait for big bass is big shiners, preferably, the native wild golden ones. However, the bigmouths also will hit commercial ones. Live bait produced for Ken Thomas of Illinois who, during a late winter visit, landed a 14-pound, 3-ounce bass from Half Moon Lake. That wasn't his only wall mount. He previously had boated an 11-pound and a 9-pound bass. Shiners really do pay off.

The shiners can be fished by trolling, a particularly effective method, or by anchoring and fishing the edges of the ponds where there is good cover. You can either use a float or freeline, depending upon the circumstances of the moment. Just remember to hang on to your rod.

You can find many of these lakes by exploring the forest roads (assuming you have the proper vehicle and boat). But unless you're an experienced woodsman, you do better to fish with a Big Scrub veteran.

If you want to hire any of the three guides with whom I've fished, they can be contacted as follows: Dick Hale, Route 2, Box 16A, Silver Springs, Fla., 32688, telephone (904) 625-2984; Lon Maas, 5137 S.E. 107th St., Belleview, Fla., 32620, telephone (904) 245-5010; and Rocky Morgan, c/o Silver Glen Springs, Route 2, Box 3000, Ft. McCoy, Fla., 32637. There are other guides, but I've not had any personal experiences with them.

You can obtain a free map of the Ocala National Forest from the various district ranger stations, or from the U.S. Forest Service, P.O. Box 1050, Tallahassee, Fla., 32302, telephone (904) 222-2120.

There are also a series of more detailed fishing information maps available in a booklet entitled "How to Fish Florida's Ocala National Forest" published by Father and Son Tackle, 5137 S.E. 107th St., Belleview, Fla., 32620. It's available in local tackle shops and bookstores or it can be ordered by mail. It costs $2.50 plus fifty cents postage and handling. The series of maps not only includes the forest lakes, but also the Oklawaha River, and such nearby lakes as Weir, Yale, and Bowers.

Fishing in the Big Scrub is different angling, indeed.

# 25

# Suwannee River
# Delta Bigmouths

Stephen Foster wrote his famous song "Way Down Upon the Suwannee River" without ever seeing the beautiful Florida stream. Of course, there were reasons. He, after all was only interested in a song title, and in the mid-nineteenth century, travel wasn't exactly easy. Reaching the Suwannee River was difficult then. However, it isn't now.

Nevertheless, today, there are hundreds of ardent bass fishermen who haven't seen the Suwannee River either, and because of the lack of national publicity are unaware of the excellent largemouth black bass fishing in the delta of this picturesque Florida stream. If you probe the winding waterways and the main channel of the Suwannee where it empties into the Gulf of Mexico after completing its twisting run to the sea across the Florida Panhandle from its headwaters in the famous Okefenokee Swamp, you can find superb fishing.

This was why Buck Bray, Jon Farmer, and I were probing the Suwannee's delta this particular day. We knew there were bass there. Jon, who knows the area like a New Yorker knows Times Square, has seen big sow bass bedding in the canals which have been dug in a helter-skelter fashion on the edge of the Gulf. The canals are far enough from salt water to afford fresh or at least brackish water for largemouth black bass, as well as for panfish.

"The bass often bed near the sea wall at the Marina," explains Jon, who manages Jon's Marina, when he isn't guiding. "You can see them easily, and there are a lot of 8 to 10-pound bass caught each spring with big shiners. And I do mean big shiners—10 to 12 inches in size."

But knowing there were bass available and hooking them are two different things. Now we had been fishing the bonnets along the main river channel unsuccessfully for several hours. We had stirred up several rolls, had a number of taps on plastic worms, but no solid hookups.

Buck, operating his eighteen-foot Ranger bass boat from the bow stick steering position, flipped another worm near the edge of the bonnets. He's a professional bass guide on the Withlacoochee River and Lake Rousseau near the little town of Dunnellon in west-central Florida. Although most of his parties prefer shiner fishing, always seeking that 10-pound or bigger wall mount, he's also an ardent and skilled worm fisherman.

While Captain Jon Farmer, who was guiding us, and I had switched to other lures unsuccessfully, Buck had stuck with his nine-inch black plastic worm. As his worm settled among the bonnets, Buck felt a slight tap. It might have been the current brushing his worm against an underwater weed. He took no chances. He set the hook hard. The resulting water explosion showed he was tied into an angry lunker. It takes a really big bass to make such a rumpus as this one was creating.

Buck immediately applied maximum pressure realizing the bigmouth intended to head deeper into the bonnet field. That's no place to let a big bass roam. The rod pressure forced his fish to halt, then slowly wallow towards the boat. Fish that size don't surrender easily, and this one was no lamb. Unable to find sanctuary in the bonnets and lily pads, Buck's fish floundered violently on the surface, churning the pads and tossing water seeking to foul his line in the debris. Fortunately, his seventeen-pound test line withstood the strain.

Now the largemouth was tiring. Slowly Buck worked the fish out of the bonnets and alongside the boat where Jon deftly netted his prize. A prize it was. The bass weighed 8 pounds, and obviously had escaped other anglers. Her jaw had been torn and healed where other hooks had pulled loose. Had we been fishing during the spawning season instead of in August, the fish easily would have weighed 10 pounds or more.

Buck's 8-pounder confirmed the tales of big bass in the Suwannee delta that we had been hearing along the fishing grapevine. It had been hard to pin down information about black bass fishing in this part of the Suwannee because most anglers operating from the little hamlet are saltwater oriented.

The little village long has been a famous saltwater angling base, and such an excellent one that only a very few fish for black bass. Most would rather fish in the Gulf for mackerel, speckled sea trout, redfish (channel bass), black drum, croaker, or even tarpon.

The guides as a result are saltwater oriented, and until Buck and I had met Captain Jon Farmer, we had been unable to locate any professional with black bass knowledge. Jon's a swing guide—both salt and fresh water depending upon the season—although the majority of his parties are briny bound. But he was a freshwater angler in Georgia before becoming a saltwater guide and marina manager in Florida. Thus he can operate either way with ease.

With Jon's help, we were able to confirm the fishing tales of big bass being caught in Suwannee's waters. We also were able to get detailed information as to the quirks of this Suwannee fishing.

As we expected, like elsewhere in Florida, Jon found that the biggest bass are caught with shiners. During the spring season, he stocks wild shiners at his marina for the anglers who are after the big bass. He also explained that not only does the Suwannee delta harbor big bass, but large quantities of big bass as well. In one 4-day period one spring, Farmer guided parties to a total of 114 bass. The fish ranged up to 4 pounds, and like most brackish water bass were scrappy ones. While most of them were caught with shiners, a number were landed with artificial lures, usually plastic worms.

Although we knew shiners would be the most effective bait, we elected to check out the angling possibilities with artificial lures. We proved that the bigmouths, while possibly a bit more difficult, weren't adverse to sampling artificial lures. And again we proved that there is a big difference between sampling and landing.

Before the day ended, Buck was somewhat frustrated when another bucketmouth in the 8-pound range picked up his worm but dove to safety before he could set the hook. A slack line when fishing among weeds, grass, and pads is a guarantee of trouble. But it's mighty hard to keep a taut line under such circumstances.

After Buck and I made several other delta fishing trips with Jon, it was obvious that there are quirks to fishing this part of the Suwannee. One major factor often overlooked by anglers accustomed to fishing inland waters is the importance and influence of the tide. The secret is fishing when tidal conditions are right, and not by the early dawn and late dusk routine. You fish by the tides, not by the sun.

Suwannee bigmouths—and all bass in tidal-influenced waters—

feed primarily when the tide is falling, although there sometimes are exceptions to this rule. But your odds are much better if you fish with a falling tide. The reason is simple. Although the Suwannee's waters are fresh but sometimes slightly brackish near the Gulf of Mexico, they respond to the tide.

High tide slows the river's flow, and forces the water into the overflow swamps where the bait fish can hide. But when the tide begins falling, the bait fish have to retreat to the deeper main river, and the creeks. The bass are well aware of the situation. They know when Mother Nature is setting up a chow line, and they wait in ambush for the bait fish.

The first of the ebb generally is the most productive, although much depends upon how far upriver you are fishing, and the type of tide. Spring tides, such as those that occur with full and new moons, bring much more violent water changes, and often the current becomes too fast to fish certain types of lures successfully.

Another factor in delta fishing is locating the good fishing holes. With the Suwannee, as with all bass waters, there are productive holes and non-productive ones. A depth finder is useful for exploring the numerous creeks, many of which go dry on a dead low, particularly a spring tide. But these creeks can fool you. Often they have deep holes where you least expect them, particularly on sharp bends.

The river, too, has a variety of depths. There are 30 and 40-foot holes, and when these (or any deep water) are located near shallow flats covered by lily or bonnet fields, or grass beds, they often are bass holding ares. Such areas are very effective during the hot months. The bass seek the cool comfort of the deep holes, but ease into the lily or bonnet fields nearby to feed in the shade.

As the tide falls, the bigmouths come out of the depths to seek food. When you are far enough upstream, a falling tide doesn't necessarily mean a radical change in depth, but it does mean improved water movement, always a factor in bass fishing.

Lures for fishing the Suwannee are typical of bass angling anywhere, although considerable simpler than on many impoundments. The best lure is the old reliable plastic worm, either black, black-grape, or chocolate. While Farmer prefers the eight-inch size, you can use any size, such as the nine-inch Bray used to land his 8-pound bass. However, if the bass refuse the big worms, don't hesitate to try a smaller size.

The most popular top-water lure is a double propeller Devils Horse. Jon favors the yellow and black, and perch colors. However, when the bass are hitting aggressively on the surface, color is of little importance.

Too, there's no reason why other propeller plugs—either single or double props—shouldn't work such as Nip-A-Diddee, Bomber, Tiny Torpedo, and similar. They all make noise, which seems to be the prime requirement for surface action.

Also very effective is a Snagless Sally with a yellow skirt with or without a pork frog. During one trip that was the only lure we could get the bass to hit. Why? Who knows? Just temperamental bass.

The yellow color is particularly effective in the tannic acid-stained water, which is clearer than you suspect. The black bottom of the creeks meandering through the cypress swamps make the water appear much darker than it really is. However, don't be pig headed if the bass are in a temperamental mood. I've also caught them with a white-skirted buzz bait (Uncle Buck's) run just under the surface, and with a white-skirted spinner bait with silver blades.

Jon also has had luck with shallow-running Rebel minnows and Bagley's Bang-O-Lures. These will work whenever the bass are hitting on top, when they don't seem to want a noisy propeller plug. Blip these minnow-type lures in an erratic fashion, duplicating the actions of an injured bait fish, and you often strike action. Stick baits such as Smith-wick's Toothpick, or Carrot Top, or Heddon's Baby Zara Spook, too, produce. Tease them along the edge of lily and bonnet beds, and watch out!

The fishing pattern for the delta is relatively simple, according to Jon. During the January-to-March period, usually cold in this part of Florida, there isn't too much bass fishing. However, those who do seek the bigmouths as a rule prefer to fish deep with black worms. If you can locate where a spring feeds the river, you find warmer water, and more fish.

The April-to-June period includes the spawning, which actually begins in late March depending upon weather. During this period, both top-water lures and worms produce. For the warm summer—July through September—Jon likes worms of various colors fished with and without sinkers, and minnow-type shallow runners.

In the final quarter of the year, October through December, the lures are Devils Horse and similar surface baits, black worms, and spinner baits with double, silver blades and yellow or yellow and black skirts.

There are two prime fishing periods, early and late in the year. During cold weather, the big bass are caught in the canals with shiners, but from March through May, action is tops with all types of lures. The other prime period is in October and November.

"The fall fishing gets good as soon as we have one or two slight cold fronts come through," explains Farmer. "The fronts cool the waters enough to cause the bass to become active. But when it gets too cold, then the bigmouths are hard to catch."

You may also encounter a surprising bass in the delta waters— the Suwannee bass (*Micropterus notius*). This bass, first recognized as a species in 1949, has been recorded as far upstream as the Suwannee River state park, 120 miles from the Gulf of Mexico, and also in the Suwannee delta within a mile of the Gulf. They also have been identified from the Ochlocknee River.

This bass closely resembles the northern smallmouth. As with the smallmouth, the upper jaw of the Suwannee bass does not extend behind the eye. Chunkier and smaller than the familiar largemouth black bass, the Suwannee bass is usually blue beneath, and most fish are marked with dark diamond-shaped blotches on their sides.

This rare bass exists only in the Suwannee watershed—the sink-hole region of North Florida and South Georgia. It is common only in the swift, rocky stretches of the Ichetucknee, Santa Fe, and Suwannee Rivers. It seldom exceeds 12 inches in length. However, this size bass will average a respectable 1 pound, 10 ounces to 2 pounds. The largest officially recognized by the state weighed 3 pounds, 8 ounces. A 4-pounder was caught from the Ochlocknee River, but was not accepted as the state record because the catch was not certified properly.

It's a good idea to have a guide on your initial Suwannee trip. A guide always can save you time on strange waters. Farmer is the only regular bass guide who I know, although more may get into the act as the freshwater bigmouths gain some recognition. Jon knows the waters. If you want to contact him you can do so at the following address: Capt. Jon Farmer, P.O. Box 315, Suwannee, Fla., 32692, telephone (904) 542-7145.

Overnight accommodations are limited. You need to make reservations, particularly whenever the saltwater fishing is hot. There are several fish camps with rental cottages. The most modern overnight accommodations are provided by the Suwannee Shores Motor Lodge, P.O. Box 443, Suwannee, Fla., 32692, telephone (904) 542-7560. This is where I stay when fishing the Suwannee delta.

There are a couple of restaurants specializing in seafood for evening meals, and usually you can make special arrangements for breakfast. There is also a small grocery store where you can get snacks for a noon lunch. Very few anglers return to shore for the noon meal.

In case you're unfamiliar with the location of Suwannee, and most people are, it's at the end of the line on the middle Florida Gulf coast. You reach the hamlet by following Florida Highway 349 for twenty-four miles from its inland junctions with U.S. 19 at Old Town, also on the Suwannee River.

If you're looking for a little-publicized bass fishing area, schedule a trip to the Suwannee delta. You won't be disappointed. The big-mouths are there, and some are real wall mounts. But the bass don't get the publicity because of much more famous saltwater angling.

# 26

# Withlacoochee—Little Ballyhooed Lunker Hole

Buck Bray flipped his fat balsa plug near the edge of a likely looking water hyacinth patch near the western edge of Lake Rousseau, and immediately began cranking fast sending his plug to maximum depth. He retrieved only a few feet, when his rod bent under the impact of a hard strike. Quickly, he leaned back setting the hook. It was a solid contact!

Buck's fish tried to make a typical power dive, but then began a series of frantic, darting movements just below the surface as the bass tried to find underwater help. These, too, failed. Shortly, Buck forced his fish top side, maneuvered it alongside, and reached down for a typical jaw landing. The bigmouth was in the 3 to 4-pound range, a welcome prize, if not exactly a wall mount.

We were fishing Lake Rousseau and the Backwaters of the Withlacoochee River west of Dunnellon on one of our many sorties onto these relatively little-publicized waters. Although you always hope for wall mounts, you gladly settle for any type of action.

Buck's bass on twelve-pound test line and spinning gear was a welcome prize. Most anglers fishing these waters won't use such light line. They're always hoping to hang (and possibly land) one of those 16-pound bass that periodically make local angling headlines. The With-lacoochee does harbor huge fish, but you don't catch them too often. However, there's always a chance of encountering a wall mount any time you wet a line in these waters.

The Withlacoochee-Lake Rousseau waters are some of the oldest bigmouth waters in Florida. Like so many good bass holes, these waters have been forced off center stage by newer areas which have had the benefits of tremendous publicity. But the lack of publicity doesn't take away from the area's fishing potential.

Like many fishermen, I had forgotten about the fishing potential of these waters, although they are right in my backyard, about twenty miles from my home in Inverness. At least I forgot them until I met Buck Bray, a professional bass guide, operating from the Anglers' Resort in Dunnellon. A few years ago, Buck, a retired civilian employee of the U.S. Air Force, and his wife moved to Citrus Springs in northern Citrus County. His ambition was to bass fish regularly, and he became so successful that full-time guiding was the next step.

He learned to fish the Withlacoochee waters prior to his retirement, and his research paid off. Too, each guide trip since retiring has pro-vided him with additional information about the quirks of the waters. Now, he regularly operates as a pro guide, mainly fishing with shiners, searching for lunker bass, and his success has resulted in his attaining national publicity and national recognition.

Operating with a special eighteen-foot custom-made Ranger bass boat with stick steering, a depth finder, a trolling motor, a bait live well, and a live well for his catch, he takes one or two anglers after the Withlacoochee "hawgs."

He generally delivers if you follow his advice, and if the fish are in a cooperative mood. Bass being bass, there are days when they have lockjaw, and there are days when they just won't leave your bait or lure alone. He's put his parties into hundreds of fish over 6 pounds. His personal record is 14 pounds, 8 ounces, which he hopes to break.

The Withlacoochee waters have never had the publicity other Flor-ida waters have had. It's understandable. Dunnellon, on the banks of the river, above the fishing grounds, is a tiny town. Tiny towns seldom are geared for publicity, and anglers (other than locals) tend to forget bass holes that have been around for years.

Another contributing factor is the confusion that sometimes arises from the name Withlacoochee. There are two rivers with this Seminole name in Florida, hence anglers from out-of-state often get confused. The stream that passes Dunnellon is the Withlacoochee of the South, which originates in the Green Swamp area in central Florida. It's one of three rivers in the state that flow north. When the river reaches a point east of Dunnellon, it makes a ninety-degree turn and heads west to the Gulf of Mexico. The other river with the same name is the Withlacoochee of the North, which originates in Georgia, and joins the Suwannee River in north Florida. Eventually, its waters, too, empty into the Gulf of Mexico.

Years ago the Withlacoochee of the South was dammed near the little hamlet of Inglis on U.S. 19. This dam was built to generate electricity, and formed a reservoir extending fourteen miles eastward towards Dunnellon. Because there was a little body of water called Lake Rousseau in the river prior to the dam's construction, the portion of the Backwaters from the dam site to the east is locally known as Lake Rousseau.

The so-called lake extends six miles east of the dam. The remaining eight miles to near Dunnellon are known generally as the Backwaters. However, for all practical purposes, they are the same body of water with two different names, and outside of local angling circles, the reservoir is more widely known as the Withlacoochee Backwaters.

Back in the 1920s, they didn't bother to clear reservoirs with the result that the Backwaters have an abundance of sunken trees for bass cover, and also a tremendous number of stobs and stumps inches under the surface. It's imperative that you watch where you're going whenever you leave the original river channel, which is well marked. Even with constant vigilance, you can expect to bump some underwater obstacles, so slow speed is the rule.

The deep water follows the old river bed, and there are holes from 15 to 60 feet deep. It's a good idea to locate these with your depth finder, for there are times when the bass congregate in deep water.

Essentially, the Backwaters are shiner-fishing country. When you dig into the background of seventy-five to eighty percent of the catches, you find live shiners were the key. Of course, this doesn't mean that you can't catch big bass with artificial lures. You can, but if you are looking for wall-mount trophy bass, then you can't beat a golden river shiner, the natural food in the river.

Normally you can catch your own bait by chumming with oatmeal and using a No. 12 hook with a tiny piece of white plastic covering the barb. However, in recent years the golden shiners have become much more difficult (impossible at times) to catch, and most anglers buy their live bait. The silver-treated commercial shiners do almost as well, but it runs up the cost of a fishing trip.

When they talk about shiner fishing, they mean big shiners. The golden river ones range from 10 to 12 inches in size. Many a first-time northern angler is amazed at their size. He's use to fishing for that size fish, not using them for bait.

Shiner anglers all use heavy tackle—twenty-five to thirty-pound test, monofilament lines on Ambassadeur reels with stiff, light, salt-water boat rods, usually six to seven feet in length. Hooks range from 1/0 to 5/0, depending upon the size of the shiner. Some use treble hooks to make certain they don't miss. These trebles range from 3/0 to 4/0, again depending upon the shiner's size. There's one disadvantage, treble hooks will foul more often as your shiner swims around in the weedy waters. And you do want your shiner to keep moving to provide maximum attraction to a bass.

Like most Florida waters, the Withlacoochee has its problems with water hyacinths and hydrilla. But the bass are there, although sometimes you bring in more grass than bass when making a landing.

Shiners are fished both with and without a float, and are also trolled. Trolling is a very effective method as Buck demonstrated one day. This trip resulted in a number of small bass in the 1 to 3-pound class, and one 6-pounder that decided it liked my shiner.

When things are slow, the veterans troll to locate the fish, then anchor to fish the area. The bass do move often in the Backwaters, and a good hole one day may be a flop three days later.

Among the artificial lures, undoubtedly the most effective is the old reliable plastic worm. They're fished with either the Texas-weedless rig, or some anglers use conventional weedless hooks with a wire-weed guard. Both systems work.

Worm colors vary. The most popular are purple, black-grape, black, and blue. Sometimes a solid color produces. At other times, a fire tail (red, blue, or chartreuse) scores. Like bigmouths everywhere, those of the Withlacoochee change their color preference from time to time.

Worm fishing is most successful when you locate deep holes, and can work your plastic deceiver slowly up the bank. Most deep holes are near the old river channel. A depth finder is very useful in locating them.

Top-water lures, both with and without props, are good, especially during the spring and fall, usually early and late in the day. They offer a means of fishing the grass beds often only a foot to three feet under the surface. If the grass and weeds are too close to the surface, you have to use weedless lures, either floating worms without sinkers; Johnson, Weedwing or similar spoons; or buzz baits retrieved rapidly across the top.

When shiner fishing in the Withlacoochee Backwaters, you want to get the bass into the boat fast with a net. The proper procedure is for the man on the rod to lead his fish into the net, then a yo heave by the netter. Here, Buck Bray is hoisting an 8-pound bucketmouth from the Withlacoochee for a client.

Shallow-running lipped plugs, such as a Rebel or Bagley make, too, are effective, particularly when the grass is some distance below the surface. Sometimes these work best when blipped along the top ala a top-water plug, but with a slightly different noise, not as loud.

Then again, they work best when retrieved rapidly. How well I know. Buck and I were plugging late one afternoon. I flipped a balsa lure alongside a patch of hyacinths where I could crank it fast in deeper water.

I barely got the lure running fast when bang!—it was a savage strike. My rod bent sharply, and my reel's drag sounded. It appeared to be the start of a first-class battle, and then my line went limp.

Reeling in, I expected to tie on another lure. But my plug was still there. The fish had hit the forward gang hook. The split-ring fastening the treble to the wire from the plug body broke. It was an ancient lure. Scratch one fish because I hadn't checked my lure.

Buck and I estimated the bigmouth would have been in the 5 to 6-pound range from the size of the swirl. It would have been a worthy foe on my ten-pound test line. I check my lures carefully now for any signs of rust weakness.

There's little opportunity to use really deep-running crank baits. On the whole, the reservoir is not very deep, except in a few places, and the abundance of submerged snags makes working deep-diving lures difficult.

There are a few places where crank downs will work at certain times of the year. Spinner baits, too, can be used deep at times, of course, with inevitable fouling problems from time to time.

For top-water plugging, the western half of Lake Rousseau starting within a quarter of a mile of the dam is best. There's excellent shoreline cover, and for some reason this area produces better when the bass are hitting on top.

Another good spot is the junction of the Rainbow and Withlacoochee Rivers to the east of Dunnellon. Sometimes the river from Dunnellon east to this junction and a short distance above produces.

Prime fishing times are much like elsewhere in the state. The biggest bass normally are caught in the cooler months—the January-to-May period being the most productive. Buck's fishing log shows this. During one eighteen-month period, eighty-five bass over 6 pounds were caught by his parties, *but* sixty-two were caught in the January-to-May period.

That's not saying you can't catch big fish at other times. You can, but the odds are best in your favor January through May. The second best time is October through November.

Accommodations are available at Dunnellon, the nearest launching point. There's an excellent, free public ramp just to the west of U.S. 41 highway bridge entering Dunnellon from the south. Several of the motels have their own docks and rental boats. There are also a few fish camps on the north and south shores of the western half of the Backwaters.

Guides are available, most of them booking through local motels and fish camps. Buck now gets most of his bookings direct. You can reach him at the following address: Buck Bray, 1489 Abbott, Citrus Springs, Dunnellon, Fl., 32630, telephone (904) 489-2139. He has top equipment for the Backwaters operating from an eighteen-foot, Ranger bass boat. Other guides either have their own boats, or use rental skiffs and motors from the various docks where they base.

Because of the stump-filled nature of this fishing area, it's a good idea to have a guide the first time out, although there are channel markers. But be careful if you get out of the channel. If you do decide to explore on your own, you'll do well to buy a copy of Buck Bray's Withlacoochee River Map. Copies are available at tackle shops, fish camps, and stores in the area.

Information on motel accommodations can be obtained from the Dunnellon Chamber of Commerce, P.O. Box 468, Dunnellon, Fl., 32640. Because accommodations are limited, it's advisable to make certain you have advance reservations if you plan more than a one-day trip. During the winter season, space often is at a premium. Rates are comparable to elsewhere in Florida, perhaps slightly lower.

They're no tub thumpers extolling the bass of the Withlacoochee, but the fish are there. It takes skill and patience, but the Backwaters and Lake Rousseau can produce.

# 27

# Cross Creek Country Bass

Meandering Cross Creek, in the upper third of Florida less than twenty miles south of Gainesville linking Orange and Lochloosa Lakes, is world famous. It's famous because of the attention paid to it by the writer Marjorie Kinnan Rawlings, whose rustic, wood home not far from the creek is now a literary museum operated by the Florida Division of State Parks. Cross Creek is also famous because of excellent largemouth black bass fishing.

Had there been no books titled "The Yearling"—a Pulitzer prize winner, also made into a movie—or "Cross Creek," the little stream today would be just another Florida "crick" known only as the twisting link between two bass lakes.

But Marjorie Kinnan Rawlings did write the famous books, and Cross Creek country enjoys a literary immortality far greater than any that could be achieved from fishing. Nevertheless, Cross Creek-country bass fishing is excellent at times. As with any bassing, your success depends upon when, where and how you fish.

Orange and Lochloosa lakes always have been famous largemouth black bass fishing waters, and also widely known for their slab-size crappie (speckled perch). Orange, the biggest lake in northeastern Florida, is the larger of the two lakes, covering 12,700 to 15,000 acres depending upon the rainfall, while Lochloosa covers from 6,000 to 7,200 acres, again depending upon the water available.

Although they are kissin' cousins as far as their geographical location is concerned, they are quite different. Orange is a much shallower lake, and is fed by the River Styx at the north end, which gets much of its water from Newnan's Lake still farther north.

Lochloosa, on the other hand, is a deeper lake, dependent largely upon rainfall, and perhaps a few springs, and drains into Orange Lake via Cross Creek.

Once Orange was also famous for its floating islands, which sailed up and down the lake at the whim of the wind, providing moving fish cover, and very unreliable landmarks. However, today, the floating islands are generally permanently anchored as a result of the infestation of both lakes by the noxious hydrilla, which covers the major parts of both lakes at the height of the blooming season.

Despite the infestation of hydrilla, which was introduced into the United States from abroad by aquarium dealers, who for a time raised the plant for sale to private aquarium owners, Orange and Lochloosa remain good bass lakes, capable of producing lunker fish.

The hydrilla is both a curse, and a blessing in disguise. It tops out in June. At maximum bloom during the peak of the summer heat, it does create navigation problems, although high-power motors usually can chop a path through the dense weeds. Also it's possible to avoid the most dense areas, and government agencies have been maintaining boat trails both by chemical and mechanical means.

The apparent blessing is that the pesky hydrilla does serve a useful purpose by providing cover for bait fish and for the small fry of gamefish until they are big enough to fend for themselves.

As John Dunn, owner-operator of John's Fish Camp on Lochloosa says: "Hydrilla is a pesky problem, *but* the lake is still fishable, and there're a lot of big fish available. It's now a lake where you have to know what you're doing to score, but if you do, you can tangle with some line breakers."

Dunn knows from practical experience that Lochloosa holds big fish. While fishing a boat tourney in May, 1981, he landed a 12½-pound bass using a Rat-L-Trap lure, bleeding shiner coloration. Now that is a real mount, and the lure was an unusual one for a hydrilla filled lake.

However, Dunn's fish was small compared to the lunker Billy Roberts of Ocala landed in the hot month of August, 1980 in Orange Lake. His fish weighed an estimated 18 pounds. Roberts was fishing with an eight-inch, black-grape-colored, plastic worm when the bass hit his lure in a hydrilla patch. The combination of the hefty fish and the hydrilla mess really made him work to land his prize.

If you talk to the various fish camp operators, they all have tales to tell of how the fishing has changed, and of lunkers landed. Chet Westergard of the South Shore Fish Camp at Orange Lake still recalls the Illinois angler—a winter resident of the trailer park—who thought there was nothing to fishing for big bass with shiners.

Shiners are deadly all right, but this angler's luck was almost unbelieveable. He landed a 14½-pound bass one day, and followed with a 13¾-pounder two days later. Many an angler never has caught a bass over 10 pounds, let alone a pair weighing over 13.

During the first week in April (1981), Westergard saw five bass brought in each weighing over 13 pounds. All were caught with shiners. During the spring 1981 season, every lunker over 10 pounds brought into the South Shore Camp was caught with shiners.

Another indication of the growing bass population, particularly in Orange Lake, which always has been known for numbers while Lochloosa has been known for size, is shown by the success of three women, all over seventy years of age, who regularly fish from South Shore Fish Camp.

"In one week," recalls Westergard, "using six-inch green worms and an open hook, they brought in strings of twenty-three, twelve, ten and twelve bass up to 5 pounds in weight. And they never went into the main lake with their four-HP motor on one of our rental skiffs. When word got out about their success with green-colored worms, I was swamped with requests for green worms. There're a lot of bass in the grass, but fishermen have to adjust to changing conditions. You have to learn to fish hydrilla!"

If you're pinpointing your trophy hunting, your best chances are in March or April, according to the Cross Creek Country experts. I prefer April because normally the March winds are gone. Both lakes are big enough that wind can be a major problem, hence March has more questionable weather. Usually by April, the winds have abated in Florida.

You can catch big fish any time of the year, but your chances of landing a big bass are best in Orange and Lochloosa lakes during the first six months of the year for two reasons. First, the spawning season occurs then, and this is always the best lunker time on any body of water. The other reason for fishing the first six months is the hydrilla. Both lakes have heavy infestations of the obnoxious weed, *but* it has

Keep your rod tip high as you haul a fighting bass out of his lair. Don't allow any slack line once you've set the hook, or a scrappy bass will get free.

not reduced the fish population. It just makes it much harder to get to the bigmouths.

By fishing the first six months, you find the hydrilla isn't quite as troublesome. During the cold weather, growth is retarded, and migrant coots have a bountiful feast. The result is that the colder months see a temporary reduction in the hydrilla. Of course, when the warm weather comes and the brilliant sunlight, the pest goes wild again.

The infestation of hydrilla has caused Orange and Lochloosa anglers to change their techniques radically. Only a few years ago, Little George tailspinners and other fast-sinking lures were widely used, but no longer except in a few isolated cases.

No longer is it generally feasible to troll in deeper Lochloosa as was customary only a few years ago, especially during the cold months. Now, trolling will only produce a tangle of hydrilla on your lure.

Today, if you want to succeed in these lakes, you've got to modify your techniques. Actually, it's resulted in a simplification of fishing. There are three effective methods now: (1) shallow-diving floating lures such as Bagley's Bang-O-Lure (balsa) with or without propellers, or Rebel's minnow (plastic), either straight or broken-back; or top-water floaters, preferably double propeller lures, fished over the top of hydrilla beds when the pesky weed is just below the surface; (2) Plastic worms, more often than not fished over and around the edges of the grass, with and without weights; (3) Spinner and buzz baits with the Snagless Sally-type apparently producing better than the safety-pin models.

Those anglers who have reverted back to Snagless Sally extensively even want a special version which has to be ordered specially from the factory. This Snagless Sally has a No. 3½ spinner blade with a 4/0 hook. Most standard models are equipped with either a No. 3, 4, or 5 blade. Weightwise, this special Sally falls between the standard ¼ and ⅓-ounce models.

The Sally regulars also have developed another trick. They clip off a portion of the wire weed guard so the wire does not extend past the hook. They've found that by leaving the hook virtually free, they have less problem setting the hook.

On regular Sallys, the weed guard extends about ⅜ths of an inch past the point of the hook. This shortening of the weed guard makes sense. Even a bass with its bucketmouth can fail to reach the hook with two wire weed guards in the way. The Sallys are fished with the regular pork frog with yellow skirts generally favored, and gold spinner blades.

The fishing pattern for the two lakes is relatively simple, much the same, except for certain physical differences. During the January-to-March period in Lochloosa you fish the edges of the lake around the cypress in water about three feet deep, particularly late in the quarter when the bass are spawning.

Hydrilla makes it difficult to fish this area, but that's where the bass are in Lochloosa, and six-inch plastic worms with 3/0 hooks are favored. Usually only small weights are used. If you can find open water along the Lochloosa shore, you also can use shallow-diving balsa lures such as Bagley's Bang-O-Lure.

However, the situation is different when you are fishing Orange Lake. Orange doesn't have deep water near cypress, unless there's been a tremendous rain during the winter. This occurs infrequently. As a result, you have to fish near lily pads, bonnets, and, of course, hydrilla in shallow water. Plastic worms—six to nine-inch lengths—are used with and without weights. The eight-inch worm is particularly popular. Shiners produce in both lakes during the cold months, but are seldom used otherwise during the year for some reason.

During the April-to-June period, you find the fish have moved away from the shore in Lochloosa and are more scattered in Orange. The bass are in 5 to 7 feet of water. Spawning is over by the end of April. Hydrilla, of course, is increasing and pothole fishing becomes effective. You cast your lure—either a worm or spinner bait—and bring it across the hydrilla until you reach a pot hole, and then let the lure sink.

This is also the period on both lakes when top-water lures become effective. Hydrilla doesn't top out until late June, which means the pesky weed is 12 to 18 inches below the surface, and you can work top-water propeller plugs over the hydrilla beds.

In Orange lake, the top-water lure choices include Devils Horse, both perch and frog colors; Tiny Torpedoes, Dalton Special frog color; and Creek Chub Darter frog color. You also can blip Bagley's black and gold Bang-O-Lure with and without propellers. Lochloosa's lure pattern is similar, except the bass seem to prefer top-water lures with white undersides such as No. 206 Devils Horse, green and white glitter.

Plastic worms are still very productive in both lakes with the favored colors being black, black with red firetail, purple, black-grape, and in Orange Lake various shades of green.

Buzz baits, too, produce usually with silver blades and white bodies and skirts. The bass during this period seem to react aggressively to noisy lures. Spinner baits, too, are used, but you have to run them just under the surface.

Although neither lake is consider crank-bait water, a few anglers do struggle to use noisy crankdowns like the Rat-L-Trap, and if you

The art of netting a fish is for the man on the rod to lead the fish into the net. The man handling the net should place the net in the water and *not* try to scoop the fish. Too often, over eager netmen knock the fish off the hook by scooping. Bob Jones correctly nets a fish for Buck Bray in Orange Lake.

can find areas to work this type of lure, the results can be explosive. Dunn's 12½ pounder was caught with a Rat-L-Trap. But to use this type of lure you have to be patient and lucky enough to retrieve maybe one time in ten without fouling in the hydrilla.

The hot weather of the July-September period finds the bass hiding in the deepest water they can find, usually 7 to 10 feet. You can succeed with top-water lures, but only early and late. Surface lures aren't much good during the mid-day heat. Then you have to use worms, usually with heavy sinkers to get the worm through the thick hydrilla.

The last quarter of the year—October through December—is a slow period. However, at times in October, top-water action is good, and it gets easier to fish as the water temperature drops causing the hydrilla to die back.

There are several fishing camps on the shores of both lakes, but overnight accommodations are limited. However, if you can't find a room on the lake, you can always base at either Gainesville or Ocala, both of which have numerous motels.

If you're willing to battle the grass, adjust your fishing techniques and fish hard, you can boat some trophy fish in Orange and Lochloosa Lakes, Florida's famous Cross Creek country.

# 28

# Florida's St. Johns River

The slow-moving St. Johns river, one of the few United States rivers flowing northward, meanders nearly 300 miles journeying to the Atlantic in the northeast quarter of Florida. The St. Johns provides nummerous fishing opportunities. There is scarcely a mile that doesn't harbor fish, especially largemouth black bass. Its fame has been generated by the fighting bigmouths, and also its panfish brigade, especially big crappie or speckled perch, with stripers adding an exotic touch.

However, if you had to pick one section of the river as the most popular, undoubtedly it would be the area from Astor on the south to Welaka on the north, which includes both Big Lake George, Little Lake George, and miles of the twisting river.

Make a few inquiries as to where the guides head most often, and the answers indicate they consistently fish Lake George, part of the middle St. Johns. Obviously, the guides go where the fish are.

The Lake George area of the St. Johns is a highly favored fishing area, and with favorable weather conditions, a knowledge of locations of fishing holes and of some of the unusual techniques used, you can catch your limit of bass. Also, you may be crying over lines broken by lunker bigmouths or hefty stripers, or you may be amazed at the aggressive antics of crappie (speckled perch), or startled by other fish.

But it's not super easy fishing. If you don't know where to fish, and the local angling quirks, the middle St. Johns can be frustrating. It's a case of decision, decision, decision. You have to make a major decision at the dock. Where do you want to fish? Even with high-speed bass boats, you don't want to spend too much time riding. Hence, your first decision is where to go.

Do you want to fish Lake George, 46,000 acres; Little Lake George, 1,400 acres; or the miles of narrow winding river? Each area can produce when conditions are right. But knowing when conditions are right isn't quite as simple as it might seem. This fact was reemphasized when three of us got to talking about the year-round productivity of the St. Johns.

Having fished it, I've a cursory knowledge but nothing like that of the Morgans, who are the real experts on the quirks and foibles of fishing this part of the river. Justin Morgan, manager of Silver Glen Springs, the camping and fishing resort on the beautiful springs whose run empties into Lake George, and his son Rocky, now a professional guide, really know these fishing waters. They should. Justin's been fishing the river for more than a quarter of a century, and Rocky learned the angling quirks from his Dad, and has spent hours expanding his own knowledge.

Both are expert anglers. They have caught big bass—real wall-mount lunkers. Justin's biggest is 17 pounds, 8 ounces. Rocky's record is 15 pounds, 8 ounces, but he isn't happy because he's low man on the totem pole in the family. His mother, Barbette, holds second place with a 16-pound, 3-ounce bucketmouth.

In planning their fishing, the Morgans pay close attention to two factors often ignored—wind direction and water temperature. These are important all year around. On Big Lake George, wind can be a big factor, and a dangerous one. A fifteen-knot wind precludes safe or successful fishing. It can hamper on smaller Little Lake George, too. Under such conditions, you have to fish protected waters which are usually in the narrow parts of the river. It's mandatory when the wind is either out of the north or south blowing the length of Big Lake George.

With north or south winds, the lake is just too rough for boating and fishing. But with either an east (fish bite least) wind or one from the west, you can fish the lee shore. For these wind conditions, you have to launch on the lee shore.

You also find lee shores on the north end of the lake around

Drayton and Hog Islands, depending upon the wind's direction. The grass flats on the west side of Drayton Island usually are productive. However, if you have to go into the narrow parts of the river, you fish the lee wherever you can, not necessarily where you prefer. The twisting St. Johns can be a problem sometimes. High wind angling is mainly a case of finding calm water first, and then worrving about how big the bass are.

There is a factor to the wind problem that many first-time anglers overlook. Current direction is important, but equally important is the direction the wind has been blowing during the previous forty-eight to seventy-two hours. Many never consider this, but the sustained direction over a period of time can radically change the fishing picture on Lake George, especially when linked with a temperature change.

Bass naturally shift their locations when the temperature changes. When the water gets cold during the winter, they concentrate on the west shore of Lake George near the mouths of Silver Glen run, Juniper Creek, and Salt Springs run. The water from the springs normally is a consistent seventy-two degrees and that's a lot more appealing to ol' bigmouth than the middle and low sixties or the high eighties.

As a result of the springs' outpourings, the west side of Lake George is always a favored hole. When the water's too cold elsewhere, the bass like the seventy-two degree range at the runs' outlets, and when it gets too hot elsewhere, again they favor the comfortable seventy-two degree range. Thus, any time of the year, your chances are good of catching fish along the western shore of Lake George.

However, wind can play havoc with their exact location. Lake George is a shallow lake, and the water responds to the wind. After three or four days of high winds from the north, the water with the temperature favored by the bass will be blown southward.

The same thing happens in reverse with a strong, direct south wind. Only this time, instead of the fish being around the south end of the lake—the Juniper-Silver Glen area—they're at the north end in the vicinity of Salt Springs run.

Obviously, knowing the wind direction prior to a fishing trip is more important here than on deep-water impoundments, where the wind is much less of a factor than is water temperature. Of course, with no wind the situation is different. Then the fish may be anywhere, assuming the proper water temperature is available over all of the lake. Even with normal water temperatures, usually you can count on finding fish on the western shore because of the spring water that continually flows into that part of the lake.

The bass can be caught anywhere under no wind problem conditions. The pilings marking the channel across the Volusia bar at the south end of Lake George are a good place for worm fishing for big-mouths.

It pays to understand the physical nature of Lake George. Basically, you are fishing a shallow-water lake. There are no real deep holes, the greatest depth being the 12-foot maintained channel. You fish waters from inches to 12 feet, a normal but not a deep water range.

You get an excellent idea of the water depths by studying NOAA Chart 11495 (St. Johns River—Dunns Creek to Lake Dexter). It's a good idea to carry this chart with you. You may be surprised at some of the water depths. They are sometimes very deceptive.

Knowing the general locations of the fish, and the wind quirks on Lake George, the next questions are just where do you fish, and at what time of year? Also, what lures produce best?

According to the Morgans, the calendar-rundown answer to these questions goes like this. During the January-to-March period, prior to and during the spawning, you fish the edge and middle of the abundant grass beds. The beds north and south of Silver Glen run are very productive. But to pinpoint the best daily locations, you have to know the wind direction for the previous forty-eight to seventy-two hours.

The eastern shore of the lake, too, is good at times depending upon weather conditions. This shore does not have any springs emptying into it. But there are fish there when water temperatures are normal.

There's one particularly good grass bed to the left of the jetties at the south end. This is an area only the veteran anglers fish. Just before reaching the jetties you turn left to pole across a shallow bar to the grass beds in slightly deeper water.

Beginning in January, the bass are moving into the grass beds either preparing to or actually spawning. From then until April is the time for big trophy fish in the St. Johns.

Bullhead minnows are the best bait, for the bigmouths hate these predators. They don't merely chase or remove them from the beds. They kill the minnows. The bullheads will feed on the bass eggs if they get the opportunity. You fish the bullheads with 3/0 size, weedless hooks. The bait is hooked through the lips. Usually a No. 5 split shot is clipped to the line about eight inches above the hook to keep the bait from surfacing.

Most fishing is casting to visible beds and the guides normally pole their boats ahead slowly looking for beds. There's an art to poling without disturbing the fish. However, when the water is stained, usually because of wind, you have to resort to blind casting.

The Morgans have learned that a Peck's Yellow Sally fished with three or four grunt worms on the hook pulled slowly through the grass is a deadly lure for blind casting. You cast into known spawning areas, let the Sally and worms settle, and then move them slowly through the grass. For some unknown reason, the bass can't resist the odd combination.

The Morgans have even rigged a Yellow Sally successfully with a plastic worm—hooked through the middle of the worm—and with grunt worms. It's a weird combination, but the bass hate it, and strike hard.

Justin and Rocky rate the Yellow Sally as a very versatile lure. They also fish the Sally with a No. 4 Hildebrandt's spinner with a No. 1-size Uncle Josh green pork frog. With this combination, they've not only caught black bass, but also rockfish (stripers), and channel bass (redfish) in the same area. The reds come into the Lake George waters after the first cold snap adding a surprising dimension to the fishing considering the distance Lake George is from the salty Atlantic.

While the Sally is the Morgan's number one lure, they are adept at using other types. They also use plastic worms, usually without weights, or at the most with only a tiny split shot for this grass bed fishing.

Their third choices are top-water and shallow-running lures such as Smithwick's Devils Toothpick, Carrot Top, Baby Zara Spook, and similar stick baits, or balsa shallow divers such as those made by Bagley and Rapala, or the Rebel plastic minnow-type. These lures score if worked slowly and carefully across the weed beds that are only inches under the surface.

The Morgans recommend looking for schools of spawning shad during the April-to-June period. The shad spawn along the edge of the eel grass around points and in coves, but they only spawn on a still morning.

The bass seem to know where the shad meals are and congregate around the spawning areas. This is not bankers' hours fishing. You have to be on the lake at daybreak, and the action generally is over by 9 A.M.

You score by casting near the shad grounds with Cordell Spots, Reflecto No. 2 spoons, or with a Yellow Sally and you retrieve all lures at high speed. The bass apparently mistake the lure for a fleeing shad, and pounce on it. The action can be fantastically fast.

Often there's deep water between the grass beds and the shore proper, and here plastic worms can be used effectively. Generally, they're most productive with small slip sinkers. Plastic worms also produce when fished without weights in gin-clear Silver Glen run. The bass in the run usually aren't lunkers, but they're scrappers, especially if you use light tackle.

During the July-to-September period, you fish the deep water. The south end of the lake around the jetties is a very good area, as is the portion of the river between the south end of the lake to south of Astor. Worm colors are a matter of personal choice. The Morgans also use Sonic lures and Reflecto Barracuda No. 2 spoons fished slow and allowed to sink. There's little surface action.

Late in this quarter, many anglers begin to use spinner baits, usually with crawdad colored skirts. Double-bladed spinners generally are preferred. The spinners are particularly effective bounced off the stumps in Juniper Cove, and around the south end of Lake George.

With the fish moving during the last quarter of the year, you fish the passes, or narrow waterways linking bodies of water. Among the producing areas are Drayton Island, the mouth of Silver Glen and Salt Springs, Jones Cove, and Nine-Mile Point area. This is also a good time to fish the middle of the lake along the maintained channel. Here deep-diving plugs sometimes work, such as the Rebel Deep Wee R series.

Of course, this is the period when sudden cold fronts begin to swing down from the north. If one does, then the place to fish is where the warmer spring water mingles with the suddenly cooled lake. Of course, the prime spots are the mouths of Juniper, Silver Glen, and Salt Spring runs.

Not only do you encounter black bass in the St. Johns, but also the famous American shad run in the spring. Too, there's a good population of crappie, and these fish are pugnacious when protecting their beds. They don't hesitate to attack a lure meant for a bass.

One trip, Charlie Keefer and I found the bass with lockjaw, but he caught three big crappie—about 2 pounds in size—all on a balsa shallow runner, basically a black bass lure. But to the crappie, it was a threat to the spawning bed, and they attacked.

The river is full of surprises, like the stripers (rockfish) that Rocky and I caught at the mouth of Silver Glen run by trolling shallow-running Rebel lures. When they hit, they meant business. They were in the 3-pound range, but the lake does have even larger ones. Tangle with one of the big boys, and you're in for a real fishing thrill.

The entire St. Johns, of course, is under tremendous pressure, as are most of Florida's waters. And the continual draining of the marshes to the south have created problems, along with the persistent ones like water hyacinths, and pollution of various types. Steps are being taken to eliminate much of the pollution, and the river is gradually getting in better shape. However, the marsh drainage continues to be a major problem.

Another problem is in the offing—the discovery that tillapia (Florida's ill-fated experiment with importing an alleged foreign gamefish) have moved into the river, and may cause problems for spawning bass.

Unfortunately, the tillapia cannot be caught with hook and line with either natural or artificial baits. They can only be removed by netting. Once established they are prolific breeders and may usurp what has been the largemouth black bass domain.

But until this or other problems become uncontrollable, the middle St. Johns will continue to offer a fish smorgasbord. Don't be surprised at any encounter, and don't forget to check the wind direction for the previous two or three days.

There are numerous fish camps with ample accommodations all along the St. Johns. We stay at Silver Glen Springs where there are both rental cabins, trailers and a beautiful campground. It's a case of taking your pick to suit your pocketbook.

# 29

# Oklawaha Chain of Lakes Has Fish

We had worked our way through the relatively narrow passage from Lake Beauclair into Carleton, part of the Oklawaha chain of lakes in central Florida. Carleton, smallest of the seven in the chain, covering about 500 acres, is a circular body of water, with perhaps a maximum depth of 12 feet. It's typical of so many Florida lakes—a shallow saucer surrounded by grass, reeds, some cypress, and a few docks, signs of civilization.

Fishing the southwest shore with sinking Rat-L-Traps and Spots, we encountered no action with the noisy crank baits. The pH was unusually high, always a bad sign, particularly during the hot months. Seeking a better pH, and wanting to explore more of the little lake, we eased over to the opposite shore and began casting again through a sparse grass bed.

Buck Bray flipped his chrome Spot rattler back into the grass and began a rapid retrieve. Bang! An unseen fish struck, and struck hard. Buck's graphite casting rod bent abruptly, and the drag on his Ambassadeur reel yielded line grudgingly.

"It's a good one!" exclaimed Buck, applying maximum pressure, holding his rod high. "It's a darned good one! Get the net!"

As he played the fish, he cautiously tightened the drag on his reel. He had it set very light, and this was no fish with which to play in the grass with a light drag. This obviously was no yearling bass. In the grass, fourteen-pound test line was none too heavy. The fish wallowed in the grass finally beginning to yield to the steady pressure of the rod, and the tighter drag. Slowly, Buck worked the fish towards the boat.

Steve Plein, owner of Lane Park Resort on Big Lake Harris of the Oklawaha Chain where we'd launched, quickly picked up the net. Steve, who was guiding us on this trip to explore the Oklawaha lakes, knew that big bass lurked in the lakes. He could tell this was no fish to hand land.

Finally Buck got the bass under control, and eased it into the net Steve has waiting in the water. As Steve lifted, we saw the reason for the commotion. It was a hefty bass, weighing 6½ pounds, definitely a trophy for a hot August day. Landing a hefty bass during the hot months is not unusual in the Oklawaha Chain. The accepted belief that the warm months will not produce good catches is flouted in the Oklawaha Chain.

These lakes produce larger catches of bass for anglers during the summer's heat than during the winter. This isn't just the random opinion of a few anglers, but is supported by statistics collected during the monthly buddy tournament sponsored by the Pine Island Campground and Fish Camp on the north end of Lake Griffin.

This tournament, begun in 1977 by Larry Fetter, operator of the fish camp, is a one-day affair held once a month with an eight-fish limit per man, 12-inch minimum size. Entry fee is $40 per boat. The twenty-four high-point men (points based on total poundage) plus any team that wins a tourney but doesn't qualify on a point basis, compete in a "classic" tournament in September. About eighteen boats compete monthly. Anglers can fish anywhere in the Oklawaha lake chain.

The tournament records show that it takes an average catch of 22.6 pounds per boat to win the monthly tournament during January, February, and March. True, this is the winter (cold-weather) period, but it's also generally regarded as a prime Florida bassing time because the bass usually are beginning to bed.

But during July, August, and September, the hottest months in Florida—the latter two months regarded generally as the Florida dog days—it takes an average of 44.6 pounds to win a tournament. Quite a difference between the cold and hot months.

There's a lot of fishing room in this chain of lakes, which consist of Lake Griffin, northernmost covering 16,505 acres; Eustis, 7,806 acres; Big and Little Lake Harris, 17,650 acres combined; Dora, 4,435 acres;

Beauclair, 1,111 acres; and Carleton, about 500 acres. The total acreage of the chain is some 48,000 acres.

Griffin is eight miles long, four wide, and has a maximum depth of 25 feet. Eustis is four and one-quarter miles long and four miles wide, while Big and Little Lake Harris are nine miles long and eleven miles wide. Lake Dora is eight miles long and four wide, while Beauclair and Carleton together are two miles long and one mile wide.

The seven lakes are interlinked. Griffin is linked to Eustis by Haines Creek, which has a lock easily transitted. From Eustis, you can go into the Harris lakes via the Dead River, or you can go from Eustis to Lake Dora via the beautiful Dora Canal, rated one of Florida's most picturesque waterways as it twists through part of a cypress swamp. Dora is directly connected to Beauclair, and the latter has an entry into Lake Carleton. Also the Apopka-Beauclair canal empties into Lake Beauclair.

With some 48,000 acres of water to fish, where do you go? It's

**Flipping is the only way at times to score on Lake Griffin. Flipping consists of gently dropping a plastic worm into likely looking bass hideouts in grass and weeds. Instead of casting, you swing your worm with a weight like a pendulum. You work close to cover, easing along with your trolling motor, and by flipping you can cover every inch of a prospective area.**

the obvious question any visiting angler asks. You can undoubtedly catch fish, sometimes real lunkers, anywhere, but probably the two most fished lakes are the Harris twins and Lake Griffin.

Although these bodies of water are about the same size, they are radically different in coloration. Big and Little Lake Harris are two of the least polluted and beautiful lakes in the chain, and their water is comparatively clear. In some areas, where streams enter, the water will be gin clear. On the whole, unless there is a wind to stir the water, the entire lake requires you fish with clear-water techniques.

Griffin, on the other hand, is not gin clear. The yellow stain can fool you, for there are big bass in the cloudy water. The biggest bass weighed in at Pine Island Fish Camp on Griffin tipped the scales at 15¾ pounds. That's a real wall mount.

None of the Oklawaha lakes can be classified as deep. The deepest water in Harris is only 28 feet, and is found where the Florida 19 bridge crosses the junction of Big and Little Lake Harris. Here you find the deepest water, and often the fish.

In Little Lake Harris, the grass beds are very productive, especially near the public beach of the little town of Howey-In-The-Hills. This western shore to the bridge is a good fishing area. Leaving Little Lake Harris, you can score by fishing the shore leading northwest along Big Lake Harris. This actually is part of the south shore of Lake Harris.

Be careful along this shoreline, for there are a number of posts barely underwater, remains of old docks that long ago disappeared. Oddly, this is a good fishing area, but it's no place for hot rodding. On calm days, you can see the posts in the clear water, but with a riffle, they're hidden.

The eastern shore of Big Lake Harris, in the vicinity of Lane Park Fishing Resort and Long Island, is also a good area. There are enormous lily fields in this area, and during the spawning period, you often can tangle with lunkers. Also the mouth of Helena Run to Lake Markham on the western shore, and where the Palatlakaha River empties into the lake are sometimes good areas.

Lake Eustis has some scattered good fishing and is making a comeback. There are a number of canals off this lake, and frequently you find the bass holding in the canals. Always check the mouth of any canal, because these seem to be natural holding areas in these lakes.

From Eustis you can do down Haines Creek and through the lock into Lake Griffin. Again you notice a number of canals leading off the main lake, and these often are bass holes.

Griffin is the site of intensive management programs. It is the only lake in the chain with significant bottom structure. This consists of ten fish attractors—artificially submerged brush piles—placed there by the Game and Fish Commission. Unfortunately, many of the attractor markers have been removed by vandals, hence you have to depend upon your depth finder. This may be a blessing in disguise, for the fishing pressure is much less on the now unmarked fish attractors.

During the spawning season, the bass generally are in the upper end of the lake where the Oklawaha River begins. The water isn't particularly deep—maybe up to 10 feet—but the bass like the abundant protection along the shore. There's plenty. The rest of the year, the bass are found all over the lake depending upon where the bait fish roam, and roam they do.

Also from Eustis you can take the Dora Canal into Lake Dora, which is connected with Beauclair which in turn is linked to Lake Carleton, where Bray landed his 6½-pound bass. The Apopka-Beauclair canal sometimes produced big fish.

One thing you immediately notice about the Oklawaha chain of lakes is the absence of the pesky grass which is almost a trademark of most Florida lakes. In these lakes, you can easily fish crank baits, as well as spinners, and plastic worms are just another useful lure, not necessarily the main one, depending upon the time of year.

After fishing the Oklawaha chain with Steve Plein, Larry Fetter, Lon Maas—all of whom guide on the lakes—and Buck Bray, who guides professionally on the Withlacoochee Backwaters at Dunnellon, the year-round fishing pattern becomes apparent.

During the January-to-March period, plastic worms are the prime lure, ranging in size from four to six inches, although there is some shiner fishing. Natural baits always produce with Florida bass, but shiners are losing their popularity with Florida anglers as the cost soars. Wild shiners, when you can get them, cost $12 a dozen, and commercial ones almost as much. Such prices dampen many angler's enthusiasm for shiner fishing. Some fish camps don't even stock shiners because of the high cost.

The preferred worm colors are blue, black-grape, and dark green. Some anglers prefer to have fire tails. It's a case of fishing your favorite lure color until you're convinced it isn't the one that day. Then try another color.

There's some use of spinner baits with both single silver blades, and tandem copper ones. Skirts are varied including white, chartreuse, and black and yellow. Some anglers prefer to use trailer hooks, and in these lakes you can do so with a minimum of fouling because of the lack of the usual super abundant grass.

At times shallow-running crank baits produce in three to four feet of water. Bomber's Model A is a very popular size in shad coloring. However, other crank baits will score, too, in the same color pattern. A few use Johnson-type spoons to fish shallow grass beds where the bass often spawn, and in Lake Harris, Plein finds that many a northern visiting angler trolls with Buck spoons.

Things change in the April-to-June period as the bass move off the beds. You find the bigmouths hitting in the eel grass, especially early in the morning with spinner baits. The same baits also can be used around the numerous docks.

All types of spinner baits are used with both single and double blades. Copper or bronze blades rate number one. Skirts are white, chartreuse, black, and yellow and black. A wide variety of crank baits can be used during this period including Mann's Razorback, black back and orange belly; Bomber's Model A and 6A in shad, chartreuse and green, and baby-bass colors.

Worms, too, are used, and this is the start of the flipping season. You can flip cane patches, tall reeds, and under the docks. Both six and seven and one-half-inch worms are used. Colors are blue, black, black-grape, and sometimes green.

The warm June-to-September period is the real flipping period. Your chances of connecting are best if you can flip into good cover, for the bass are not about to roam in the bright sun. Blue is the most popular worm color, but now bigger worms are preferred up to nine inches. The bigger worms are more successful because the bass now are feeding on larger bait fish.

Early and late in the day, crank baits of the same colors as those used earlier in the year often produce. There's some use of buzz baits across grass beds again early and late. Less popular, but sometimes used, particularly early and late in the day, are various top-water lures with and without propellers, and shallow divers such as Bagley and Rebel manufacture. Rebel broken-back minnows are used as well as straight-back models. Colors are black and gold, or black and silver.

The October-to-December period is regarded as the most difficult to fish on this lake chain. Why? Experts can't say why, but they can testify that the fish are hard to locate. In this period, your best chances of finding bass are in the numerous canals, particularly around where they empty into the lakes. These seem to be very good holding areas, apparently because the bait fish move in and out, and often there's moving water. Wherever you can find moving water, your chances of hooking up with a bass are much better.

Again you have your choice of lures. You can use crank baits, spinner baits, or worms, and most anglers use all three before a trip is over. The bass are very erratic as to their likes and dislikes. With the worms, it's a case of casting rather than flipping, and using a variety of retrieves depending upon where you're fishing.

The Oklawaha chain has been stocked with Sunshine Bass (hybrids) resulting from the cross-breeding of white bass and stripers. These scrappers tend to roam open water, and you often encounter them when fishing open-water fish attractors. How big they will grow is unknown. However, in other states, the hybrids have surpassed 20 pounds.

There are numerous fishing resorts around the lakes, and if you can't find a cottage or room at one of them, you can always find motel space in the towns of Leesburg, Tavares, Mt. Dora, and Eustis. All are adjacent to the chain of lakes.

The Oklawaha Chain is surprising. Don't be afraid to test it during the hot months. You may be more successful when the sweat drips off your brow than when your teeth chatter in the cold.

# 30

# Headline Grabbing
# West Lake Toho

Wherever fishermen gather to discuss Florida lakes noted for producing lunker, largemouth black bass, you're always certain to hear the name Toho mentioned sooner or later. For those unfamiliar with the name, when a bass fisherman speaks of Florida's Toho, sometimes with a bit of awe in his voice, he is referring to West Lake Tohopekaliga in central Florida near the town of Kissimmee.

There are two lakes with the jawbreaking Indian name—East and West Tohopekaliga. But it's West Toho that has gained the greatest publicity in bass-fishing circles. West Toho has gained the national publicity because of fabulous catches of lunker bass, and for its role in experimental drawdowns for management purposes by the Florida Game and Freshwater Fish Commission.

West Toho, more often referred to merely as Toho, is a big lake covering about 22,750 acres. It's approximately twelve miles long and two to three miles wide, depending upon where you measure it. It's got a hard sandy bottom, with no stumps and no fallen timber or other underwater structures which hold bass in many Florida lakes. It is really a shallow saucer with a maximum depth of about 15 feet.

Toho is the northernmost lake in the Kissimmee River chain. Eventually its waters drain into Lake Okeechobee after passing through Cypress Lake, Lake Hatchineha, and Lake Kissimmee, and down the canal that has replaced the original winding Kissimmee River.

It's a typical central Florida lake. It's a case of fishing in a hayfield, just as you do in Lake Okeechobee farther south. Toho has an abundance of vegetation, mostly desirable plants for good bass and panfish habitat, including reeds, eel grass, lily pads, bull rushes, pepper grass, and sawgrass. It also has water hyacinths, which can cause fishing problems. On the whole, you fish in grass for lunker bass.

Toho's history in the last ten years has been fascinating. After being one of the premier Florida bass lakes for years, Toho got into pollution trouble in the 1960s, as man began to dump wastes helter skelter with no thought as to the impact on the waters.

By 1969, the lake was in dismal shape, giving every indication of becoming another Jolly Green Giant as had Apopka years earlier when pollution overwhelmed a fabulous fishing lake. The situation was so bad the Florida Game and Freshwater Fish Commission decided to gamble on a drawdown to dry out part of the lake's bottom.

The Commission drew down the water level in the lake in 1971 exposing much of the shallow bottom. Drawdowns have proved numerous times that they can give a hard-pressed lake a chance to revive. Man is doing artificially what nature did normally before man began tinkering with nature's cycle under the guise of flood control.

The first Lake Toho drawdown was a tremendous success. Bass grew rapidly to lunker size with an abundant food supply, and 10-pound and larger fish were consistently caught. The lake's record now is over 17 pounds. Now that's a hefty bass.

By six years after the drawdown, big bass were commonplace in Toho. The most spectacular example of the drawdown's success was achieved in February, 1977, by Dick and Elaine Hengl of Princeton, Ia., who landed twenty bass—two ten-fish limits—having a total weight of 148.23 pounds. Eleven of the bigmouths weighed 8 pounds or more. Of these eleven, two weighed 8 pounds, four weighed 9 pounds, four weighed 10 pounds, and one ranked in the 11-pound bracket. Their two-limit string averaged 7.41 pounds a fish. What a record!

The Hengl's caught their fabulous string using a crawdad-colored Rebel Deep R. They were fishing the deeper water below the gates at the upper end of the Southport Canal which connects Toho with Cypress Lake. The Hengl string was an amazing catch. Toho veterans regarded it as one in a million bonanza. The bass apparently were concentrated in the deep water ambushing bait fish that were coming through the open canal locks.

Despite the fantastic Hengl catch, you won't catch too many fish in what deep water Toho has. The majority of the bass are caught in and around grass beds in three to five feet of water.

Too, veteran guides recommend using big shiners if you're actively seeking a wall-mount bigmouth. Artificial lures produce on Toho, but there's nothing like a hefty shiner to lure the bigmouths into action, particularly during the cooler months when the bass are sluggish.

Shiner fisherman use a variety of systems. Some use a sliding float with a bead stopper for depth control, usually fishing shiners in from 1 to 3 feet of water. At times, freelining a shiner without a float is the best way. And there are anglers who prefer to use fixed position floats. All of the systems work when conditions are right.

Although shiners are highly productive, the most glamorous way to seek the bigmouth lunkers is with artificial lures, and big bass consistently are landed with them. Depending upon the water level and the grass, you can use a variety of lures on Toho, although not as wide a variety as on some lakes. After all, basically you're after bass in the grass.

Most experts rate the Johnson-type spoon (including the Weed Wing and the Skitter Buzz) and the plastic worm as the most productive for day-in and day-out fishing. Most anglers fish a black spoon with a yellow skirt across the top of grass or through the reeds and weeds. They also favor fishing a black worm—six to nine-inch—on top through the vegetation. Of course, there are always certain situations when other lures are the answer. There also are times when top-water or shallow-diving lures (balsa types especially) are effective. The success of the propeller top-waters or the shallow divers depends upon the density of the grass. Top-water lures often are successful when you encounter schooling bass.

Toho, too, is perhaps one of the state's finest waters for fly fishermen. Because of the shallow depth, and pothole-type fishing, a popping bug can be cast into the open water surrounded by aquatic vegetation, and worked slowly until a strike results.

Most flyrod anglers use medium-size poppers to entice both large bream and average-size bass into hitting. If you want bigger bass, you can use bigger poppers, but you may have less action.

While the lake is shallow, most of the wading is done in waist-deep water—ideal depth for bass and bream. During cold weather, a pair of chest-high waders are necessary. However, for seven to eight months a year all you need for wading is a pair of old pants and sneakers.

But where do you fish in a lake covering almost 23,000 acres which lacks the usual structure and holding areas such as creek mouths, rocks, sunken trees, and similar? Locating the bass is a bit more difficult than you'd assume. Grass beds, of course, are the first key, but with acres and acres of grass, what is the tip-off?

Tom Howerton of Lakeland, who guides and fishes Toho, says: "I like to look for anything that's the least bit unusual as a tip-off— grass near a little deeper water, grass with tall reeds, or anything that might provide a bit different cover. Bass have to hold differently in Toho than they do in a lot of lakes," he explains.

If you observe Toho's surface closely, you immediately notice there are clumps of tall reeds growing from the abundant grass. These are particularly good areas, whether you use artificial lures (spoons or worms) or live bait. The bass seem to have an affinity for this type of cover.

After several lengthy discussion with Howerton, and also with Lee McDonald, and other anglers it's apparent Toho, like all lakes, has to be fished differently at various times of the year. The fishing calendar goes like this. During the winter—January through March—shiners, of course, are the most productive. However, artificial lures also score. Eight and ten-inch black worms rigged Texas weedless-style produce when fished in two to six feet of water in the grass around bedding areas. A few use hooks with wire weed guards.

You need a sensitive rod to feel the worm pickup, and one with plenty of backbone for bringing the bass out of the grass. One cast into an area isn't sufficient. Make several because the bass (if bedding) may first only move the worm out of the bed. But if you keep tormenting long enough, the buckemouth may hit trying to kill the interloper.

You also can use single and double-blade spinner baits in the same areas, depending upon how thick the grass is. With these lures, you often have to vary your speed of retrieve. Sometimes you zip across the top of the grass (buzz baits are good for such situations). At other times, you run your spinner bait slowly across the bottom. Yellow and chartreuse skirts are favored for the spinner baits.

Along the outer edges of the weed and grass beds, you sometimes can score with crank baits. Colors vary, ranging from conventional black and silver to the more exotic such as chartreuse and crawdad. It's a case of experimenting to find what color is wanted on a given day.

Just before the spawning season, spoons—both Johnson and Weed-Wing types—are very effective skittered across the top of the grass. Black is the preferred color with either yellow, yellow and white, or chartreuse skirts.

Cagey Toho veterans often encounter short strikers when skittering spoons fast. They have two solutions to the problem. First, they trim the spoon's skirts to a minimum length, barely extending past the hook. Thus when a bass grabs at the skirt, he's also grabbing at the hook. None of this nipping at a long skirt.

Also when conditions permit, i.e. minimal grass, Toho anglers use a trailer hook. With a trailer hook, the length of the skirt isn't as important, for the bigmouth can hardly avoid contacting the trailer hook. With a trailer, a longer skirt is somewhat of an advantage because it makes the lure a little more weedless.

Buzz baits, too, produce when zipped over the top of vegetation. Generally skirts for these baits are yellow or white, the skirt color matching the color of the lure's body.

In the April-to-June period, spoons and worms remain the top lures. Black, of course, is the preferred spoon color regardless of the type of day, but there are variations in worm colors. Depending upon the water temperature, and the amount of sunlight, Toho anglers use black, blue, or ice blue worms, usually eight to ten-inches in length. Black works best on dark days. Blue is used on clear days, and exceptionally sunny ones call for the lighter, ice blue-colored worm.

Basically, you are fishing the same general areas, except you look for heavy cover with deeper water of about six feet. Again you can use crank baits along the edges of the grass beds in open water.

During the hot months of July, August, and September, Johnson-type spoons and buzz baits are fished over thick grass standing in four to six feet of water. Worm fishing during this hot period is best early and late in the day, or whenever you can locate a deeper hole.

At dawn, and again at sundown, sometimes you can tease bass into hitting with top-water lures, but this is strictly a hit and miss proposition. Early morning offers the best opportunity because the lake has had a chance to cool a bit during the night.

During the fall—October through December—worms are rated the number one lure, again black-colored ones being preferred on dark days with blue on bright ones. However, you also can use spoons and buzz baits. All of these lures score when the bass are feeding.

Water depths are the same, and again when fishing deep water that isn't full of grass, you can use crank baits. Once in awhile, you can use sinking baits such as Rat-L-Traps or Spots.

Considering the size of Toho, a guide is advisable for your initial trips. Guides operate out of the four fish camps on the lake. If you want to go without a guide, you'll do well to get a map of the lake to orient yourself. A Toho map is published by Southern Guide Maps, P.O. Box 1326, 500 Gulf Shore Drive, Destin, Fl., 32541.

There are several camps where you can stay on the lake, or there are motels in Kissimmee. The area is full of motels since the town of Kissimmee, and the north end of the lake are only a short distance from Disney World. Hence, motel reservations are advisable.

I've based at Scotty's Camp on Lake Toho, which has modern, clean accommodations along with covered boat stalls and a good launching ramp. The address is Scotty's Fish Camp, Rt 1, Box 56, Kissimmee, Fl., 32741, telephone (305) 847-3840.

Scotty's also has a campground if you're hauling a camping rig. You also can utilize Southport Campground on the south end of the lake, which has a small store, and a good launching ramp. Southport camping reservations can be made c/o Manager, Southport Park, 2001 Southport Road, Kissimmee, Fl, 32741, telephone (305) 348-5822.

Although Toho is a superior bass lake, perhaps not quite as good after the second drawdown that took place in 1979-80, it faces an uncertain future because of the continued introduction of excessive quantities of nutrients from surrounding cities.

Fish biologists monitoring Lake Toho report the 22,750-acre lake will not be able to support a sportfish population by 1990 unless things are changed. As Vince Williams, Florida Game and Fish biologist says in the report titled *Impact of Sewage Plant Discharge on Lakes of the Upper Kissimmee Basin*: "There is little doubt in the minds of biologists familar with Lake Tohopekaliga that it probably will suffer a Lake Apopka-like collapse within the next decade.

"By this, we mean that the lake no longer will be capable of supporting a recreational sportfishery, which presently generates millions of dollars of revenue to the local economy. . . .

"The lake *cannot* be maintained through any management technique including periodic drawdowns if massive nutrient discharges from sewage plants are allowed to continued unabated. . . .

"If Lake Toho does collapse, other downstream lakes in the chain including Cypress, Hatchineha, and Kissimmee undoubtedly will do the same."

The source of pollution has been pinpointed for years. Four major sewage treatment plants discharge into Lake Toho. They are the City of Orlando's McLeod Road plant (discharges into Shingle Creek); Southwest Orange County Road plant; City of Kissimmee Martin Street plant (discharges directly into Lake Tohopekaliga via the Kissimmee "city ditch"); and the St. Cloud plant. Sewage discharge has increased from seven million gallons per day in 1971 to an estimated twenty-two million gallons per day in 1980, and growing.

The input of nutrients speeds up the growth of excessive aquatic plants. Phosphorous, which has proven to be one of the major problem-causing nutrient materials in lakes throughout the country, is being dumped into Toho at an alarming rate.

On February 11, 1980, the four plants were dumping 2,094 pounds of phosphate into the lake. The figure is meaningless until compared with what happened to Lake Apopka. Apopka, which no longer supports a sportfishery, received 1,956 pounds of phosphate daily when the pollution there was at its peak.

Apopka died receiving a smaller daily phosphate than Toho is receiving, *yet* Apopka is the larger body of water. Toho is twenty-seven percent smaller, and has twenty-one percent less volume of water. Toho is receiving up to twice the amount of phosphate that contributed to Apopka's destruction. Can Toho survive? Time holds the answer, but unless the pollution problem is solved, Toho may be going down the tube. Even so, the developers, especially in the Orlando area, could care less.

Lake Toho is one of Florida's premier bass lakes, but if you want to seek wall mounts you'd better do it soon unless the polluters are curbed. With the frantic emphasis the Orlando-Disney World area puts on more and more development (meaning more and more sewage) the chances of Toho surviving until 1990 aren't too bright.

# 31

# Lake Kissimmee—
# Ready To Explode

Lake Kissimmee, sprawling over nearly 40,000 acres in central Florida, is being closely watched by bass fishermen in anticipation of an angling explosion. Fishermen are asking will Kissimmee be the Florida lunker hole of the 1980s, just as Lake Jackson was during the 1960s, and West Lake Tohopekaliga in the 1970s?

It could well happen. Already reports of 10-pound largemouth, black bass have become common, and the stage has been set. To understand why the feeling of imminent explosion exists, you have to know something of the lake's immediate past.

Kissimmee always has been an excellent bass lake. Now a link in the Kissimmee river flood-control chain, it's linked to Lake Hatchineha to the north, and to Lake Okeechobee to the south via the channelized river.

Kissimmee is a typical Florida flatland lake dotted with an abundance of grass and weeds, including water hyacinths and lily pads. It's some eighteen miles long, and five miles at its widest point and has a surface area of more than fifty-five square miles. Yes, there is lots of room for largemouth bass to roam, not to forget speckled perch, bream, and shellcrackers.

Like so many Florida lakes, Kissimmee has a grass problem, which is fine for bass but tough for the fisherman. Overenrichment, as a result of the channelization of the Kissimmee River for flood control purposes, has been a major factor in the expansion of the grass problem.

Grass became such a problem that after studying the problem the Florida Game and Fish Commission decided in the late 1970s to create a drawdown of Kissimmee patterned after the earlier, highly successful drawdown of Lake Tohopekaliga, more widely known as Lake Toho.

Toho's drawdown in the early 1970s reduced the grass problem, and also set the stage for several years of spectacular fishing with bass in the 10-pound and heavier brackets caught routinely. The fish biologists hoped for comparable results with Kissimmee. The drawdown began in December, 1976, and was completed in March, 1977, and the program ended officially in December, 1977.

The drawdown was expected to reduce the grass problem by drying out much of the lake bottom, making possible the growth of grasses favored by bass. It was expected this change would increase the food supply, which naturally would expand the bass population.

The drawdown dropped the lake's level to 44 feet above sea level. Normally, Kissimmee's depth fluctuates between 52.5 and 48.5 feet above sea level. The plan was to expose forty-five percent of the lake's bottom, or some 18,500 acres. The program called for the lake to remain at low stage until June. Then refilling would begin. Water was to be supplied from above Kissimmee where a plug had been inserted temporarily in the channelization project canal, also from normal summer rains, and possibly from a wet hurricane.

The Kissimmee River basin lakes normally are drawn down from January until June to attain the minimum depths in June to provide emergency storage capacity if heavy rains sweep Florida during the hurricane period.

The drawdown didn't work as planned—nature intervened by providing less than normal rainfall. Kissimmee actually was drawn down to 43.5 feet. Abnormally low in June, it refilled very slowly because of the lack of normal rain. By October, 1977, the lake had only risen to its normal June low point of 48.5 feet.

According to the fish biologists monitoring the lake, there is now an excellent bass population, but too many of the bass are holding in unfishable waters. According to Jerry Lunsford, who has been fishing the Kissimmee for years from the Oasis Marina where Florida Highway 60 crosses the beginning of the Kissimmee river: "There're lots of bass. They're getting bigger and bigger with plenty of food. But you can't get to them. When the lake gets three more feet of water then you'll be able to get a boat back into the grass fields.''

Buck Bray, my regular fishing partner, and I learned the grass problem in a couple exploratory trips. Without higher water, you're confined to a few areas, and, of course, the bass aren't necessarily there. Off in the distance we could see the shallow grass beds affording excellent bass cover. There obviously was a more than ample food supply, but reachable? No way! But with water, hang onto your rods.

There's ample evidence that the fish are there and growing bigger. A 12-pound, 1-ounce bass was weighed at the Oasis Marina in 1981 caught with a 9¼-inch, blue Fliptail worm. Numerous fish weighing between 10 and 11 pounds have been landed. Of course, the best evidence is the Oasis' fish tank where you can see eight bass from 7½ to 11 pounds lazily swimming or finning. They all were caught in Kissimmee.

After Buck and I fished with Lunsford a couple of times, and held several "hot stove" league discussions, the year-round fishing pattern for the Big K became apparent. Even with normal water depths, the lake is a challenging fishing hole, more difficult than some lakes because of the abundant grass. However, the grass affords cover for the bait fish, and for the bigmouths, and actually is an asset, even if anglers often swear at it.

Obviously, Lake Kissimmee is a lake where a plastic worm is useful most of the time, although there are a few periods when other lures will work. Shiners, of course, are the number one big bass producer if you're looking for wall mounts in Kissimmee, just as they are in every other Florida lake. But the worm is the number one artificial.

The calendar rundown on the Big K goes like this. The first quarter of the year—January through March—is the major spawning period. The bass are in the heavy grass, around lily pads, and cattails in water ranging from six inches to three feet in depth.

The most popular artificial, lure of course, is the plastic worm. Kissimmee anglers prefer the larger worms, ranging in size from seven to nine inches. Colors are black, blue, or violet. When fished near a bass bed, the plastic enticers are deadly, but make more than one cast. Often the bass will merely pick up the worm and move it out of the bed. But eventually you can provoke the bigmouth into killing the worm, and when this happens strike, and set the hook hard!

Another effective lure is a Johnson-type weedless spoon. Black, gold, and silver are the preferred colors in that order with a variety of skirts. Black with a green skirt is particularly effective. You also can score using a chartreuse, black and yellow, or yellow skirt. Big K bass can be temperamental, and changing skirt colors often is the key to success.

Some anglers also use spinner baits both single- and double-blade models with silver- or copper-colored blades. Again a variety of skirt colors are used including, white, chartreuse, or black and yellow. Another producer is a yellow Snagless Sally with a pork frog chunk. With these various spinner baits, the rule for success is to impart as much action to the bait as possible while moving the bait as slowly as you can. This method of retrieving sounds odd, but it can be done.

By the second quarter—April-to-June—the bass generally have moved off the beds, and you find the largemouths on the outside edges of the numerous grass beds and in the pepper-grass patches. If you locate an area where water is emptying into the lake, you are almost sure to find bass in the vicinity. Bass like moving water. During this period, you fish water five to seven feet deep.

Plastic worms again are rated the number one lure, although there are other lures used. Again, worm colors are black, blue, and violet, or purple-grape. However, if the water is discolored, then use worms with flourescent tails either chartreuse, red, or blue.

When you can find open water near the grass beds, you often can score with top-water lures. Among the most popular top waters on Kissimmee are black and yellow Devils Horse, silver flash Nip-A-Diddee, Dalton Special, both frog back and silver flash; and Boone's Long A.

Both single- and double-propeller lures produce depending upon fishing conditions. The noisy plugs seem to do best when there's a slight chop on the water because they're heard better by the bass. Of course, with the abundant grass, you don't want to overlook the weed-less Johnson and Strike King spoons, either black, gold, or silver in color. A variety of skirts are used including green and white, chartreuse, black and yellow, and yellow.

You also have success blipping Rebel and Bagley minnow-types along the edges of the grass beds like injured bait fish. This type of lure is good all year around in Kissimmee, as long as there is enough water to cover part of the grass, but these lures probably produce best during the spring.

Few spinner baits are used during this period for some unknown reason. Of course, they're difficult to work through the dense grass, and with the bass off the beds, you can do very little spot casting. The bass are found everywhere. But it never hurts to experiment.

During the hot months of July through September, the fish are

Tom Howerton displays a pair of West Lake Toho bass that couldn't resist a plastic worm. This famous bass lake is loaded with weeds and grass, and a plastic worm rigged weedless is one of the most effective lures.

either deep or seeking shade in the dense grass. A plastic worm is the most efficient lure as usual rigged weedless with slip sinkers of various weights. Worm colors are the same, and again you can use weedless spoons. Black, gold, or silver spoons can be used with a variety of skirt colors.

With the water temperature cooling in the last quarter of the year— October through December—you find the bass more active. They're usually around the outside edge of the grass, and around pepper-grass patches. Again the same color worms are rated number one. However, if the water is discolored, as sometimes happens during heavy rains that often accompany the last of the hurricane season, then amber-colored worms are very good. Again you can use weedless spoons with various skirt combinations.

During the fall, the bass often school, and when you encounter them chasing bait schools on the surface, you can score using most standard top-water lures, either single- or double-propeller ones. Lure color doesn't seem too important as long as you can cast your lure into the middle of the frantic feeding action. It is a good idea, however, to try and match the color of your lure to the color of the bait on which the school bass are feeding.

Kissimmee being a big, shallow lake can have a wind problem, and white cap quickly. A north or south wind can sweep the entire lake, and create dangerous boating conditions. Watch the wind directions. A north wind, which often occurs as weather fronts move through during the winter, is a real headache on Kissimmee.

With windy conditions, sometimes you can find protected waters to fish behind 5,500-acre Brahama Island, and smaller Bird Island. If these don't afford enough protection, you can find sheltered waters at the south end of the lake by going through Lock No. S-65 and into the Kissimmee River. The locks are in operation from 7 A.M. to 7 P.M. daily, and there are stretches of the now channelized river which are very productive, especially where old ox-bows have been cut across leaving sloughs and pockets where fish can hide.

As with any lake, it's wise to orient yourself before fishing the first time. A map of Lake Kissimmee is published by Southern Guide Fishing Maps, P.O. Box 1326, 500 Gulfshore Drive, Destin, Fl., 32541. You also can obtain a topographical map from the District Engineer, U.S. Corps of Engineers, P.O. Box 4970, Jacksonville, Fl., 32201.

There are several fish camps on Lake Kissimmee. I've stayed at the Oasis on the south end, and have no experience with the others. Guides are available at all camps.

Time holds the answer to whether or not Kissimmee will be the fabulous lunker hole of Florida during the 1980s. All signs indicate it can be if man or Mother Nature doesn't interfere, but the lake will have to have normal water depths to grab the fishing spotlight. Otherwise the lunkers will be unreachable.

# 32

# Beautiful Blue Cypress Lake

If lakes were designated as either masculine or feminine, Blue Cypress in the boondocks east of Yeehaw Junction, Florida, definitely would be classified as feminine. The adjectives generally used to describe this beautiful cypress-rimmed lake always seem to have a feminine connotation. Blue Cypress is as bewitching as any brunette, as baffling as any blonde, and as unpredictable as any redhead.

Nevertheless, the lake is an excellent bass hole if you can decipher its whims. The fish are there. It's a matter of luring them into striking. Blue Cypress' black bass record is 18 pounds, 1 ounce, a mark not too many other bodies of water can claim. Yet in typical feminine fashion, the lake can be red hot one day, and frigid the next. No wonder it leaves many bassmen bewildered. Blue Cypress is a tease.

Definitely, Blue Cypress has me bewildered. The lake always does the unexpected. One trip Buck Bray and I made, the bass drove us up a wall with their antics. They dashed at our top-water lures with submarine wakes, only to prove to be short sighted. Too, they ignored our plastic worms. However, they provided enough action to tease us into coming back again and again.

Another trip was a typical tease, although we did manage to have top-water action when guided by Joe Middleton. But the irony of one evening sortie was that Joe's young son, Gary, landed a 6-pound largemouth with a plastic worm while taking his girl for a boat ride.

Buck, who guides on the Withlacoochee near the little town of Dunnellon, and I trailered his eighteen-foot Ranger bass boat from Inverness to Blue Cypress during the heat of the summer. It wasn't the best time of year by any means, and Blue Cypress gave us the typical tease treatment.

We were fishing the northwest corner among the cypress—one of our favorite locations because of the scenic beauty—when I flipped a top-water plug (Buck 'n Brawl by Smithwick) near a lonesome tree. The water exploded as the lure landed, but the bass missed. Undoubtedly the fish would have weighed more than 7 pounds. It had to be that hefty to create such a disturbance. But that bass also needed glasses badly.

The next evening in the same area, Joe Middleton tossed a shallow-running, lipped propeller plug (Bang-O-Lure) and the same thing happened. Possibly this was the same old cantankerous, near-sighted bass, or perhaps an even bigger one. Unfortunately, it missed.

I wasn't watching the cast from the other boat, but the bass made such an explosion that momentarily I thought that a huge branch or log had fallen from the cypress. Glancing around, I saw it was no log. It was a bass of trophy proportions that missed his lure. Just some more of Blue Cypress' feminine antics. Tease and torment, and sometimes relent.

After being tantalized and tormented several times and talking at length with Joe, who's been operating the only fish camp on Blue Cypress since 1965, I'm convinced the secret of getting the lake to quit playing tricks depends upon when and how you fish.

You run the risk of encountering a hulking bass any time you toss your lure into Blue Cypress, *but* you can increase the odds in favor of scoring if you study the lake's yearly track record, and learn some of the quirks of fishing it.

Unlike so many Florida lakes, Blue Cypress has no major weed problems. There's no sign of hydrilla. There's no major water hyacinth problem, and the lake rises and falls naturally as nature intended. The result is that during the year, you have to fish a variety of locations and change your lure technique.

Here's the rundown Joe gives you on fishing the lake. During the January-to-March period, the best angling is found around the lily pads at the southeast and southwest ends of the lake. For some reason, the lily fields are concentrated in that area. Unless you know this, you may wander off in the wrong direction, for the cypress at the north end of the lake looks interesting. However, this area is not a prime bass hangout during these months.

During the first quarter, you can use worms with slip sinkers, spinner baits, and Johnson spoons—silver and gold—with various skirts. The most productive worm colors are black, black with firetail, and blue. Joe has found black and blue are the most productive colors, and he won't use any other.

With spinner baits, they key is the color of the skirts. Chartreuse is number one, unless the lake's water is stained. Then Joe recommends a white skirt. Blades can either be silver or gold. Some prefer single-blade spinners (which do sink faster and run deeper), while others opt for double blades. It's a personal choice, and also depends upon the depth at which the fish are holding.

The best time to fish Blue Cypress is the period of March through June. Joe rates May as the best of these months, although he can't bad-mouth June. Why? Because he caught his largest bigmouth then—a 14-pound, 1-ounce lunker. He was using ten-pound test line on an open-face spinner, and a top-water lure (Bagley 007).

There's a reason for this period's number one rating, of course. It's the spawning season, and during and after always are prime times for Florida bassing. Although the Blue Cypress bass begin spawning as early as March (sometimes in February, depending upon the type of winter), they are still bedding in May.

During this time of year, you score by fishing the grass shoreline on the east side, and among the trees on the south end of the lake. Joe's favorite lure is a four-inch Bang-O-Lure with a propeller, either black and silver, or shad color. Although Blue Cypress has tannic acid water, stained at times but clear, gold is not the recommended color unless you're going to fish the Big M canal which drains northeast, or the creek that feeds the lake from the southeast. There definitely are color quirks with these boondock bass.

Although Joe has a definite preference for top-water lures, that doesn't mean that other single- and twin-propeller lures won't work. They will. Buck and I know that from personal experience, since neither of us had Bagley propeller Bang-O-Lures in our boxes. We've stirred up as much action with Tiny Torpedoes, Devils Horse, Spin-A-Diddee, and similar lures. For top-water fish, the balsa lures may be best, but the others are close behind. Probably just as important is your lure-handling technique.

During the hot months of July through September, you have to

If you're going to hand land a bass as Gary Middleton is doing be certain you get a good grip on the bucketmouth's lower jaw, and swing the fish aboard fast. It's a tricky procedure, and much safer with small fish and with fish hooked with only one hook.

change your fishing tactics again. Then the bass are in the deepest
water, which isn't very deep in this lake. Deepest holes are only 20
feet, and there aren't very many. But the bass head for the deepest
water they can find for cool comfort. The best times to fish the shallows
is just after sunrise and just after sunset. You only have about an hour
of good fishing time.

This is the worm period, when you have to get your lure down
deep. Most anglers fish their plastics with a slip sinker, varying the
weight according to their own whims. Again Joe believes in the same
colors, blue or black. For early and late top-water fishing, the favored
lures are Bang-O-Lures, Rapalas, Rebels, Devils Horse, Tiny Torpedo,
Spin-A-Diddee and similar plugs.

Crank baits, too, are used, although until recently they haven't
been given too much consideration. But there's no reason they shouldn't
work. The lake has an unusually clean and sandy bottom, and there
are fewer underwater hazards.

Fish attractors have been built in the lake, a joint project of the
Florida Game and Freshwater Fish Commission and the Blue Cypress
Sportsman's Club. Even here a crank down can be fished without too
many fouling problems.

The October-to-December period is the second best time to fish
this tantalizing bass hole. But again you have to know where. During
these months, the Big M canal is the most productive as long as the
water is running. This canal was dug in the 1950s to deepen a natural
northward drainage and to enable citrus growers to irrigate. There's
also a lateral canal that affords fine fishing at times.

The main canal is uniformly 10 to 11 feet deep with ledges along
the bank. Plastic worms are the prime lure, but crank baits are gaining
steadily in popularity. During cool weather you can fish the canal successfully all day long. Of course, you also can score by fishing live
shiners in Blue Cypress. As with all Florida lakes, shiners are almost
certain to provoke the bass into feeding. Live shiners are available at
Middleton's camp.

Blue Cypress isn't huge, but it isn't a pond. It's three miles wide
and seven miles long. Nevertheless, Joe swears there's a new world
record bass in the lake. He may be right. He never has forgotten
encountering a bass weighing at least 18-pounds one day when running
a trot line. This bass had swallowed a small catfish that was caught on
the trot line's hook. The bigmouth became impaled on the catfish's
dorsal spine. When Joe attempted to haul in the trot line, the bass broke
loose in the ensuing ruckus.

"That was the biggest bass I've ever seen," he recalls. "It was a monster. But you can't catch a bass with a catfish spine. What a fish! I'd like to tie into that monster on hook and line someday. It could be a new record.''

Not only is Blue Cypress noted for its black bass, but it's also noted for its bluegills, shellcrackers, and lunker crappie. Three-pound speckled perch are common—too common, as Joe learned early in his fish camp career. When he first opened the Blue Cypress Lake Fish Camp, he offered a $25 prize for every 3-pound crappie brought in and weighed. The idea became too expensive. One woman brought in two 3-pounders in one day. They cost Joe $50, and he was glad to drop the promotion.

You can rent fiberglass 14-foot skiffs available with seven and one-half HP rental motors. But most anglers trailer their own boats, preferring the comfort of a modern bass boat. The lake is large enough that a big motor and speed can be useful, particularly when running away from a squall.

Blue Cypress is out in the boondocks. It's located east of Yeehaw Junction of Florida 60, the Lake Wales to Vero Beach highway. You reach it by driving six miles east on Florida 60, and then north four and one-half miles over a dirt road. If you aren't alert for the small fish camp sign on Florida 60, you can miss your turn.

The lake can hardly be classed as one that rubbs elbows with civilization. Among the few facilities available are: Middleton's Blue Cypress Fish Camp; one launching ramp at the little Indian River County park; a small trailer park of retirees and weekend escapees from the concrete canyons. Electricity is available.

The Middleton's don't have RFD service. They pick up their mail every two or three days in Vero Beach. The mailing address is Middleton's Blue Cypress Fish Camp, P.O. Box 1649, Vero Beach, Fl., 32698. There is a telephone at the camp, number (305) 562-9971. Middleton has six trailers and two cabins for rent. There are 40 primitive campsites for self-contained campers. You are really in the boondocks.

You can also stay at Yeehaw Junction at the junction of Florida 60, the Sunshine Parkway (toll), and U.S. 441. There is a Holiday Inn with a restaurant. If you're going to fish early or late (before or after closing of the Holiday Inn restaurant) you can utilize Horne's restaurant, not far from the motel, which is open 24 hours.

Tantalizing, teasing Blue Cypress in the boondocks is a bassing challenge few can resist once they know of this beautiful body of water. The big bass are there, but they tease and bewilder you as well as clobber your lures. Try Blue Cypress sometime, and expect to be surprised.

# 33

# Angling Changes on
# Florida's Big O

"They're signalling us to come over there," remarked Fred Wilson to Buck Bray, who was operating our 18-foot Ranger bass boat. "Bet they've found a school of bass," he added as Buck turned our boat towards a sawgrass point in Florida's famous Lake Okeechobee where Jim Fowler, Chip Campbell, and Doc Henderson were fishing.

As we approached, we could see they were in the midst of frantic action. Everyone seemed to be hooking fish on every cast. "What're you throwing?" called Fred, when we got within hailing distance.

"Chartreuse, fire tiger, Model A Bomber," replied Fowler, holding up a weird-looking plug as he unhooked a small school bass and released it. I knew the lure only by accident. A friend had given me the plug a couple of weeks before and said it was a good one. Out of courtesy, I'd stuck it in my tackle box.

I dug it out in a hurry, tied it onto my 10-pound test spinning line, and hurriedly cast. Nothing happened. I retrieved and cast again. Bingo! Action, and shortly I was boating a 2-pound school bass that didn't like the idea of being suckered into hitting the lure.

Meanwhile, Fred was beginning to score with the same lure, while

Buck tried to find something in his tackle box resembling the oddball color combination. Fred and I scored on almost every cast as did the three in the other boat, while Buck tested every lure in his box unsuccessfully. He didn't get into action until Jim loaned him a sinking chartreuse Spot—not exactly the same lure, but the same color. Then Buck, too, began boating fish.

For the next hour or so, fishing was frantic. It was almost unbelieveable for mid-July on Florida's Big O. It was as near as one can get to being in angling heaven.

At the end of the day, when we tallied our score, we estimated we had encountered more than 100 bass. They were school fish, top weights being in the 4-pound range, and they provided the wildest sort of action with a lure featuring the wildest color combination.

Naturally, the question is, What's so unusual about schooling bass wanting a particular color even if it is an oddball one? Normally, nothing, but in this case, the incident summarized one of the facets of the radical change in Lake Okeechobee fishing techniques.

Depending upon how recently you've sampled the Big O fishing, you may or may not be surprised at what has been happening. There have been some surprising changes in how you fish the Big O, since the 720-odd square miles of water have been completely encircled by the huge earthen dike.

To understand what's happening, it's necessary to know the history of the Okeechobee dike. After the raging hurricanes of 1926 and 1928, which killed hundreds along the shallow shores of the Big O, a program was begun by the U.S. Corps of Engineers to enclose the huge inland sea. Enclosing the 720-odd square miles of water was a major project, and the construction stretched over a period of 40 years.

Initially, the dike was built around the south shore, roughly from near Moore Haven to Belle Glade. This actually blocked the normal southward flow of the lake's waters, and later was to create problems for the Shark River in the Everglades National Park. Instead of the waters flowing south, they were diverted east by the St. Lucie canal, and west, via the Caloosahatchee River.

Then the northern end around Okeechobee City was diked. But until the 1970s, the lake was not completely encircled with the huge dirt wall. As a result, maximum storage capacity was estimated at 15.5 feet of water for handling hurricane flood waters.

Now completely surrounded, the lake's holding capacity is estimated at 17.5 feet, and this increased depth is the major cause of some of the surprising changes in fishing techniques.

At its maximum height, Okeechobee now is a larger lake. There's more water to spread out, and the bass have more room to roam, and roam they do. As a result, there has been a gradual change in lures, techniques, and fishing locations.

Only a few years ago, if you'd suggested using crank baits such as Bagley's Killer B-II, or Rebel's Wee R series, Bomber's Model As, or sinking lures such as Rat-L-Trap or Spot, veteran Okeechobee fishermen would have emphatically declared: "It can't be done. Too much grass!" They were correct then.

The Big O had grass then, and it has it now, but the situation is different. For years, there were only two consistently recommended lures used on Okeechobee. One was the black, weedless spoon with a variety of skirts, the other the old, faithful plastic worm, rigged weedless.

Infrequently, a top-water propeller plug would work. But it was not a standby. Generally an Okeechobee angler's tackle box didn't have to contain a large variety of lures. Of course, it was a good idea to have an ample supply of lures, for it's easy to lose them in the grass.

But, today, it's a different situation, startlingly different as was demonstrated by that unforgetable day when we encountered more than a hundred bass. That's a lot of bass to encounter during a single outing, but the most surprising facet was the lure that we used.

It wasn't the weedless spoon, the old Big O standby. Instead, we caught 80 percent of the bass with the weird looking Model A Bomber, a shallow-running crank bait, a lure every angler would have spurned a few years ago.

"We discovered when they raised the lake's maximum level you could score with shallow crank baits," recalls Fred Wilson Jr., a close friend, who guides on the lake. "You could score if you have the right color combination, and if you modify your techniques.

"For some reason, this chartreuse/tiger stripe is a deadly lure on Okeechobee, although we can't figure out what it's suppose to represent to a bass. But it catches fish. Almost as good at times are Bagley's Honey B in black and white color, or any crank bait that's white or bone color.

"These colors, of course, make more sense," he continues. "After all, they could look like shad. Anyway, the bass will hit these colors."

The black and white and bone colors didn't seem too unusual to me. Black spoons with white skirts have been effective lures on the Big O. But the chartreuse combination amazed me. Of all the lures on a tackle shop shelf, that was the color scheme I'd never have chosen. That crank-bait sortie was no fluke. Today, as a result of the change in Big O methods, you can use crank and other baits, of course, with modified techniques.

There's more use of top-water lures such as Tiny Torpedoes, Devils Horse, Dalton Special, Devils Toothpick, or Baby Zara Spook, lures with and without propellers, as well as some use of spinner and buzz baits.

But probably the biggest change in Okeechobee fishing is the adoption of the crank baits. However, there's a difference in methods. While normally you cast these lures long distances and retrieve them fast to attain maximum depth, this isn't the Big O system.

Instead, you make short casts, and crank the lures shallow. If you score with a crank down, you do so within the first few feet of the landing site. After that you're usually merely retrieving a plug, often with too much grass if you make the mistake of going too deep.

Not only will floating crank baits work, but also fast sinkers such as the Rat-L-Trap and Spot. But again you don't make long casts, and long, deep retrieves. Instead you spot cast to open water, retrieve a few feet, and if you get no action, bring back your lure and cast again. Action is either immediate or nonexistent.

The Big O is still a giant hayfield, greatly expanded at maximum water height. The bass are found around the peppei grass beds, reeds, water hyacinths, and the spreading hydrilla. There's a trick to using a crank or sinking bait around such cover.

You have to spot cast to patches of open water, and tease a bass into coming from the cover to sock your lure. Of course, such a technique is really only efficient when the lake is calm, and you can spot clear areas. You also need to be an accurate caster, for some of the target areas are mightly small, but that's where the bass are laying.

You find top-water floaters, both propeller and stick baits, are very effective for spot casting to small areas of open water. You also can work the minnow-type lures, either balsa or plastic, successfully if you fish them slowly on top, and don't let them run too deep. Often there's grass within a few inches of the surface under the apparent open area, and the bass hide in the grass to ambush passing meals.

Another change Okeechobee experts have noticed is that the schooling season for bass is longer. With the changing water level, the bass have begun to school in mid-July and continue as late as early December. What once was a few-week season, now sometimes stretches into six months.

What causes the change in schooling tactics is unknown. Many anglers theorize the lake's water is cooler. With more water being retained, the deeper water doesn't heat as quickly. The resulting lower temperature may cause the bass to be more active. It's a theory, but the guides don't care too much whether it's true or not, as long as the fishing is better. Theories are fine, but fish in the boat are better.

Another thing the professional lake guides have discovered is that the school bass can fool you. "We use to assume that when they quit schooling on top, they scattered," explains Wilson. "But those fish don't scatter. They just sound and stay in the same area. We've finally learned that when they quit hitting on top, you still can catch them with plastic worms fished deep."

However, the use of new lures doesn't mean the old reliable weedless spoon skittered across the pepper grass or weeds won't produce. "A spoon is still mighty important," declared Jim Fowler and Chip Campbell, another pair of expert Big O guides. "But we find so many customers don't have the proper tackle. You need a stiff rod, twenty-pound test line, and a fast, retrieving reel to keep the spoon skipping across the water. Too many of our customers have rods that lack the backbone to work a spoon correctly."

Black and silver are still the most effective spoon colors, usually with all black, black and yellow, and all white skirts. Depending upon the time of year, most spoon fishing is done in 5 to 6 feet of water.

Plastic worms, too, continue to be effective in a variety of colors. Most Big O veterans prefer the black-grape color. However, there are times when the fish are temperamental, and blue, black, and even reddish brown are more successful, and who knows what oddball hue will produce in the future?

Another development has been the importance of line test. At one time, twenty-pound test line was standard for the Big O, but not any longer. "We've found that you have to carry several line tests," explains Wilson. "It makes a big difference sometimes. Jim Fowler and I proved this to my sorrow.

"We were fishing together. Jim was using fourteen-pound test, while I had twenty-pound on my worm outfit. We found fish, and Jim was putting it to me landing fish after fish, while I couldn't even get a tap, We were both using the same color and size worm.

"The only difference was my heavier line, and it was the difference! I changed to fourteen-pound test and began matching him fish for fish.

"If you're going to fish Okeechobee, and don't have any luck fishing a plastic worm with twenty-pound test, then change to seventeen, fourteen, or even twelve. You may lose some fish in the grass, but I'd rather have fish on and lose them, than no strikes at all. Line test makes a much bigger difference now than it did a few years ago.''

As with all worm fishing, it pays to experiment when the bass are performing erratically. The worms are fished with and without a sinker, either rigged weedless Texas-style, or with a wire weed-guard hook, depending upon the grass situation.

The spreading hydrilla, which is infecting the Big O as it is so many other Florida waterways, is also bringing about a change in the worm fishing. The pesky weed affords a form of structure fishing. The Okeechobee anglers find they catch more bass by dropping their plastic worms along the edge of the thick mess. The bass roam the edge of the hydrilla seeking freshwater shrimp, and the small bait fish hiding in the hydrilla. Dropping your worm along the edge of the mass of hydrilla can bring results, sometimes lunkers as big as 9 pounds.

With the new water-level schedule, you find the fish are holding in different locations, some that never before were fishing holes. You have to be willing to explore new areas at different times. You have to pick your fishing locations on the basis of how much water is in the Big O. Mother Nature, of course, has the final say, despite the Engineers' water level schedules.

With the completion of the lake's dikes, the South Florida Water Management District and the U.S. Corps of Engineers anticipate being able to hold two and one-half feet more water in the Big O.

The revised lake schedule calls for 15.5 feet of water by June 1 in preparation for possible flood waters during the hurricane season. Then the plan calls for a gradual increase in depth to 17.5 feet by October 1. This depth is maintained until January 1.

The first of the year marks the beginning of the gradually lowering of the lake to meet the 15.5 foot depth by June 1. No wonder the fish shift locations, and you have to readjust your fishing thinking according to the calendar.

With such radical change in fish locations as well as techniques, it's wise to hire a guide for your first few trips. If you want to contact any of the three experts with whom I've fished the new locations, they can be reached at the following addresses: Chip Campbell, P.O. Box 247, Okeechobee, Fl., 33472; Jim Fowler, P.O. Box 1255, Okeechobee, Fl., 33472; and Fred Wilson Jr., 1305 S.E. 8th Ave., Okeechobee, Fl., 33472.

If you prefer to sample the Big O without guidance, be sure you get a map to orient yourself. There's an awful lot of water to explore. For navigation, get NOAA chart No 11428 (formerly listed as 855-SC).

It's published by the federal government. For a map with fishing information, you can use the Lake Okeechobee map published by Southern Guide Fishing Maps, P.O. Box 1326, 500 Gulfshore Drive, Destin, Fl., 32541.

Florida had an extreme drougth in 1980–81, and Lake Okeechobee dropped to a record low during the June low-water period of less than than 10½ feet. Thousands of acres of normally flooded lake were exposed for months, and the bottom dried out.

While the drougth was a hardship on farmers and those dependent upon water in South Florida, it probably was a blessing in disguise as far as fishing the Big O. The long exposure to the sun dried out a large area of the lake, which will permit new grasses to grow and remove much of the unwanted sediment.

The odds are good that during the next few years, assuming the Big O returns to its normal water levels, the bass population will explode and superb fishing will be available. Fred Wilson Jr., a guide friend who remembers when the lake underwent a low-water period in early 1971, also recalls that fishing became excellent after the lake regained water.

"Bass fishing was fantastic for several years after the 1971 drougth," recalls Fred. "The bass multiplied like fleas, and you could catch your limit in a few hours. The fishing was so good it was unreal. I suspect the same thing will happen again this time when the lake gets back to normal. A natural drawdown is always helpful."

There are fish camps scattered all around the Big O, so you have no problem in establishing a fishing base. Some of the camps are medicore, while others are good. I've stayed in motels in Okeechobee City most of the time. There also are motels in Clewiston, Moore Haven, Belle Glade, and Pahokee.

Fishing techniques have changed on the Big O, and the bass are still there, with every indication there will be more bigmouths in the future. Too, they'll have more room to roam, and undoubtedly grow.

# 34

# Lake Trafford—The Lake That Came Back

Bill DeLisle and I were making our final casts late in the afternoon after another successful sortie on Lake Trafford in southwestern Florida. I flipped my shallow-running balsa minnow-type lure towards a hydrilla line where we had been encountering rapid-fire action. Landing, the lure was greeted by a violent swirl.

Fishing from the bow, Bill didn't see the strike, but he heard the rumpus. Without turning, he called: "You gotta a good one now!"

I was too busy at the moment to engage in any small talk. This fish definitely was larger than the 2 and 3 pounders that had been walloping our top-water lures. My rod bent perilously, and the reel gave line grudgingly. This fish was so big it wallowed instead of jumping, always a sign of a hefty bass. While the smaller ones invariably take to the air, the bigger ones don't as often. This fish was not engaging in any aerial acrobatics.

"Bill," I called. "Better get the net. This one's too big to hand land on 6-pound line."

"What?" he exclaimed, stumbling off the front casting deck. "You're using 6-pound test in this grass?"

"Yeah, Bill," I answered. "Get the net and can the chatter."

Bill's a professional guide on Lake Trafford, specializing in big fish, and he likes to use shiners for bait. He's an advocate of stout line—twenty and thirty-pound test. Of course, he has a reason. Trafford not only has big bass, but it also has plenty of hydrilla and hyacinths, not exactly the type of water for light tackle.

Bill scrambled aft, kicking over his tackle box in his excitement to find the net, then stood panting at my side, beginning to wave the net in the water. I didn't need that added hazard.

"Get that damned net out of the water, Bill," I hollered. "This fish isn't nearly ready."

The bigmouth was still plenty green. Although the steady pressure of the light rod was forcing the bass towards the boat, the battle wasn't over. Nearing the boat, the bigmouth dove under, but by sticking my rod beneath the surface. the maneuver was thwarted.

Meanwhile, Bill hurriedly pulled the motor just as the cantankerous bass decided to see what was on the other side of the boat. Holding my rod out as far as possible, I kept the six-pound test line from dragging on the motor. That would have been disastrous.

Now the bass sulked as I maintained steady pressure with the light spinning rod. For once, I wished I had a lunker stick, but there was no changing now. Obviously, the bass was tiring, and slowly, steadily I forced him nearer and nearer the boat. At last the fish was within netting range. With one quick pass, Bill netted the bass, and hoisted my prize aboard. Then we both collapsed.

"You'll be the death of me yet," mournfully remarked Bill as our nerves quieted. "You and that thread line. That ball will go well over seven pounts. Why, oh why, won't you listen to me?"

I chuckled, responding, "It's more fun on light tackle, Bill. It's more of a challenge."

Placing the fish in the live well, Bill started the motor and headed for the dock. That was a good fish with which to end a trip. Back at the little marina, the bass weighed an even 8 pounds—not the biggest that Trafford can produce, but a mighty nice fish on six-pound test line. Then we released the fish.

Afterwards I couldn't help but think how Trafford had changed in the last few years. Now I rate it as one of the most consistent big bass producers in the Florida and that's covering a lot of territory. But it does produce big bass. The lake record is 13 pounds, 11 ounces, caught with a shiner.

But if you know the history of Trafford, which is located near the little farming town of Immokalee in Collier County, you know the days

Unhappy at being conned into hitting a plastic worm, a Lake Trafford bass attempts to throw the lure with a leap. When you feel your prize starting to surface, retrieve your line to avoid giving slack which will enable the bass to throw your lure.

of the big bass are comparatively recent. Trafford is a shallow saucer sitting in the middle of the flat lands of Collier County, located about forty miles southwest of Fort Myers.

It's a lake that depends entirely upon rainfall, and it overflows towards the Corkscrew Swamp to the south. By normal standards, it's not a lake where you expect to find big bass, nor a plentiful bass population. But it has both.

You get an idea of how productive Trafford is when you consider some of the records. For example, when they were keeping close records at the Lake Trafford Marina, the only one on the lake, from March, 1976, until March, 1977, 250 bass weighing 7 pounds or more were caught and photographed.

However, this was by no means the total number of lunkers caught during this period. Nobody knows how many were hauled out at the nearby public ramp, and the Marina closed at 6 p.m.

Wouldn't you have liked to have been fishing one August only a couple of years ago when, in one week, Bill DeLisle fishing with Bill Kerfoot and Bill Adams really hit a bass bonanza?

As DeLisle says: "We tore 'em up. Landed a 7, 7½, 8,9, and 10¼ in three days plus twenty-seven from 3 to 6 pounds, all while fishing with shiners, and all during the heat of the day with blue-bird sky conditions."

Wow! Who'd argue that Trafford doesn't have big bass, lots of 'em, and that they won't hit during the dog days? Despite the fishing success, Trafford isn't widely ballyhooed. Most of the fishermen come from within a fifty-mile radius, although slowly the lake's fame is spreading.

You have to know the lake's history to really appreciate what has happened. Back in the 1940s, this 1,400-acre lake was one of the hottest, if not the hottest, bass lakes in Florida. Then it was nothing for as many as sixteen bass over 10 pounds to be boated in a single day. Even back then such catches were unusual in the Sunshine State.

But then Trafford went into a decline. Gizzard shad and mudfish took over, and this shallow saucer with an average maximum depth of 10 feet fell into disrepute. Most anglers forgot it. Newcomers never fished it, the lake's reputation was so bad.

Florida Game and Fish Commission biologists studied the lake and discovered that the bass comprised only one-tenth of one percent of the fish population. No wonder you couldn't catch bass, there were practically none.

Trafford had fallen to the lowest of the fish lows. Seventy-nine percent of the fish consisted of rough fish, mainly gizzard shad. Efforts were made to seine and remove the rough fish, but although thousands of pounds were netted, the black bass population didn't come back.

Then selective poisoning was tried. It was only partly successful. At last in 1962, it was decided to poison the entire lake and restock it with a new supply of bass. The lake was poisoned, and restocking began in 1963. Trafford was reopened to the public in 1964.

The restocking was successful, but the lake's poor reputation persisted. A few local anglers sampled the lake, and had success, but they didn't beat any publicity drums for Trafford. Gradually other Florida lakes grabbed the angling headlines.

Like most anglers, I'd forgotten about Trafford until Kit and I stopped there while on a trip into southwest Florida in 1975. Bill, then managing the Marina, and his fish tales aroused my interest. They intrigued me so much that I persuaded Buck Bray, my angling buddy, a professional bass guide on the Withlacoochee River at Dunnellon, to trailer his boat to Immokalee to check out Trafford.

As any angler knows, the fish tales have a habit of being slightly exaggerated, and while I didn't disbelieve Bill, I still had some doubts. They disappeared in a hurry when Buck and I checked out the lake with DeLisle.

In a day and a half of fishing, the three of us boated and released forty-five bass. Now that's no reason to bad-mouth a lake. Our biggest bucketmouth was a 6-pounder that Buck enticed into hitting a plastic worm. We did miss fish that could have gone 8 to 10 pounds, when we couldn't set the hooks fishing plastic worms in the grass. Yes, Trafford had come back.

Since then I've been back frequently, always with good luck, and sometimes with thrilling experiences as witness the 8-pounder on six-pound test line. One of these days I'll stumble onto a 10-pounder.

Although there're plenty of fish in this sawgrass saucer, it does take a little know-how to catch them. After a number of successful trips, and picking DeLisle's brains, I've learned some of the quirks. Hydrilla, of course, is one of the major problems, and small motors have problems if used away from the boat trails. Big motors usually can hack their way through the mess. This pesky grass is a major influence on how you fish the lake, and it can confuse you if you're accustomed to fishing relatively clear waters.

For example, you normally don't fish the shore but fish away from it. There's a reason. The shore is very shallow, muddy, and not an area that bass like to roam. Also you have to be selective where you fish away from the banks. The governing factor is the thickness of the hydrilla.

Lake Trafford is noted for its huge bass caught primarily with big shiners. Here, Bill DeLisle is shown netting a 10-pound bass for one of his clients.

The secret is fishing the edge of the thick patches, and that's where the bass like to lurk. Why? The bait fish are there naturally, and the bass follow the bait. You can entice the bigmouths into coming out to hit your lures or your shiners, but you have very little luck casting across or into the thickest hydrilla. That's a no-no.

If you're shiner fishing, you don't want your bait to burrow back into the hydrilla. Bass don't want a salad with their meal. So you must be constantly alert for this hydrilla burrowing by your shiner.

There's another Trafford oddity—simplicity of lures. You don't need a huge tackle box. It's really a two-lure lake. You can catch bigmouths with top-water propeller lures, or with very shallow runners blipped on the surface, or you can use plastic worms.

Deep-diving lures such as crank baits will only work if there's a heavy hydrilla kill during the winter. This has happened, and I've caught fish with Rebel's medium running crank baits, black and silver color. However, it's an exception rather than the rule.

Spinner and buzz baits can be used only if the hydrilla is sufficiently below the surface to permit them being run shallow. But this type of lure seldom finds favor with the few Trafford regular fishermen.

The worm colors, too, are simple. Bill's found that purple and black are the producing colors. The key to the worm color is the type of light. He prefers purple when the sun is shining brightly, but black when the day is overcast. He's found the bass apparently can see the black worms more easily on dark days. Probably other worm colors will work, but few Trafford anglers want to experiment when such a successful color pattern has been established. Size doesn't seem to make much difference, although the eight-inch is the most popular.

Although Trafford isn't a huge lake, there is a quirk as to fish locations. The local experts have found that the most bass are caught in the south end, *but* the biggest come from the north end. My 8-pounder came from the northern half of the lake. Of course, if you really want to seek trophy bass, undoubtedly shiners are the bait to use. However, this doesn't mean you can't catch big bass with artificials. You can.

Bill swears he's lost bass in the 14 to 15-pound class worm fishing. He just couldn't handle the fish with twenty and twenty-five-pound test line. He's seen enough big bass in the water to be an expert at judging their size. Who knows? Trafford might produce the next world's record largemouth.

Although traditionally shiner fishing is best during the winter, Bill isn't entirely married to this theory since his success with Bill Kerfoot. And Kerfoot is another who doubts the heat-slump theory. Both are convinced that shiners will produce lunkers during the so-called dog days, and they've caught enough fish to prove the theory.

If you're interested in sampling this little ballyhooed lake, here's the way to reach Immokalee, three miles from the "glory hole."

The little farming town is astride Florida 29 highway, which intersects U.S. 41 on the south, and U.S. 27 on the north. You also can drive from Fort Myers (on U.S. 41) via Florida 82 highway.

Accommodations are limited. There's one motel, the Frontier Lodge, 504 E. Main St., Immokalee, Fl, 33934. It's a long way from a Holiday Inn. There are several restaurants serving home-style meals. You won't starve, neither will you have to contend with a maitre d'.

A guide is advisable on your initial trips, for the fish do move, and there's no use in wasting time trying to locate them when a guide can put you on the spot. The only guide with whom I've fished is Bill DeLisle. You can reach him at the following address: Bill DeLisle, 1102 New Market Road, Immokalee, Fl., 33934, telephone (813) 657-4284. He guides from a modern bass boat fishing with either shiners or artificial lures.

If you're looking for trophy bass, try Trafford sometime. The odds are good you'll tangle with some line stretchers there. Whether you can land them is another matter.

# Appendix

*Licenses and Limits*

As with all states, freshwater fishing licenses are required to fish the impoundments, lakes, and rivers discussed in this book.

Fishing licenses and bag limits for the various states are as follows.

## FLORIDA

Annual, resident license $6.50.

Nonresident, annual license, $10.50; 14-day continuous, $7.50; and 5-day continuous, $5.50.

Bag limits for gamefish are: ten black bass; fifteen chain pickerel; fifty panfish (bream, speckled perch, and red-finned pike, individually or in aggregate); six sunshine (hybrid) bass, no minimum length. Total possession limit, two days bag limit after first day of fishing. You are allowed six striped bass (minimum length fifteen inches). The total possession limit is six.

There are special bag limits in certain waters. In Lakes George and Crescent and the St. Johns River between State Road 40 and 100, no more than four black bass may be under twelve inches in length. The limit for the Jim Woodruff reservoir (Lake Seminole) and the St. Mary's River is ten black bass, thirty white bass, fifteen chain pickerel, fifty panfish, and fifty of all gamefish in aggregate.

Licenses are issued from the offices of county tax collectors and their subagents, i.e. tackle shops, fish camps, and other places of business catering to fishermen. All licenses are valid from July 1 until June 30 of the following year.

## GEORGIA

Annual, resident fishing license, $5.50.

Nonresident, annual fishing license, $12.50; 5-day, nonresident, $5.50.

Creel and possession limits are as follows: bream (bluegill, redbreast and other species of bream), fifty; crappie (white or black speckled perch), fifty; white bass, thirty; largemouth, black bass, smallmouth bass, redeye bass, spotted bass, shoal bass, and/or Suwannee bass, ten; striped bass or white/striped hybrid, six; chain pickerel, red/fin, and/or grass pickerel, fifteen.

Resident Georgia fishing licenses are available in all parts of the state from approximately 2,000 license dealers in hardware stores, sporting goods stores, marinas, and other places of business catering to fishermen. Many license dealers, but not all, sell nonresident licenses.

All licenses may be purchased in person or by mail from the Department of Natural Resources, License Office, 2258 Northlake Parkway, Suite 100, Tucker, Ga, 30084. Orders by mail must include a complete physical description and address of the applicant with the proper payment. All licenses are valid from April 1 until March 31 of the following year.

## NORTH CAROLINA

Annual, resident license, statewide, $9.50; county fishing only, $4.50; comprehensive daily, $4; sportsman's $27.50.

Nonresident, annual, $15.50; comprehensive daily, $6; sportsman's, $55.

Creel and possession limits are as follows: bass (including black, spotted, smallmouth, and largemouth) eight, minimum length twelve inches; white bass, twenty-five; striped bass and hybrids, eight, minimum length twelve inches; panfish, no daily or size limit.

Annual licenses expire with the calendar year.

## SOUTH CAROLINA

Annual, statewide license, $7.50; 14-day resident, $3.25. Lake and reservoir permits are $1.75. (One permit only required of all residents, using *only* cane poles in Lakes Marion, Moultrie, and the Diversion and Tailrace Canals).

Nonresident, annual, $20.50. Ten-day, non-resident, $7.50.

Creel limits: No more than a total of forty gamefish may be caught in one day. This total shall not include more than ten largemouth black bass; ten striped bass and/or hybrids; thirty other gamefish—white bass, crappie (speckled perch), chain pickerel (or jackfish), redfin pike, yellow perch, bream (shellcrackers and warmouth).

Licenses are valid from July 1 until June 30 of the following year.

## ALABAMA

Annual, resident, $6; hook and line in county of residence, $1. Nonresident, annual $10. Seven-day, nonresident, $4.

Creel limits: black bass (including largemouth, smallmouth, Kentucky or spotted, redeye or Coosa) ten; walleye and sauger, fifteen; white and yellow bass, thirty; striped bass (rockfish) or hybrids, six; crappie (speckled perch), fifty; bream, fifty. No size limits.

### Additional Information

Additional information can be obtained from the following sources: Department of Conservation and Natural Resources, Division of Game and Fish, Montgomery, Al, 36130; Florida Game and Freshwater Fish Commission, Farris Bryant Building, Tallahassee, Fl., 32301; Georgia Department of Natural Resources, Information Office, 270 Washington St, S.W., Atlanta, Ga., 30334.

N.C. Wildlife Resources Commission, 512 N. Salisbury St., Raleigh, NC, 27611; S.C. Wildlife and Marine Resources Dept., P.O. Box 167, Columbia, SC 29202; Duke Power Co., P.O. Box 2178, 422 S. Church St., Charlotte, NC, 28242; Pendleton District Historic and Recreation Commission, P.O. Box 234, Pendleton, SC 29670; Santee Cooper Country, P.O. Drawer 40-F, Santee, SC, 29142; Historic Chattahoochee Commission, P.O. Box 33, Eufaula, AL, 36027.

Florida Chambers of Commerce generally have fishing information, especially when they are located near famous fishing waters. The following are associated with or near the fishing areas listed in this book:

Walton County, P.O. Box 29, DeFuniak Springs, Fl, 32433; Apalachicola, P.O. Box 39, Apalachicola, Fl., 32320; Gadsen County, P.O. Box 389, Quincy, Fl, 32351; Tallahassee, P.O. Box 1639, Tallahassee, Fl, 32302; Gainesville, P.O. Box 1187, Gainesville, Fl., 32601; Crescent City, 115 N. Summit St., Crescent City, Fl, 32012; Marion County, P.O. Box 1210, Ocala, Fl., 32670; Putnam County, P.O. Box 550, Palatka, Fl., 32077; Eustis, P.O. Drawer AZ, Eustis, Fl, 32726; Leesburg, P.O. Box 629, Leesburg, Fl., 32748; Tavares, P.O. Box 697, Tavares, Fl., 32778; Citrus County, P.O. Box 416, Inverness, Fl., 32650; Kissimmee-Osceola, P.O. Box 776, Kissimmee, Fl., 32741; Immokalee, P.O. Drawer C, Immokalee, Fl., 33934; Bell Glade, 9 E. Canal St., Belle Glade, Fl., 33430; Clewiston, P.O. Box 275, Clewiston, Fl., 33440; St. Cloud, Rt 1, Box 790-D, St. Cloud, Fl, 32769;

Glades County, P.O. Box 788, Moore Haven Fl, 33471; Okeechobee County, 55 South Parrott Ave, Okeechobee, Fl, 33472; Pahoke, 115 E. Main St., Pahokee, Fl, 33476; Dunnellon, P.O. Box 468, Dunnellon, Fl, 32640.